THE CENTRALIA CASE

A Da Capo Press Reprint Series

CIVIL LIBERTIES IN AMERICAN HISTORY

GENERAL EDITOR: LEONARD W. LEVY

Claremont Graduate School

THE CENTRALIA CASE

Three Views of the Armistice Day Tragedy at
Centralia, Washington, November 11, 1919

The Centralia Conspiracy
By Ralph Chaplin

Centralia: Tragedy and Trial
By Ben Hur Lampman

The Centralia Case
A Joint Report

DA CAPO PRESS • NEW YORK • 1971

A Da Capo Press Reprint Edition

The following three pamphlets are reproduced
in this volume without abridgement:

The Centralia Conspiracy by Ralph Chaplin
(3rd ed., revised; Chicago, 1924)

Centralia: Tragedy and Trial by Ben Hur Lampman
(Centralia and Tacoma, Washington, 1920)

The Centralia Case: A Joint Report (New York,
Baltimore, Washington, D.C., 1930); reprinted by
permission from a copy of the original edition
in the collection of the Harvard Law School Library.

Library of Congress Catalog Card Number 77-160845
ISBN 0-306-70211-8

Published by Da Capo Press, Inc.
A Subsidiary of Plenum Publishing Corporation
227 West 17th Street, New York, N.Y. 10011

THE CENTRALIA CASE

CONTENTS

The Centralia Conspiracy

By Ralph Chaplin

A Tongue of Flame

The martyr cannot be dishonored. Every lash inflicted is a tongue of flame; every prison a more illustrious abode; every burned book or house enlightens the world; every suppressed or expunged word reverberates through the earth from side to side. The minds of men are at last aroused; reason looks out and justifies her own, and malice finds all her work is ruin. It is the whipper who is whipped and the tyrant who is undone.—Emerson.

The CENTRALIA CONSPIRACY

The Truth About the Armistice Day Tragedy

by RALPH CHAPLIN

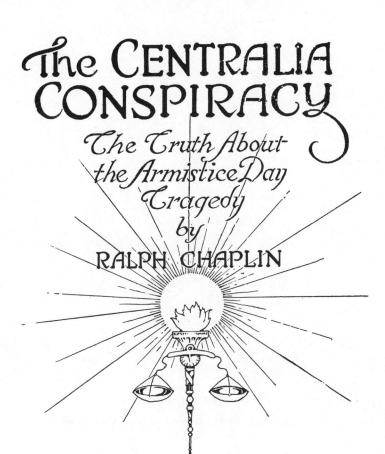

Chicago, Illinois.
GENERAL DEFENSE COMMITTEE

Introduction

The Centralia case is a part of the backwash of the world war. It marks the peak of the black wave of hysteria, hatred and intolerance that has swept the world since the beginning of hostilities. This wave, fortunately, shows signs of receding. Slowly but surely the war-born animosities are dying down, common sense if not real fellowship seems to be returning. The people are stirring restlessly and reaching out for priceless liberties that were taken from them under the excuse of "war necessity." The clutch of reaction upon the throat of the nation is weakening. The right of free speech, free press and free assembly are becoming something more than mere ornaments for political oratory. But the fight is not over, the final bulwarks are still unscaled. Victories of this kind are not conceded until they are won. Only the united and stubbornly persistent efforts of forward-looking men and women can undo the wrongs that were done and tear down the edifices of lies and oppression that were erected during the dark days. It is our hope that this book will not only help you to discover a mass of suppressed facts about the famous Centralia case but will also inspire you with a real determination to fight for well deserved and belated justice.

For members of the advanced working class movement in America the war period was an exceedingly bitter one. From the beginning the war was used by American plutocrats as an excuse to muzzle dissenting opinion and to destroy nonconformist labor organizations. Such a movement confronted them in the form of the Industrial Workers of the World—the hated I. W. W. Its philosophy, always unpopular with the exploiters of labor, was exceptionally so during the war. The I. W. W. claimed that that war was fundamentally the same as all other wars, that it was inspired by the same sinister influences and that it would have identically the same ending as other wars. This was its crime. As a menace to the prosecution of the war the I. W. W. was negligible; but as a challenge to oppression, exploitation and injustice it was formidable. At least it was considered formidable enough to merit the most atrocious legal and extra legal persecution ever visited upon any movement in American history. Only the attempted suppression of the Abolitionists is comparable in any way.

In the Centralia case are summed up all of the class arrogance, hatred and intolerance that characterized the war period. The raid of the Legionaires and business men on the union hall was the culmination of a long series of similar outrages. The defense of this hall by the loggers was an act of desperate protest and not an act of vindictiveness or deliberate lawlessness. It called the attention of the nation to many hitherto unknown acts of mob violence.

The loggers who defended their union hall in Centralia were tried during the period of war hysteria. They were convicted by an intimidated jury and sentenced by a bitterly biased judge. The customary rules of courtroom procedure and legal ethics were set aside by a wealthy and powerful prosecution in order to obtain a conviction that could not have been obtained at any other time. The trial was full of errors and irregularities. Even the plea of the jury for clemency was ignored by the black robed gentleman on the bench. To call this trial a miscarriage of justice is to speak mildly. A dispassionate perusal of the court records will show that it was a disgrace to American jurisprudence. Six of the jurors have since made affidavits exonerating the loggers and complaining about the evidence withheld from them at the trial.

All things considered we feel that so much injustice was done in this case and with such terrible consequences to the victims that it now concerns every worker and thinker in America. We believe that you are seeking the light and are willing to investigate and find out the truth about this case. We believe also that you will be willing to spread the truth far and wide once you are convinced that it is the truth. In this book Ralph Chaplin relates the detailed story of the trial and the events which led up to the tragedy on Armistice Day, 1919. We want everyone to know the facts about this case. We believe the prison doors will swing open for the survivors of the Centralia mob just as soon as the people know the truth. The Centralia case is one of the big cases of the generation. If the horror and injustice of it were fully known it would so touch the hearts and minds of men and women that the entire country would resound with demands for the release of the victims.

GENERAL DEFENSE COMMITTEE.

The Centralia Conspiracy

MURDER OR SELF-DEFENSE?

THIS BOOKLET is not an apology for murder. It is an honest effort to unravel the tangled mesh of circumstances that led up to the Armistice Day tragedy in Centralia, Washington. The writer is one of those who believe that the taking of human life is justifiable only in self-defense. Even then the act is a horrible reversion to the brute—to the low plane of savagery. Civilization, to be worthy of the name, must afford other methods of settling human differences than those of blood letting.

The nation was shocked on November 11, 1919, to read of the killing of four American Legion men by members of the Industrial Workers of the World in Centralia. The capitalist newspapers announced to the world that these unoffending paraders were killed in cold blood—that they were murdered from ambush without provocation of any kind. If the author were convinced that there was even a slight possibility of this being true, he would not raise his voice to defend the perpetrators of such a cowardly crime.

But there are two sides to every question and perhaps the newspapers presented only one of these. Dr. Frank Bickford, an ex-service man who participated in the affair, testified at the coroner's inquest that the Legion men were attempting to raid the union hall when they were killed. Sworn testimony of various eyewitnesses has revealed the fact that some of the "unoffending paraders" carried coils of rope and that others were armed with such weapons as would work the demolition of the hall and bodily injury to its occupants. These things throw an entirely different light on the subject. If this is true it means that the union loggers fired only in self-defense and not with the intention of committing wanton and malicious murder as has been stated. Now, as at least two of the union men who did the shooting were ex-soldiers, it appears that the tragedy must have resulted from something more than a mere quarrel between

7

loggers and soldiers. There must be something back of it all that the public generally doesn't know about.

There was one body of men in the Northwest which hated a union hall enough to have it raided—the lumber "interests." And now we get at the kernel of the matter, which is the fact that the affair was the outgrowth of a struggle between the lumber trust and its employees—between Organized Capital and Organized Labor.

A LABOR CASE

And so, after all, the famous trial at Montesano was not a murder trial but a labor trial in the strict sense of the word. Under the law, it must be remembered, a man is not committing murder in defending his life and property from the felonious assault of a mob bent on killing and destruction. There is no doubt whatever but what the lumber trust had plotted to "make an example" of the loggers and to destroy their hall on this occasion. And this was not the first time that such atrocities had been attempted and actually committed. Isn't it peculiar that, out of many similar raids, you only heard of the one where the men defended themselves? Self-preservation is the first law of nature, but the preservation of its holy profits is the first law of the lumber trust. The organized lumber workers were considered a menace to the super-prosperity of a few profiteers— hence the attempted raid and the subsequent killing.

What is more significant is the fact that the raid had been carefully planned three weeks in advance. There is a great deal of evidence to prove this point.

There is no question that the whole affair was the outcome of a struggle—a class struggle, if you please—between the union loggers and the lumber interests; the former seeking to organize the workers in the woods and the latter fighting this movement with all the means at its disposal.

In this light the Centralia affair does not appear as an isolated incident but rather an incident in an eventful industrial conflict, little known and less understood, between the lumber barons and loggers of the Pacific Northwest. This viewpoint will place Centralia in its proper perspective and enable one to trace the tragedy back to the circumstances and conditions that gave it birth.

But was there a conspiracy on the part of the lumber interests to commit murder and violence in an effort to drive organized labor from its domain?

8

Weeks of patient investigating in and around the scene of the occurrence has convinced the present writer that such a conspiracy existed. A considerable amount of startling evidence has been unearthed that has hitherto been suppressed. If you care to consider Labor's version of this unfortunate incident you are urged to read the following truthful account of this almost unbelievable piece of mediæval intrigue and brutality.

The facts will speak for themselves. Credit them or not, but read!

THE FORESTS OF THE NORTHWEST

The Pacific Northwest is world famed for its timber. The first explorers to set foot upon its fertile soil were awed by the magnitude and grandeur of its boundless stretches of virgin forests. Nature has never endowed any section of our fair world with such an immensity of kingly trees. Towering into the sky to unthinkable heights, they stand as living monuments to the fecundity

WITNESSES SAY MEN IN PARADE ATTACKED HALL

Testimony at Inquest Over Centralia Shooting Influences Jury's Verdict.

By Associated Press.

CENTRALIA, Nov. 13.—Testimony tending to show that the marching ex-service men started toward the I. W. W. hall before shots were fired from the building or from the Avalon hotel opposite, featured the coroner's inquest over the bodies of the four former soldiers killed here last Tuesday and is said to have been responsible for the failure of the jury in rendering its verdict to fix responsibility for the shooting.

Dr. Frank Bickford, one of the marchers, testified that the door of the I. W. W. hall was forced open by participants in the parade before the shooting began through the doorway or from the Avalon hotel opposite. Dr. Bickford said he was immediately in front of the I. W. W. hall at the time, and that during a temporary halt some one suggested a raid on the hall.

Ready to Lead.

"I spoke up and said I would lead if enough would follow," he stated, "but before I could take the lead there were many ahead of me. Some one next to me put his foot against the door and forced it open, after which a shower of bullets poured through the opening about us."

Dr. Bickford told how he

—From Seattle Post Intelligencer.

THE TRUTH LEAKS OUT!

First statement to reach the world about reason for Armistice Day shooting. Dr. Bickford's sensational "slip" created a furor among reactionaries in the northwest. The A. P. reporter who wrote this story left Centralia by request in a hurry; suitcase and typewriter were left behind. After this the persecution started immediately to "manufacture" its case.

9

of natural life. Imagine, if you can, the vast wide region of the West coast, hills, slopes and valleys, covered with millions of fir, spruce and cedar trees, raising their verdant crests a hundred, two hundred or two hundred and fifty feet into the air.

When Columbus first landed on the uncharted continent these trees were already ancient. There they stood, straight and majestic with green and foam-flecked streams purling here and there at their feet, crowning the rugged landscape with superlative beauty, overtopped only by the snow-capped mountains—waiting for the hand of man to put them to the multitudinous uses of modern civilization. Imagine, if you can, the first explorer, gazing awe-stricken down those "calm cathedral aisles," wondering at the lavish bounty of our Mother Earth in supplying her children with such inexhaustible resources.

But little could the first explorer know that the criminal clutch of Greed was soon to seize these mighty forests, guard them from the human race with bayonets, hangman's ropes and legal statutes; and use them, robber-baron like, to exact unimaginable tribute from the men and women of the world who need them. Little did the first explorer dream that the day would come when individuals would claim private ownership of that which prolific nature had travailed through centuries to bestow upon mankind.

But that day has come and with it the struggle between master and man that was to result in Centralia—or possibly many Centralias.

LUMBER—A BASIC INDUSTRY

It seems the most logical thing in the world to believe that the natural resources of the Earth, upon which the race depends for food, clothing and shelter, should be owned collectively by the race instead of being the private property of a few social parasites. It seems that reason would preclude the possibility of any other arrangement, and that it would be considered as absurd for individuals to lay claim to forests, mines, railroads and factories as it would be for individuals to lay claim to the ownership of the sunlight that warms us or to the air we breathe. But the poor human race, in its bungling efforts to learn how to live in our beautiful world, appears destined to find out by bitter experience that the private ownership of the means of life is both criminal and disastrous.

Lumber is one of the basic industries—one of the industries mankind never could have done without. The whole structure of

10

what we call civilization is built upon wooden timbers, ax-hewn or machine finished as the case may be. Without the product of the forests humanity would never have learned the use of fire, the primitive bow and arrow or the bulging galleys of ancient commerce. Without the firm and fibrous flesh of the mighty monarchs of the forest men might never have had barges for fishing or weapons for the chase; they would not have had carts for their oxen or kilns for the fashioning of pottery; they would not have had dwellings, temples or cities; they would not have had furniture nor fittings nor roofs above their heads. Wood is one of the most primitive and indispensable of human necessities. Without its use we would still be groping in the gloom and misery of early savagery, suffering from the cold of outer space and defenseless in the midst of a harsh and hostile environment.

FROM PIONEER TO PARASITE

So it happened that the first pioneers in the northern forests were forced to bare their arms and match their strength with the wooded wilderness. At first the subjugation of the forests was a social effort. The lives and future prosperity of the settlers must be made secure from the raids of the Indians and the inclemency of the elements. Manfully did these men labor until their work was done. But this period did not last long, for the tide of emigration was sweeping westward over the sun-baked prairies to the promised land of the golden West.

Towns sprang up like magic, new trees were felled, saw-mills erected and huge logs in ever increasing numbers were driven down the foaming torrents each year at spring time. The country was new, the market for lumber constantly growing and expanding. But the monopolist was unknown and the lynch-mobs of the lumber trust still sleeping in the womb of the future.

So passed the not unhappy period when opportunity was open to everyone, when freedom was dear to the hearts of all. It was at this time that the spirit of real Americanism was born, when the clean, sturdy name "America" spelled freedom, justice and independence. Patriotism in these days was not a mask for profiteers, and murderers were not permitted to hide their bloody hands in the folds of their nation's flag.

But modern capitalism was creeping like a black curse upon the land. Stealing, coercing, cajoling, defrauding, it spread from its plague-center in Wall Street, leaving misery, class antagonism and resentment in its trail. The old free America of our fathers

11

was undergoing a profound change. Equality of opportunity was doomed. A new social alignment was being created. Monopoly was loosed upon the land. Fabulous fortunes were being made as wealth was becoming centered into fewer and fewer hands. Modern capitalism was intrenching itself for the final and inevitable struggle for world domination. In due time the social parasites of the East, foreseeing that the forests of Maine, Michigan and Wisconsin could not last forever, began to look to the woods of the Northwest with covetous eyes.

STEALING THE PEOPLE'S FOREST LAND

The history of the acquisition of the forests of Washington, Montana, Idaho, Oregon and California is a long, sordid story of thinly veiled robbery and intrigue. The methods of the lumber barons in invading and seizing its "holdings" did not differ greatly, however, from those of the steel and oil kings, the railroad magnates nor any of the other industrial potentates who acquired great wealth by pilfering America and peonizing its people. The whole sorry proceeding was disgraceful, highhanded and treacherous, and only made possible by reason of the blindness of the generous American people, drugged with the vanishing hope of "success" and too confident of the continued possession of its blood-bought liberties. And so the lumber barons were unhindered in their infamous work of debauchery, bribery, murder and brazen fraud.

As a result the monopoly of the Northwestern woods became an established fact. The lumber trust came into "its own." The new social alignment was complete, with the idle, absentee landlord at one end and the migratory and possessionless lumberjack at the other. The parasites had appropriated to themselves the standing timber of the Northwest; but the brawny logger whose labor had made possible the development of the industry was given, as his share of the spoils, a crumby "bindle" and a rebellious heart. The masters had gained undisputed control of the timber of the country, three-quarters of which is located in the Northwest; but the workers who felled the trees, drove the logs, dressed, finished and loaded the lumber were left in the state of helpless dependency from which they could only extricate themselves by means of organization. And it was this effort to form a union and establish union headquarters that led to the tragedy at Centralia.

The lumber barons had not only achieved a monopoly of the woods but a perfect feudal domination of the woods as well.

12

Within their domain banks, ships, railways and mills bore their private insignia — and politicians, Employers' Associations, preachers, newspapers, fraternal orders and judges and gunmen were always at their beck ánd call. The power they wield is tremendous and their profits would ransom a kingdom. Naturally, they did not intend to permit either power or profits to be menaced by a mass of weather-beaten slaves in stag shirts and overalls. And so the struggle waxed fiercer just as the lumberjack learned to contend successfully for decent living conditions and adequate remuneration. It was the old, old conflict of human rights against property rights. Let us see how they compared in strength.

THE TRIUMPH OF MONOPOLY

The following extract from a document entitled "The Lumber Industry," by Herbert Knox Smith, federal Commissioner of Corporations, and published by the U. S. Department of Commerce and Labor (Bureau of Corporations) in 1911 will give some idea of the holdings and influence of the lumber trust:

"Ten monopoly groups, aggregating only one thousand eight hundred and two holders, monopolized one thousand, two hundred and eight billion eight hundred million (1,208,800,000,000) board feet of standing timber—each a foot square and an inch thick. These figures are so stupendous that they are meaningless without a hackneyed device to bring their meaning home. These one thousand, eight hundred and two timber business monopolists held enough standing timber, an indispensable natural resource, to yield the planks necessary (over and above manufacturing wastage) to make a floating bridge more than two feet thick and more than five miles wide from New York to Liverpool.

"It would supply one inch planks for a roof over France, Germany and Italy. It would build a fence eleven miles high along our entire coast line. All monopolized by one thousand, eight hundred and two holders, or interests more or less interlocked. One of those interests—a grant of only three holders—monopolized at one time two hundred and thirty-seven billion, five hundred million (237,500,000,000) feet which would make a column one foot square and three million miles high. Although controlled by only three holders, that interest comprised over eight per cent of all the standing timber in the United States at that time."

13

FIR AND SPRUCE TREES

The woods of the West coast abound
with tall fir trees. Spruce was a war
necessity and the lumber trust profiteered
hugely during the late unpleasantness.
Its patriotism paid.

Opposing this colossal aggregation of wealth and cussedness were the thousands of hard-driven and exploited lumber workers in the woods and sawmills. These had neither wealth nor influence—-nothing but their hard, bare hands and a growing sense of solidarity. And the masters of the forests were more afraid of this solidarity than anything else in the world—and they fought it more bitterly, as events will show. Centralia is only one of the incidents of this struggle between the owner and worker. But let us see what this hated and indispensable logger —the productive and human basis of the lumber industry, the man who made all these things possible, is like.

THE HUMAN ELEMENT—
"THE TIMBER BEAST"

Lumber workers are, by nature of their employment, divided into two categories—the sawmill hand and the logger. The former, like his brothers in the Eastern factories, is an indoor type while the latter is essentially a man of the open air. Both types are necessary to the production of finished lumber, and to both union organization is an imperative necessity.

Sawmill work is machine work—-rapid, tedious and often dangerous. There is the monotonous repetition of the same act of motions day in and day

14

out. The sights, sounds and smells of the mill are never varied. The fact that the mill is permanently located tends to keep mill workers grouped about the place of their employment. Many of them, especially in the shingle mills, have lost fingers or hands in feeding the lumber to the screaming saws. It has been estimated that fully a half of these men are married and remain settled in the mill communities. The other half, however, are not nearly so migratory as the lumberjack. Sawmill workers are not the "rough-necks" of the industry. They are of the more conservative "home-guard" element and characterized by the psychology of all factory workers.

The logger, on the other hand, (and it is with him our narrative is chiefly concerned), is accustomed to hard and hazardous work in the open woods. His occupation makes him of necessity migratory. The camp, following the uncut timber from place to place, makes it impossible for him to acquire a family and settle down. Scarcely one out of ten has ever dared assume the responsibility of matrimony. The necessity of shipping from a central point in go-

CEDAR TREES OF THE NORTHWEST

With these giants the logger daily matches his strength and skill. The profit-greedy lumber trust has wasted enough trees of smaller size to supply the world with wood for years to come.

15

ing from one job to another usually forces a migratory existence upon the lumberjack in spite of his best intentions to live otherwise.

WHAT IS A CASUAL LABORER?

The problem of the logger is that of the casual laborer in general. Broadly speaking, there are three distinct classes of casual laborers: First, the "harvest stiff" of the middle West who follows the ripening crops from Kansas to the Dakotas, finding winter employment in the North, Middle Western woods, in construction camps or on the ice fields. Then there is the harvest worker of "the Coast" who garners the fruit, hops and grain, and does the canning of California, Washington and Oregon, finding out-of-season employment wherever possible. Finally there is the Northwestern logger, whose work, unlike that of the Middle Western "jack," is not seasonal, but who is compelled nevertheless to remain migratory. As a rule, however, his habitat is confined according to preference or force of circumstances, to either the "long log" country of Western Washington and Oregon as well as California, or to the "short log" country of Eastern Washington and Oregon, Northern Idaho and Western Montana. Minnesota, Michigan and Wisconsin are in what is called the "short log" region.

As a rule the logger of the Northwest follows the woods to the exclusion of all other employment. He is militantly a lumberjack and is inclined to be a little "patriotic" and disputatious as to the relative importance of his own particular branch of the industry. "Long loggers," for instance, view with a suspicion of disdain the work of "short loggers" and vice versa.

"LUMBERJACK" THE GIANT KILLER

But the lumberjack is a casual worker and he is the finished product of modern capitalism. He is the perfect proletarian type—possessionless, homeless, rebellious. He is the reverse side of the gilded medal of present day society. One the one side is the third generation idle rich—arrogant and parasitical, and on the other, the actual producer, economically helpless and denied access to the means of production unless he "beg his lordly fellow worm to give him leave to toil," as Robert Burns has it.

The logger of the Northwest has his faults. He is not any more perfect than the rest of us. The years of degradation and struggle he has endured in the woods have not failed to leave

16

their mark upon him. But, as the wage workers go, he is not the common but the uncommon type both as regards physical strength and cleanliness and mental alertness. He is generous to a fault and has all the qualities Lincoln and Whitman loved in men.

In the first place, whether as faller, rigging man or on the "drive," his work is muscular and out of doors. He must at all times conquer the forest and battle with the elements. There is a tang and adventure to his labor in the impressive solitude of the woods that gives him a steady eye, a strong arm and a clear brain. Being constantly close to the great green heart of Nature, he acquires the dignity and independence of the savage rather than the passive and unresisting submission of the factory worker. The fact that he is free from family ties also tends to make him ready for an industrial frolic or fight at any time. In daily matching his prowess and skill with the products of the earth he feels in a way, that the woods "belong" to him and develops a contempt for the unseen and unknown employers who kindly permit him to enrich them with his labor. He is constantly reminded of the glaring absurdity of the private own-

"TOPPING" A TREE

After one of these huge trees is "topped" it is called a "spar tree"—very necessary in a certain kind of logging operations. As soon as the chopped-off portion falls, the trunk vibrates rapidly from side to side—sometimes shaking the logger to certain death below.

17

ership of natural resources. Instinctively he becomes a rebel against the injustice and contradictions of capitalist society.

Dwarfed to ant-like insignificance by the verdant immensity around him, the logger toils daily with ax, saw and cable. One after another forest giants of dizzy height crash to the earth with a sound like thunder. In a short time they are loaded on flat cars and hurried across the stump-dotted clearing to the river, whence they are dispatched to the noisy, ever-waiting saws at the mill. And always the logger knows in his heart that this is not done that people may have lumber for their needs, but rather that some overfed parasite may first add to his holy dividends. Production for profit always strikes the logger with the full force of objective observation. And is it any wonder, with the process of exploitation thus naked always before his eyes, that he should have been among the very first workers to challenge the flimsy title of the lumber barons to the private ownership of the woods?

THE FACTORY WORKER AND THE LUMBERJACK

Without wishing to disparage the ultimate worth of either, it might be well to contrast for a moment the factory worker of the East with the lumberjack of the Pacific Northwest. To the factory hand the master's claim to the exclusive title of the means of production is not so evidently absurd. Around him are huge, smoking buildings filled with roaring machinery—all man-made. As a rule he simply takes for granted that his employers—whoever they are—own these just as he himself owns, for instance, his pipe or his furniture. Only when he learns, from thoughtful observation or study, that such things are the appropriated products of the labor of himself and his kind, does the truth dawn upon him that labor produces all and is entitled to its own.

It must be admitted that factory life tends to dispirit and cow the workers who spend their lives in the gloomy confines of the modern mill or shop. Obedient to the shrill whistle they pour out of their clustered grey dwellings in the early morning. Out of the labor ghettos they swarm and into their dismal slave-pens. Then the long monotonous, daily "grind," and home again to repeat the identical proceeding on the following day. Almost always tired, trained to harsh discipline or content with low comfort, they are all too liable to feel that capitalism is invincibly colossal and that the possibility of a better day is hopelessly remote. Most of them are unacquainted with their neighbors. They live in small family or boarding house units and, having no common meeting place, realize only with difficulty the mighty potency of their vast numbers. To them organization appears desirable at times but unattainable. The dickering conservatism of craft unionism appeals to their cautious natures. They act only en masse, under awful compulsion and then their release of repressed slave emotion is sudden and terrible.

Not so with the weather-tanned husky of the Northwestern woods. His job life is a group life. He walks to his daily task with his fellow workers. He is seldom employed for long away from them. At a common table he eats with them, and they all sleep in common bunkhouses. The trees themselves teach him to scorn his master's adventitious claim to exclusive ownership. The circumstances of his daily occupation show him the need of class solidarity. His strong body clamours constantly for the sweetness and comforts of life that are denied him, his alert brain urges him to organize and his independent spirit gives him the courage and tenacity to achieve his aims. The union hall is often his only home and the One Big Union his best-beloved. He is fond of reading and discussion. He resents industrial slavery as an insult. He resented filth, overwork and poverty, he resented being made to carry his own bundle of blankets from job to job; he gritted his teeth together and fought until he had ground these obnoxious things under his iron-caulked heel. The lumber trust hated him just in proportion as he gained and used his industrial power; but neither curses, promises nor blows could make him budge. He knew what he wanted and he knew how to get what he wanted. And his bosses didn't like it very well.

The lumberjack is secretive and not given to expressed emotion—except in his union songs. The bosses don't like his songs either. But the logger isn't worried a bit. Working away in the woods every day, or in his bunk at night, he dreams his dream of the world as he thinks it should be—that "wild wobbly dream" that every passing day brings closer to realization—and he wants all who work around him to share his vision and his determination to win so that all will be ready and worthy to live in the New Day that is dawning.

In a word the Northwestern lumberjack was too human and too stubborn ever to repudiate his red-blooded manhood at the behest of his masters and become a serf. His union meant to him all that he possessed or hoped to gain. Is it any wonder that he endured the tortures of hell during the period of the war rather than yield his Red Card—or that he is still determined and still undefeated? Is it any wonder the lumber barons hated him

19

and sought to break his spirit with brute force and legal cunning—or that they conspired to murder it at Centralia with mob violence—and failed?

WHY THE LOGGERS ORGANIZED

The condition of the logger previous to the period of organization beggars description. Modern industrial autocracy seemed with him to develop its most inhuman characteristics. The evil plant of wage slavery appeared to bear its most noxious blossoms in the woods.

The hours of labor were unendurably long, ten hours being the general rule—with the exception of the Grays Harbor district, where the eleven or even twelve hour day prevailed. In addition to this men were compelled to walk considerable distances to and from their work and meals through the wet brush. Not infrequently the noon lunch was made almost impossible because of the order to be back on the job when work commenced. A ten hour stretch of arduous labor, in a climate where incessant rain is the rule for at least six months of the year, was enough to try the strength and patience of even the strongest. The wages too were pitiably inadequate.

The camps themselves, always more or less temporary affairs, were inferior to the cow-shed accommodations of a cattle ranch. The bunkhouses were over-crowded, ill-smelling and unsanitary. In these ramshackle affairs the loggers were packed like sardines. The bunks were arranged tier over tier and nearly always without mattresses. They were uniformly vermin-infested and sometimes of the "muzzle-loading" variety. No blankets were furnished, each logger being compelled to supply his own. There were no facilities for bathing or the washing and drying of sweaty clothing. Lighting and ventilation were, of course, always poor.

In addition to these discomforts the unorganized logger was charged a monthly hospital fee for imaginary medical service. Also it was nearly always necessary to pay for the opportunity of enjoying these privileges by purchasing employment from a "job shark" or enlisting the good graces of a "man catcher." The former often had "business agreements" with the camp foreman and, in many cases, a man could not get a job unless he had a ticket from a labor agent in some shipping point..

It may be said that the conditions just described were more prevalent in some parts of the lumber industry than in others. Nevertheless, these prevailed pretty generally in all sections of the industry before the workers attempted to better them by organizing. At all events such were the conditions the lumber barons sought with all their power to preserve and the loggers to change.

ORGANIZATION AND THE OPENING STRUGGLE

A few years before the birth of the Industrial Workers of the World the lumber workers had started to organize. By 1905, when the above mentioned union was launched, lumberworkers were already united in considerable numbers in the old Western, afterwards

A LOGGER OF THE PACIFIC NORTHWEST

This is a type of the men who work in the "long log" region of the West coast. His is a man's sized job, and his efforts to organize and better the working conditions in the lumber industry have been manly efforts—and bitterly opposed.

the American Labor Union. This organization took steps to affiliate with the Industrial Workers of the World and was thus among the very first to seek a larger share of life in the ranks of that militant and maligned organization. Strike followed strike with varying success and the conditions of the loggers began perceptibly to improve.

Scattered here and there in the cities of the Northwest were many locals of the Industrial Workers of the World. Not until 1912, however, were these consolidated into a real industrial unit. For the first time a sufficient number of loggers and saw mill men were organized to be grouped into an integral part of the One Big Union. This was done with considerable success. In the following year the American Federation of Labor attempted a similar task but without lasting results, the loggers preferring the industrial to the craft form of organization. Besides this, they were predisposed to sympathize with the ideal of solidarity and Industrial Democracy for which their own union had stood from the beginning.

21

The "timber beast" was starting to reap the benefits of his organized power. Also he was about to feel the force and hatred of the "interests" arrayed against him. He was soon to learn that the path of labor unionism is strewn with more rocks than roses. He was making an earnest effort to emerge from the squalor and misery of peonage and was soon to see that his overlords were satisfied to keep him right where he had always been.

Strange to say, almost the first really important clash occurred in the very heart of the lumber trust's domain, in the little city of Aberdeen, Grays Harbor County—only a short distance from Centralia, now of mob fame!

This was in 1912. A strike had started in the saw mills over demands for a $2.50 daily wage. Some of the saw mill workers were members of the Industrial Workers of the World. They were supported by the union loggers of Western Washington. The struggle was bitterly contested and lasted for several weeks. The lumber trust bared its fangs and struck viciously at the workers in a manner that has since characterized its tactics in all labor disputes.

The jails of Aberdeen and adjoining towns were filled with strikers. Picket lines were broken up and the pickets arrested. When the wives of the strikers with babies in their arms, took the places of their imprisoned husbands, the fire hose was turned on them with great force, in many instances knocking them to the ground. Loggers and saw mill men alike were unmercifully beaten. Many were slugged by mobs with pick handles, taken to the outskirts of the city in automobiles and told that their return would be the occasion of a lynching. At one time an armed mob of business men at Hoquiam dragged 150 of the strikers from their homes or boarding houses, herded them into waiting box-cars, sealed up the doors and were about to deport them en masse. The sheriff, getting wind of the unheard-of proceeding, stopped it at the last moment. Many men were badly scarred by beatings they received. One logger was crippled for life by the brutal treatment accorded him.

But the strikers won their demands and conditions were materially improved. The Industrial Workers of the World continued to grow in numbers and prestige. This event may be considered the beginning of the labor movement on Grays Harbor that the lumber trust sought finally to crush with mob violence on a certain memorable day in Centralia seven years later.

Following the Aberdeen strike one or two minor clashes occurred. The lumber workers were usually successful. During

22

this period they were quietly but effectually spreading One Big Union propaganda throughout the camps and mills in the district. Also they were organizing their fellow workers in increasing numbers into their union. The lumber trust, smarting under its last defeat, was alarmed and alert.

A MASSACRE AND A NEW LAW

But no really important event occurred until 1916. At this time the union loggers, organized in the Industrial Workers of the World, had started a drive for membership around Puget Sound. Loggers and mill hands were eager for the message of Industrial Unionism. Meetings were well attended and the sentiment in favor of the organization was steadily growing. The A. F. of L. shingle weavers and longshoremen were on strike and had asked the I. W. W. to help them obtain free speech in Everett. The ever-watchful lumber interests decided the time to strike had again arrived. The events of "Bloody Sunday" are too well known to need repeating here. Suffice to say that after a summer replete with illegal beatings and jailings five men were killed in cold blood and forty wounded in a final desperate effort to drive the union out of the city of Everett, Washington. These unarmed loggers were slaughtered and wounded by the gunfire of a gang of business men and plug-uglies of the lumber interests. True to form, the lumber trust had every union man in sight arrested and seventy-four charged with the murder of a gunman who had been killed by the cross-fire of his own comrades. None of the desperadoes who had done the actual murdering was ever prosecuted nor even reprimanded. The charge against the members of the Industrial Workers of the World was pressed. The case was tried in court and the industrialists declared "not guilty." George F. Vanderveer was the attorney for the defense.

The lumber interests were infuriated at their defeat, and from this time on the struggle raged in deadly earnest. Almost everything from mob law to open assassination had been tried without avail. The execrated One Big Union idea was gaining members and power every day. The situation was truly alarming. Their heretofore trustworthy "wage plugs" were showing unmistakable symptoms of intelligence. Workingmen were waking up. They were, in appalling numbers, demanding the right to live like men. Something must be done—something new and drastic—to split asunder this on-coming phalanx of industrial power.

But the gunman-and-mob method was discarded, temporarily at least, in favor of the machinations of lumber trust tools in

23

the law making bodies. Big Business can make laws as easily as it can break them—and with as little impunity. So the notorious Washington "criminal syndicalism" law was devised. This law, however, struck a snag. The honest-minded governor of the state, recognizing its transparent character and far-reaching effects, promptly vetoed the measure. After the death of Governor Lister the criminal syndicalism law was passed, however, by the next State Legislature. Since that time it has been used against the American Federation of Labor, the Industrial Workers of the World, the Socialist Party and even common citizens not affiliated with any of these organizations. The criminal syndicalism law registers the high water mark of reaction. It infringes more on the liberties of the people than any of the labor-crushing laws that blackened Russia during the dynasty of the Romanoffs.

THE 8 HOUR DAY AND "TREASON"

Nineteen hundred and seventeen was an eventful year. It was then the greatest strike in the history of the lumber industry occurred—the strike for the eight hour day. For years the logger and mill hand had fought against the unrestrained greed of the lumber interests. Step by step, in the face of fiercest opposition, they had fought for the right to live like men; and step by step they had been gaining. Each failure or success had shown them the weakness or strength of their union. They had been consolidating their forces as well as learning how to use them. The lumber trust had been making huge profits the while, but the lumber workers were still working ten hours or more and the logger was still packing his dirty blankets from job to job. Dissatisfaction with conditions was wider and more prevalent than ever before. Then came the war.

As soon as this country had taken its stand with the allied imperialists the price of lumber, needed for war purposes, was boosted to sky-high figures. From $16.00 to $116.00 per thousand feet is quite a jump; but recent disclosures show that the government paid as high as $1,200.00 per thousand for spruce that private concerns were purchasing for less than one-tenth of that sum. Gay parties with plenty of wild women and hard drink are alleged to have been instrumental in enabling the "patriotic" lumber trust to put these little deals across. Due to the duplicity of this same bunch of predatory gentlemen the airplane and ship building program of the United States turned

24

LOGGING OPERATIONS

Look around you at the present moment and you will see wood used for many different purposes. Have you ever stopped to think where the raw material comes from or what the workers are like who produce it? Here is a scene from a lumber camp showing the loggers at their daily tasks. The lumber trust is willing that these men should work—but not organize.

out to be a scandal instead of a success. Out of 21,000 feet of spruce delivered to a Massachusetts factory, inspectors could only pass 400 feet as fit for use. Keep these facts and figures in mind when you read about what happened to the "disloyal" lumber workers during the war—and afterwards.

Discontent had been smouldering in the woods for a long time. It was soon fanned to a flame by the brazen profiteering of the lumber trust. The loggers had been biding their time —rather sullenly it is true—for the day when the wrongs they had endured so patiently and so long might be rectified. Their quarrel with the lumber interests was an old one. The time was becoming propitious.

In the early summer of 1917 the strike started. Sweeping through the short log country it spread like wild-fire over nearly all the Northwestern lumber districts. The tie-up was practically complete. The industry was paralyzed. The lumber trust, its mouth drooling in anticipation of the many millions it was about to make in profits, shattered high heaven with its cries of rage.

Immediately its loyal henchmen in the Wilson administration rushed to the rescue. Profiteering might be condoned, moralized over or winked at, but miltant labor unionism was a menace to the government and the prosecution of the war. It must be crushed. For was it not treacherous and treasonable for loggers to strike for living conditions when Uncle Sam needed the wood and the lumber interests the money? So Woodrow Wilson and his coterie of political troglodytes from the slave-owning districts of the old South, started out to teach militant labor a lesson. Corporation lawyers were assembled. Indictments were made to order. The bloodhounds of the Department of "Justice" were unleashed. Grand Juries of "patriotic" business men were impaneled and did their expected work not wisely but too well. All the gunmen and stoolpigeons of Big Business got busy. And the opera bouffe of "saving our government" was staged.

INDUSTRIAL HERETICS AND THE WHITE TERROR

For a time it seemed as though the strikers would surely be defeated. The onslaught was terrific, but the loggers held out bravely. Workers were beaten and jailed by the hundreds. Men were herded like cattle in blistering "bull-pens," to be freed after months of misery, looking more like skeletons than human beings. Ellensburg and Yakima will never be forgotten in Washington. One logger was burned to death in a wooden jail in Troy, Montana. In the Northwest the military was used and the bayonet of the soldier could be seen glistening beside the cold steel of the hired thug. Union halls were raided all over the land. Thousands of workers were deported. Dozens were tarred and feathered and mobbed. Some were even taken out in the dead of night and hanged to railway bridges. Hundreds were convicted of imaginary offenses and sent to prison for terms of from one to twenty years. Scores were held in filthy jails for as long as twenty-six months awaiting trial. The Espionage Law, which never convicted a spy, and the Criminal Syndicalism Laws, which never convicted a criminal, were used savagely and with full force against the workers in their struggle for better conditions. By means of newspaper-made war hysteria the profiteers of Big Business entrenched themselves in public opinion. By posing as "100% Americans" (how stale and trite the phrase has become from their long misuse of it!) these social parasites sought to convince the nation that they, and not the truly American unionists whose backs they were

26

trying to break, were working for the best interests of the American people. Our form of government, forsooth, must be saved. Our institutions must be rescued from the clutch of the "reds." Thus was the war-frenzy of their dupes lashed to madness and the guarantees of the constitution suspended so far as the working class was concerned.

So all the good, wise and noisy men of the nation were induced by diverse means to cry out against the strikers and their union. The worst passions of respectable people were appealed to. The hoarse blood-cry of the mob was raised. It was echoed and re-echoed from press and pulpit. The very air quivered from its reverberations. Lynching parties became "respectable." Indictments were flourished. Hand-cuffs flashed. The clinking feet of workers going to prison rivaled the sound of the soldiers marching to war. And while all this was happening, the head of the American Federation of Labor glared through his thick spectacles and nodded his approval. But the lumber trust licked its fat lips and leered at its swollen dividends. All was well and the world was being made "safe for democracy."

AUTOCRACY VERSUS UNIONISM

This unprecedented struggle was really a test of strength between industrial autocracy and militant unionism. The former was determined to restore the palmy days of peonage for all time to come, the latter to fight to the last ditch in spite of hell and high water. The lumber trust sought to break the strike of the loggers and destroy their organization. In the ensuing fracas the lumber barons came out only second best—and they were bad losers. After the war-fever had died down—one year after the signing of the Armistice—they were still trying in Centralia to attain their ignoble ends by means of mob violence.

But at this time the ranks of the strikers were unbroken. The heads of the loggers were "bloody but unbowed." Even at last, when compelled to yield to privation and brute force and return to work, they turned defeat into victory by "carrying the strike onto the job." As a body they refused to work more than eight hours. Secretary of War Baker and President Wilson had both vainly urged the lumber interests to grant the eight hour day. The determined industrialists gained this demand, after all else had failed, by simply blowing a whistle when the time was up. Most of their other demands were won as well. In spite of even

27

EUGENE BARNETT

The prosecution tried desperately to prove that this man fired the shot which killed Warren O. Grimm. Barnett's alibi remained unshaken to the end. His frankness and candor on the witness stand were damaging to the prosecutor's case.

the Disque despotism, mattresses, clean linen and shower baths were reluctantly granted as the fruits of victory.

But even as these lines are written the prisons of America are filled with men whose only crime is loyalty to the working class—victims of "criminal syndicalism laws." The war profiteers are still wallowing in luxury. None has ever been placed behind the bars. Before he was lynched in Butte, Frank Little had said, "I stand for the solidarity of labor." That was enough. The vials of wrath were poured on his head for no other reason. And for no other reason was the hatred of the employing class directed at the valiant workers who now rot in prison for longer terms than those meted out to felons. And like procurers and thieves America still deports workingmen for the crime of thought. The boys at Centralia were conspired against because they too stood "for the solidarity of labor." It is simply lying and camouflage to attempt to trace such persecutions to any other source. These are things America will be ashamed of when she comes to her senses. Such grewsome events are paralleled in no other country save the Germany of Kaiser Wilhelm or the Russia of the Czar.

The picture of labor persecution in free America—terrible but true—will serve as a background for the dramatic history of the events leading up to the climacteric tragedy at Centralia on Armistice Day, 1919.

WHILE IN WASHINGTON . . .

All over the state of Washington the mobbing, jailing and tar and feathering of workers continued the order of the day until long after the cessation of hostilities in Europe. The organization had always urged and disciplined its members to avoid violence as an unworthy weapon. Usually the loggers had left their halls to the mercy of mobs when they knew a raid was contemplated. Centralia was the one exception. Here the outrages heaped upon them could no longer be endured.

In Yakima and Sedro Woolley, among other places in 1918, union men were stripped of their clothing, beaten with rope ends and hot tar was applied to bleeding flesh. They were then driven half naked into the woods. A man was hanged at night in South Montesano about this time and another had been tarred and feathered. As a rule the men were taken unaware before being treated in this manner. In one instance a stationary delegate of the Industrial Workers of the World received word that he was to be "decorated" and ridden out of town on a rail. He slit a pillow open and placed it in the window with a note attached stating that he knew of the plan; would be ready for them, and would gladly supply his own feathers. He did not leave town either on a rail or otherwise.

In Seattle, Tacoma and many other towns, union halls and print shops were raided and their contents destroyed or burned. In the former city in 1919, men, women and children were knocked insensible by policemen and detectives riding up and down the sidewalks in automobiles, striking to right and left with "billy" and night stick as they went. These were accompanied by auto trucks filled with hidden riflemen and an armored tank bristling with machine guns. A peaceable meeting of union men was being dispersed.

In Centralia, Aberdeen and Montesano, in Grays Harbor County, the struggle was more local but not less intense. No fewer than twenty-five loggers on different occasions were taken from their beds at night and treated to tar and feathers. A great number were jailed for indefinite periods on indefinite charges. As an additional punishment these were frequently locked in

EUGENE BARNETT
(After the man-hunt)

Coal miner. Born in North Carolina. Member of U. M. W. A. and I. W. W. Went to work underground at the age of eight. Self-educated, a student and philosopher. Upon reaching home Barnett, fearful of the mob, took to the woods with his rifle. He surrendered to the posse only after he had convinced himself that their purpose was not to lynch him.

their cells and the fire hose played on their drenched and shivering bodies. "Breach of jail discipline" was the reason given for this "cruel and unusual" form of lumber trust punishment.

In Aberdeen and Montesano there were several raids and many deportations of the tar and feather variety. In Aberdeen in the fall of 1917 during a "patriotic" parade, the battered hall of the union loggers was again forcibly entered in the absence of its owners. Furniture, office fixtures, victrola and books were dumped into the street and destroyed. In the town of Centralia, about a year before the tragedy, the union secretary was kidnaped and taken into the woods by a mob of well dressed business men. He was made to "run the gauntlet" and severely beaten. There was a strong sentiment in favor of lynching him on the spot, but one of the mob objected, saying it would be "too raw." The victim was then escorted to the outskirts of the city and warned not to return under pain of the usual penalty. On more than one occasion loggers who had expressed themselves in favor of the Industrial Workers of the World, were found in the morning dangling from trees in the vicinity. No explanation but that of "suicide" was ever offered. The whole story of the atrocities perpetrated during these days of the White Terror, in all probability, will never be published . The criminals are well known but their influence is too powerful to ever make it expedient to expose their crimes. Besides, who would care to get a gentleman in trouble for killing a mere "wobbly"? The few instances noted above will, however, give the reader some slight idea of the grewsome events that were leading inevitably to that grim day in Centralia in November, 1919.

WEATHERING THE STORM

EUGENE BARNETT'S FAMILY
Mrs. Barnett and son, Clifford.

Through it all the industrialists clung to their Red Cards and to the One Big Union for which they had sacrificed so much. Time after time, with incomparable patience, they would refurnish and reopen their beleaguered halls, heal up the wounds of rope, tar or "billy" and proceed with the work of organization as though nothing had happened. With union cards or credentials hidden in their heavy shoes they would meet secretly in the woods at night. Here they would consult about members who had been mobbed, jailed or killed, about caring for their families—if they had any—about carrying on the work of propaganda and laying plans for the future progress of their union. Perhaps they would take time to chant a rebel song or two in low voices. Then, back on the job again to "line up the slaves for the New Society!"

Through a veritable inferno of torment and persecution these men had refused 'to be driven from the woods or to give up their union—the Industrial Workers of the World. Between the two dreadful alternatives of peonage or persecution they chose the latter—and the lesser. Can you imagine what their peonage must have been like?

BERT FAULKNER

American. Logger. 21 years of age. Member of the Industrial Workers of the World since 1917. Was in the hall when raid occurred. Faulkner personally knew Grimm, McElfresh and various others who marched in the parade. He is an ex-soldier himself. The prosecution used a great deal of pressure to make this boy turn state's evidence. He refused stating that he would tell nothing but the truth. After the state had concluded/its testimony, Faulkner was discharged by the court for lack of any evidence against him.

SINISTER CENTRALIA

But Centralia was destined to be the scene of the most dramatic portion of the struggle between the entrenched interests and the union loggers. Here the long persecuted industrialists made a stand for their lives and fought to defend their own, thus giving the glib-tongued lawyers of the prosecution the opportunity of accusing them of "wantonly murdering unoffending paraders" on Armistice Day.

Centralia in appearance is a creditable small American city —the kind of city smug people show their friends with pride from the rose-scented tranquility of a super-six in passage. The streets are wide and clean, the buildings comfortable, the lawns and shade trees attractive. Centralia is somewhat of a coquette but she is as sinister and cowardly as she is pretty. There is a shudder lurking in every corner and a nameless fear sucks the sweetness out of every breeze. Song birds warble at the outskirts of the town but one is always haunted by the cries of the human beings who have been tortured and killed within her confines. Main Street is the name of the chief thoroughfare.

A red-faced business man motors leisurely down the wet street. He shouts a laughing greeting to a well dressed group at the curb who respond in kind. But the roughly dressed lumberworkers drop their glances in passing one another. The Fear is always upon them. As these lines were written several hundred discontented shingle-weavers were threatened with deportation if they dared to strike. They did not strike, for they knew too well the consequences. The man-hunt of November, 1919, was not forgotten and the terror of it gripped their hearts whenever they thought of opposing the will of the Moloch that dominates their every move.

Around Centralia are wooded hills; men have been beaten beneath these trees and lynched from them. The beautiful Chehalis River flows near by; Wesley Everest was left dangling from one of its bridges. But Centralia is provokingly pretty for all that. It is small wonder that lumber trust henchmen wish to keep it all for themselves.

Well tended roads lead in every direction, bordered with clearings of worked out camps and studded with occasional tree stumps of great age and truly prodigious size. At intervals are busy saw mills with thousands of feet of odorous lumber piled up in orderly rows. In all directions stretches the pillared immensity of the forests. The vistas through the trees seem enchanted rather than real—unbelievably green and of form and depth that remind one of painted settings for a Maeterlinck fable rather than matter-of-fact timber land.

THE HIGH PRIESTS OF LABOR HATRED

Practically all of this land is controlled by the trusts; much of it by the Eastern Railway and Lumber Company, of which F. B. Hubbard is the head. The strike of 1917 almost ruined this worthy gentleman. He has always been a strong advocate of the open shop, but during the last few years he has permitted his rabid labor-hatred to reach the point of fanaticism. This Hubbard figures prominently in Centralia's business, social and mob circles. He was one of the moving spirits in the Centralia conspiracy. The Eastern Railway and Lumber Company, besides large tracts of land, owns sawmills, coal mines and a railway. The Centralia newspapers are its mouthpieces while the Chamber of Commerce and the Elks' Club are its general headquarters. The

32

Farmers' & Merchants' Bank is its local citadel of power. In charge of this bank is a sinister character, one Uhlman, a German of the old school and a typical Prussian junker. At one time he was an officer in the German army but at present is a "100% American"—an easy metamorphosis for a Prussian in these days. His native born "brother-at-arms" is George Dysart whose son led a posse in the man-hunt that followed the shooting. In Centralia this bank and its Hun dictator dominates the financial, political and social activities of the community. Business men, lawyers, editors, doctors and local authorities all kow-tow to the institution and its Prussian president. And woe be to any who dare do otherwise! The power of the "interests" is a vengeful power and will have no other power before it. Even the mighty arm of the law becomes palsied in its presence.

The Farmers' & Merchants' Bank is the local instrumentality of the invisible government that holds the nation in its clutch. Kaiser Uhlman has more influence than the city mayor and more power than the police force. The law has always been a little thing to him and his clique. The inscription on the shield of this bank is said to read "To hell with the Constitution; this is Lewis County." As events will show, this inspiring maxim has been faithfully adhered to. It has been the rallying cry for the reactionaries throughout years of effort to crush the union movement among loggers and sawmill workers.

THE LOVED AND HATED UNION HALL

Now the loggers, being denied the luxury of home and family life, have but three places they can call "home." The bunkhouse in the camp, the cheap rooming house in town, and the union hall. This latter is by far the best loved of all. It is here the men can gather around a crackling wood fire, smoke their pipes and warm their souls with the glow of comradeship. Here they can, between jobs or after work, discuss the vicissitudes of their daily lives, read their books and magazines and sing their songs of solidarity, or merely listen to the "tinned" humor or harmony of the much-prized victrola. Also they here attend to affairs of their union —line up members, hold business and educational meetings and a weekly "open forum." Once in awhile a rough and wholesome "smoker" is given. The features of this great event are planned for weeks in advance and sometimes talked about for months afterwards.

These halls are at all times open to the public and induce-

RAY BECKER

Logger. American born. Twenty-five years of age. Studied four years for the ministry before going to work in the woods. His father and brother are both preachers. Becker joined the Industrial Workers of the World in 1917 and has always been a strong believer in the cause of the solidarity of Labor. He has the zeal of a prophet and the courage of a lion. Defended himself inside the hall with an Ivor Johnson, 38, until his ammunition was exhausted. He surrendered to the authorities—not to the mob.

ments are made to get workers to come in and read thoughtful treatises on industrial questions. The latch-string is always out for people who care to listen to a lecture on economics or similar subjects. Inside the hall there is usually a long reading table littered with books, magazines or papers. In a rack or case at the wall are to be found copies of the 'Seattle Union Record," "Industrial Solidarity," "The Industrial Worker," "The Liberator," the "New Republic" and "The Nation." Always there is a shelf of thumb-worn books on history, science, economics and socialism. On the walls are lithographs or engravings of noted champions of the cause of Labor, a few photographs of local interest and the monthly bulletins and statements of the union. Invariably there is a blackboard with jobs, wages and hours written in chalk for the benefit of men seeking employment. There are always a number of chairs in the room and a roll top desk for the secretary. Sometimes at the end of the hall is a plank rostrum—a modest altar to the Goddess of Free Speech and open discussion. This is what the loved and hated I. W. W. halls are like—the halls that were raided and destroyed by the hundreds during the years of the White Terror.

Remember, too, that in each of these raids the union men were not the aggressors and that there was never any attempt at reprisal. In spite of the fact that the lumber workers were within their legal right to keep open their halls and to defend them from felonious attack, it had never happened until November 11, that active resistance was offered the marauders. This fact alone speaks volumes for the long-suffering patience of the logger and for his desire to settle his problems by peaceable

34

means wherever possible. But the Centralia raid was the straw that broke the camel's back. The lumber trust went a little too far on this occasion and it got the surprise of its life. Four of its misguided dupes paid for their lawlessness with their lives, and a number of others were wounded. There has not since been a raid on a union hall in the Northwestern District.

It is well that workingmen and women throughout the country should understand the truth about the Armistice Day tragedy in Centralia and the circumstances that led up to it. But in order to know why the hall was raided it is necessary first to understand why this, and all similar halls, are hated by the oligarchies of the woods.

The issue contested is whether the loggers have the right to organize themselves into a union, whether they must remain chattels—mere hewers of wood and helpless in the face of the rapacity of their industrial overlords—or whether they have the right to keep open their halls and peacefully to conduct the affairs of their union. The lumber workers contend that they are entitled by law to do these things and the employers assert that, law or no law, they shall not do so. In other words, it is a question of whether organized labor shall retain its foothold in the lumber industry or be driven from the woods.

PIONEERS OF UNIONISM

It is hard for workers in most of the other industries—especially in the East—to understand the problems, struggles and aspirations of the husky and unconquerable lumber workers of the Northwest. The reason is that the average union man takes his union for granted. It seldom enters his mind that the privileges and benefits that surround him and the protection he enjoys are the result of the efforts and sacrifices of the nameless thousands of pioneers that cleared the way. But these unknown heroes of the great struggle of the classes did precede him with their loyal hearts and strong hands; otherwise workers now organized would have to start the long hard battle at the beginning and count their gains a step at a time, just as did the early champions of industrial organization, or as the loggers of the West Coast are now doing.

The working class owes all honor and respect to the first men who planted the standard of labor solidarity on the hostile frontier of unorganized industry. They were the men who made possible all things that came after and all things that are still to come. They were the trail blazers. It is easier to follow them than to have gone before them—or with them. They established the outposts of unionism in the wilderness of industrial autocracy. Their voices were the first to proclaim the burning message of Labor's power, of Labor's mission and of Labor's ultimate emancipation. Their breasts were the first to receive the blows of the enemy; their unprotected bodies were shielding the countless thousands to follow. They were the forerunners of the solidarity of Toil. They fought in a good and a great cause; for without solidarity, Labor would have attained nothing yesterday, gained nothing today nor dare to hope for anything tomorrow.

THE BLOCK HOUSE AND THE UNION HALL

In the Northwest today the rebel lumberjack is a pioneer. Just as our fathers had to face the enmity of the Indians, so are these men called upon to face the fury of the predatory interests that have usurped the richest timber resources of the richest nation in the world. Just outside Centralia stands a weatherbeaten landmark. It is an old, brown, dilapidated block house of early days. In many ways it reminds one of the battered and wrecked union halls to be found in the heart of the city.

The evolution of industry has replaced the block house with the union hall as the embattled center of assault and defense. The weapons are no longer the rifle and the tomahawk but the boycott and the strike. The frontier is no longer territorial but industrial. The new struggle is as portentous as the old. The stakes are larger and the warfare even more bitter.

The painted and be-feathered scalp-hunter of the Sioux or Iroquois were not more heartless in maiming, mutilating and killing their victims than the "respectable" profit-hunters of today—the type of men who conceived the raid on the union hall in Centralia on Armistice Day—and who fiendishly tortured and hanged Wesley Everest for the crime of defending himself from their inhuman rage. It seems incredible that such deeds could be possible in the twentieth century. It is incredible to those who have not followed the bloody trail of the lumber trust and who are not familiar with its ruthlessness, its greed and its lust for power.

As might be expected the I. W. W. halls in Washington were hated by the lumber barons with a deep and undying hatred. Union halls were a standing challenge to their hitherto undisputed right to the complete domination of the forests. Like the block houses of early days, these humble meeting places were the outposts of a new and better order planted in the stronghold

36

of the old. And they were hated accordingly. The thieves who had invaded the resources of the nation had long ago seized the woods and still held them in a grip of steel. They were not going to tolerate the encroachments of the One Big Union of the lumber workers. Events will prove that they did not hesitate at anything to achieve their purposes.

THE FIRST CENTRALIA HALL

In the year 1918 a union hall stood on one of the side streets in Centralia. It was similar to the halls that have just been described. This was not, however, the hall in which the Armistice Day tragedy took place. You must always remember that there were two halls raided in Centralia; one in 1918 and another in 1919. The loggers did not defend the first hall and many of them were manhandled by the mob that wrecked it. The loggers did defend the second and were given as reward a hanging, a speedy, fair and impartial conviction and sentences of from 25 to 40 years. No member of the mob has ever been punished or even taken to task for his misdeed. Their names are known to all. They kiss their wives and babies at night and go to church on Sundays. Yet they are a greater menace to this country's institutions than all the "reds." In a world where Mammon is king the king can do no wrong. But the question of "right" or "wrong" did not concern the lumber interests when they raided the union hall in 1918. "Yes, we raided the hall; what are you going to do about it?" is the position they took in the matter.

During the 1917 strike the two lumber trust papers in Centralia, the "Hub" and the "Chronicle" were bitter in their denunciation of the strikers. Repeatedly they urged that most drastic and violent measures be taken by the authorities and "citizens" to break the strike, smash the union and punish the strikers. The war-frenzy was at its height and these miserable sheets went about their work like Czarist papers inciting a pogrom. The lumber workers were accused of "disloyalty," "treason," "anarchy"—anything that would tend to make their cause unpopular. The Abolitionists were spoken about in identical terms before the Civil War. As soon as the right atmosphere for their crime had been created the employers struck and struck hard.

It was in May, 1918. Like many other cities in the land Centralia was conducting a Red Cross drive. Among the feat-

37

ures of this event were a bazaar and a Memorial Day parade.

The profits of the lumber trust were soaring to dizzy heights at this time and its patriotism was proportionately exalted. There was the usual brand of hypocritical and fervid speech-making. The flag was waved, the Government was lauded and the Constitution praised. Then, after the war-like proclivities of the stay-at-home heroes had been sufficiently worked upon; flag, Government and Constitution were forgotten long enough for the gang to go down the street and raid the "wobbly" hall.

Dominating the festivities was the figure of F. B. Hubbard, at that time President of the Employers' Association of the State of Washington. This is neither Hubbard's first nor last appearance as a terrorist and mob-leader—usually behind the scenes, however, or putting in a last minute appearance.

THE 1918 RAID

It had been rumored about town that the union hall was to be wrecked on this day but the loggers at the hall were of the opinion that the business men, having driven their secretary out of town a short time previously, would not dare to perpetrate another atrocity so soon afterwards. In this they were sadly mistaken.

Down the street marched the parade, at first presenting no unusual appearance. The Chief of Police, the Mayor and the Governor of the State were given places of honor at the head of the procession. Company G of the National Guard and a gang of broadcloth hoodlums disguised as "Elks" made up the main body of the marchers. But the crafty and unscrupulous Hubbard had laid his plans in advance with characteristic cunning. The parade, like a scorpion, carried its sting in its rear.

Along the main avenue went the guardsmen and the gentle-men of the Elks Club. So far nothing extraordinary had happened. Then the procession swerved to a side street. This must be the right thing for the line of march had been arranged by the Chamber of Commerce itself. A couple of blocks more and the parade had reached the intersection of First Street and Tower Avenue. What happened then the Mayor and Chief of Police probably could not have stopped even had the Governor himself ordered them to do so. From somewhere in the line of march a voice cried out, "Let's raid the I. W. W. Hall!" And the crowd at the tail end of the procession broke ranks and leaped to their work with a will.

In a short time the intervening block that separated them from the union hall was covered. The building was stormed with clubs and stones. Every window was shattered and every door was smashed, the very sides of the building were torn off by the mob in its blind fury. Inside the rioters tore down the partitions and broke up chairs and pictures. The union men were surrounded, beaten and driven to the street where they were forced to watch furniture, records, typewriter and literature demolished and burned before their eyes. An American flag hanging in the hall, was torn down and destroyed. A victrola and a desk were carried to the street with considerable care. The former was auctioned off on the spot for the benefit of the Red Cross. James Churchill, owner of a glove factory, won the machine. He still boasts of its possession. The desk was appropriated by F. B. Hubbard himself. This was turned over to an expressman and carted to the Chamber of Commerce. A small boy picked up the typewriter case and started to take it to a nearby hotel office. One of the terrorists detected the act and gave warning. The mob seized the lad, took him to a nearby light pole and treatened to lynch him if he did not tell them where books and papers were secreted which somebody said had been carried away by him. The boy denied having done this, but the hoodlums went into the hotel, ransacked and overturned everything. Not finding what they wanted, they left with a notice that the proprietor would have to take the sign down from his building in just twenty-four hours. Then the mob surged around the unfortunate men who had been found in the union hall. With cuffs and blows these were dragged to waiting trucks where they were lifted by the ears to the body of the machine and knocked prostrate one at a time. Sometimes a man would be dropped to the ground just after he had been lifted from his feet. Here he would lie with ear drums bursting and writhing from the kicks and blows that had been freely given. Like all similar mobs this one carried ropes, which were placed about the necks of the loggers. "Here's an I. W. W.," yelled someone. "What shall we do with him?" A cry was given to "lynch him!" Some were taken to the city jail and the rest were dumped unceremoniously on the other side of the county line.

Since that time the wrecked hall has remained tenantless and unrepaired. Grey and gaunt like a house in battle-scarred Belgium, it stands a mute testimony of the labor-hating ferocity of the lumber trust. Repeated efforts have since been made to destroy the remains with fire. The defense tried without avail to introduce a photograph of the ruin as evidence to prove that the second hall was raided in a similar manner on Armistice

39

LOREN ROBERTS

American. Logger. 19 years old. Loren's mother said of him at the trial: "Loren was a good boy, he brought his money home regularly for three years. After his father took sick he was the only support for his father and me and the three younger ones." The father was a sawyer in a mill and died of tuberculosis after an accident had broken his strength. This boy, the weakest of the men on trial, was driven insane by the unspeakable "third degree" administered in the city jail. One of the lumber trust lawyers was in the jail at the time Roberts signed his so-called "confession." "Tell him to quit stalling," said a prosecutor to Vanderveer, when Roberts left the witness stand. "You cur!" replied the defense attorney in a low voice, "You know who is responsible for this boy's condition." Roberts was one of the loggers on Seminary Hill.

Day, 1919. Judge Wilson refused to permit the jury to see either the photographs or the hall. But in case of another trial . . . . ? Evidently the l u m b e r t r u s t thought it better to have all traces of its previous crime obliterated.

The raid of 1918 did not weaken the lumber workers' union in Centralia. On the contrary it served to strengthen it. But not until more than a year had passed were the loggers able to establish a new headquarters. This hall was located next door to the Roderick Hotel on Tower Avenue, between Second and Third Streets. Hardly was this hall opened when threats were circulated by the Chamber of Commerce that it, like the previous one, was marked for destruction. The business element was lined up solid in denunciation of and opposition to the union hall and all that it stood for. But other anti-labor matters took up their attention and it was some time before the second raid was actually accomplished.

There was one rift in the lute of lumber trust solidarity in Centralia. Business and professional men had long been groveling in sycophantic servility at the feet of "the clique." There was only one notable exception.

A LAWYER—AND A MAN

A young lawyer had settled in the city a few years previous to the Armistice Day tragedy. Together with his parents and four brothers he had left his home in Minnesota to seek fame and fortune in the woods of Washington. He had worked his way through McAlester College and the Law School of the University of Minnesota. He was young, ambitious, red-headed and husky, a loving husband and the proud father of a beautiful baby girl. Nature had endowed him with a dangerous combination of gifts,— a brilliant mind and a kind heart. His name was just plain Smith— Elmer Smith—and he came from old rugged American stock.

Smith started to practice law in Centralia, but unlike his brother attorneys, he held to the assumption that all men are equal under the law—even the hated I. W. W. In a short time his brilliant mind and kind heart had won him as much hatred from the lumber barons as love from the down-trodden,—which is saying a good deal. The "interests" studied the young lawyer carefully for awhile and soon decided that he could be neither bullied nor bought. So they determined either to break his spirit or to break his neck. Smith was thrown into prison charged with murder. This is how it happened:

AFTER THE TORTURE

This is possibly one of the most dramatic photographs ever taken. The poor boy had been so tortured by the fiendish "third degree" that for a while he was a mental and physical wreck. His suffering is plainly visible on his face.

Smith established his office in the First Guarantee Bank Building, quite the proper thing to do. Then he began to handle law suits for wage-earners, which was altogether the reverse. Caste rules in Centralia, and Elmer Smith was violating its most sacred mandatories by giving the "working trash" the benefit of his talents instead of people really worth while.

Warren O. Grimm, who was afterwards shot while trying to break into the union hall with a mob, once cautioned Smith of the folly and danger of such a course. "You'll get along all right," said he, "if you will come in with us." Then he continued:

"How would you feel if one of your clients would come up to you in public, slap you on the back and say 'Hello, Elmer'?"

"Very proud," answered the young lawyer.

Some months previous Smith had taken a case for an I. W. W. logger. He won it. Other cases in which workers needed legal advice came to him. He took them. A young girl was working at the Centralia "Chronicle." She was receiving three dollars a week, which was a violation of the minimum wage law of the state for women. Smith won the case. Also he collected hundreds of dollars in back wages for workers whom the companies had sought to defraud. Workers in the clutches of loan sharks were extricated by means of the bankruptcy laws, hitherto only used by their masters. An automobile firm was making a practice of replacing Ford engines with old ones when a machine was brought in for repairs. One of the victims brought his case to Smith, and a lawsuit followed. This was an unheard-of proceeding, for heretofore such little business tricks had been kept out of court by common understanding.

A worker, formerly employed by a subsidiary of the Eastern Lumber & Railway Company, had been deprived of his wages on a technicality of the law by the corporation attorneys. This man had a large family and hard circumstances were forced upon them by this misfortune. One of his little girls died from what the doctor called malnutrition—plain starvation. Smith filed suit and openly stated that the lawyers of the corporation were responsible for the death of the child. The indignation of the business and professional element blazed to white heat. A suit for libel and disbarment proceedings were started against him. Nothing could be done in this dirction as Smith had not only justice but the law on his side. His enemies were waiting with great impatience for a more favorable opportunity to strike him down. Open threats were beginning to be heard against him.

A union lecturer came to town. The meeting was well attended. A vigilance committee of provocateurs and business men was in the audience. At the close of the lecture those gentlemen started to pass the signal for action. Elmer Smith sauntered down the aisle, shook hands with the speaker and told him he would walk to the train with him.

The following morning the door to Smith's office was ornamented with a cardboard sign. It read: "Are you an American? You had better say so. Citizens' Committee." This was lettered in lead pencil. Across the bottom were scrawled these words: "No more I. W. W. meetings for you."

In 1919 an event occurred which served further to tighten the noose about the stubborn neck of the young lawyer. On this occasion the terrorists of the city perpetrated another shameful crime against the working class—and the law.

Tom Lassiter made his living by selling newspapers at a little stand on a street corner. Tom is blind, a good soul and well liked by the loggers. But Tom has vision enough to see that there is something wrong with the hideous capitalist system we live under; and so he kept papers on sale that would help enlighten the workers. Among these were the "Seattle Union Record," "The Industrial Worker" and "Solidarity." To put it plainly, Tom was a thorn in the side of the local respectability because of his modest efforts to make people think. And his doom had also been sealed.

Early in June the news stand was broken into and all his clothing, literature and little personal belongings were taken to a vacant lot and burned. A warning sign was left on a short pole stuck in the ashes. The message, "You leave town in 24 hours, U. S. Soldiers, Sailors and Marines," was left on the table in his room.

BLIND MAN STANDS HIS GROUND

With true Wobbly determination, Lassiter acquired a new stock of papers and immediately re-opened his little stand. About this time a Centralia business man, J. H. Roberts by name, was heard to say, "This man (Lassiter) is within his legal rights and if we can't do anything by law we'll take the law into our own hands." This is precisely what hapened.

On the afternoon of June 30th, Blind Tom was crossing Tower Avenue with hesitating steps when, without warning, two business men seized his groping arms and yelled in his ear, "We'll get you out of town this time!" Lassiter called for help. The good Samaritan came along in the form of a brute-faced creature known as W. R. Patton, a rich property owner of the city. This Christian gentleman sneaked up behind the blind man and lunged him forcibly into a waiting Oakland automobile. The machine is owned by Cornelius McIntyre, who is said to have been one of the kidnaping party.

"Shut up or I'll smash your mouth so you can't yell," said one of his assailants as Lassiter was forced, still screaming for help, into the car. Turning to the driver one of the party said, "Step on her and let's get out of here." About this time Constable Luther Patton appeared on the scene. W. R. Patton walked over to where the constable stood and shouted to the bystanders, "We'll arrest the first person that objects, interferes or gets too loud."

"A good smash on the jaw would do more good," suggested the kind-hearted official.

LUMBERWORKERS' UNION HALL, RAIDED IN 1918

The first of the two halls to be wrecked by Centralia's terrorists. This picture was not permitted to be introduced as evidence of the conspiracy to raid the new hall. Judge Wilson didn't want the jury to know anything about this event.

"Well, we got that one pretty slick and now there are two more we have to get," stated W. R. Patton, a short time afterwards.

Blind Tim was dropped helpless in a ditch just over the county line. He was picked up by a passing car and eventually made his way to Olympia, capital of the state. In about a week he was back in Centralia. But before he could again resume his paper selling he was arrested on a charge of "criminal syndicalism.

Before his arrest, however, Lassiter had engaged Elmer Smith as counsel. Smith appealed to County Attorney Herman Allen for protection for his client. After a half-hearted effort to locate the kidnapers—who were known to everybody—this official gave up the task saying he was "too busy to bother with the affair, and, besides, the offense was only third degree assault which is punishable with a fine of one dollar and costs." The young lawyer did not waste any more time with the County authorities. Instead he obtained sworn statements of the facts in the case and submitted them to the Governor. These were duly acknowledged and placed on file in Olympia. But up to date no action has been taken by the executive to prosecute the criminals who committed the crime.

"Handle these I. W. W. cases if you want to," Smith was warned by an attorney for one of the local banks, "but sooner or later they're all going to be hanged or deported anyway."

Smith was feathering a nest for himself—feathering it with steel and stone and a possible coil of hempen rope The shadow of the prison bars was falling blacker on his red head with every passing moment. His fearless championing of the cause of the "under dog" had won him the implacable hatred of his own class. To them his acts of kindness and humanity were nothing less than treason. Smith had been ungrateful to the clique that had offered him every inducement to "come in with us." A lawyer with a heart is as dangerous as a working man with brains. Elmer Smith yould be punished all right; it would just be a matter of time.

THE SCENE OF THE ARMISTICE DAY TRAGEDY

This is what is left of the union hall the loggers tried to defend on Nov. 11, 1919. Three of the raiders, Grimm, McElfresh and Casagranda, were killed in the immediate vicinity of the doorway. Several others were wounded while attempting to rush the doors.

The indifference of the county and state authorities regarding the kidnaping of Blind Tom gave the terrorists renewed confidence in the efficacy and "legality" of their methods. Also it gave them a hint as to the form their future depredations were to take. And so, with the implied approval of everyone worth considering, they went about their plotting with still greater determination and a soothing sense of security.

THE CONSPIRACY DEVELOPS

The cessation of hostilities in Europe deprived the gangsters of the cloak of "patriotism" as a cover for their crimes. But this cloak was too convenient to be discarded so easily. "Let the man in uniform do it" was an axiom that had been proved both profitable and safe. Then came the organization of the local post of the American Legion and the now famous Citizens' Protective League—of which more afterwards.

With the signing of the Armistice, and the consequent almost

45

imperceptible lifting of the White Terror that dominated the country, the organization of the loggers began daily to gather strength. The Chamber of Commerce began to growl menacingly, the Employers' Association to threaten and the lumber trust papers to incite open violence. And the American Legion began to function as a cat's paw for the men behind the scenes.

Why should the beautiful city of Centralia tolerate the hated union hall any longer? Other halls had been raided, men had been tarred and feathered and deported—no one had ever been punished! Why should the good citizens of Centralia endure a lumber workers' headquarters and their despised union itself right in the midst of their peaceful community? Why indeed! The matter appeared simple enough from any angle. So then and there the conspiracy was hatched that resulted in the tragedy on Armistice Day. But the forces at work to bring about this unhappy conclusion were far from local. Let us see what these were like before the actual details of the conspiracy are recounted.

There were three distinct phases of this campaign to "rid the woods of the agitators." These three phases dovetail together perfectly. Each one is a perfect part of a shrewdly calculated and mercilessly executed conspiracy to commit constructive murder and unlawful entry. The diabolical plan itself was designed to brush aside the laws of the land, trample the Constitution underfoot and bring about an unparalleled orgy of unbridled labor hatred and labor repression that would settle the question of unionism for a long time.

THE CONSPIRACY—AND A SNAG

First of all comes the propaganda stage with the full force of the editorial virulence of the trust-controlled newspapers directed against labor in favor of "law and order," i. e., the lumber interests. All the machinery of newspaper publicity was used to villify the lumber worker and to discredit his union. Nothing was left unsaid that would tend to produce intolerance and hatred or to incite mob violence. This is not only true of Centralia, but of all the cities and towns located in the lumber district. Centralia happened to be the place where the tree of anti-labor propaganda first bore its ghastly fruit. Space does not permit us to quote the countless horrible things the I. W. W. was supposed to stand for and to be constantly planning to do. Statements made by General Wood and young Theodore Roosevelt to the effect that citizens should not argue with Bolshevists but meet them "head on," were conspicuously displayed. Any addle-headed mediocrity, in or out of uniform, who had anything particularly atrocious to say against the labor movement in general or the "radicals" in particular, was afforded every opportunity to do so. The papers were vying with one another in devising effectual, if somewhat informal, means of dealing with the "red menace."

Supported by, and partly the result of this barrage of lies, misrepresentation and incitation, came the period of attempted repression by "law." This was probably the easiest thing of all because the grip of Big Business upon the law making and law-enforcing machinery of the nation is incredible. At all events a state "criminal syndicalism law" had been conveniently passed and was being applied vigorously against union men, A. F. of L. and I. W. W. alike, but chiefly against the Lumber Workers' Industrial Union, No. 500, of the Industrial Workers of the World, the basic lumber industry being the largest in the North-west and the growing power of the organized lumberjack being therefore more to be feared.

No doubt the lumber interests had great hope that the execution of these made-to-order laws would clear up the atmosphere so far as the lumber situation was concerned. But they were doomed to a cruel and surprising disappointment.

Arrests of workers were made in Washington, Oregon, Idaho, Montana and even Nevada. Fifty or sixty men all told were arrested and their trials rushed as test cases. During this period from April 25 to October 20, 1919, the lumber trust saw with chagrin and dismay each of the state cases in turn either won outright by the defendants or else dismissed in the realization that it would be impossible to win them. By October 20, so George F. Vanderveer, chief attorney for the defense, declared, there was not a single member of the I. W. W. in custody in Washington, Idaho or Montana under this charge. In Seattle, Washington, an injunction was obtained restraining the mayor from closing down the new union hall in that city under the new law. Thus it appeared that the nefarious plan of the employers and their subservient lawmaking adjuncts, to outlaw the lumber workers' union and to penalize the activities of its members, was to be doomed to an ignominious failure.

RENEWED EFFORTS—LEGAL AND OTHERWISE

Furious at the realization of their own impotency the "interests" launched forth upon a new campaign. This truly machiavellian scheme was devised to make it impossible for accused men to obtain legal defense of any kind. All labor cases were to be tried simultaneously, thus making it impossible for the defendants to employ adequate counsel. George F. Russell, Secretary-Manager of the Washington Employers' Association, addressed meetings over the state urging all Washington prosecuting attorneys to organize that this end might be achieved. It is reported that Governor Hart, of Washington, looked upon the scheme with favor when it was brought to his personal attention by Russell.

However, the fact remains that the lumber trust was losing and that it would have to devise even more drastic measures if it were to hope to escape the prospect of a very humiliating defeat. And, all the while the organization of the lumber workers continued to grow.

In Washington the situation was becoming more tense, momentarily. Many towns in the heart of the lumber district had passed absurd criminal syndicalism ordinances. These prohibited membership in the I. W. W.; made it unlawful to rent premises to the organization or to circulate its literature. The Employers' Association had boasted that it was due to its efforts that these ordinances had been passed. But still they were faced with the provocative and unforgettable fact, that the I. W. W. was no more dead than the cat with the proverbial nine lives. Where halls had been closed or raided the lumber workers were transacting their union affairs right on the job or in the bunkhouses, just as though nothing had happened. What was more deplorable a few union halls were still open and doing business at the same old stand. Centralia was one of these; drastic measures must be applied at once or loggers in other localities might be encouraged to open halls also. As events prove these measures were taken—and they were drastic.

THE EMPLOYERS SHOW THEIR FANGS

That the Employers' Association was insidiously preparing its members for action suitable to the situation is evidenced by the following quotations from the official bulletin addressed privately "to Members of the Employers' Association of Washington." Note them carefully; they are published as "suggestions to members" over the written signature of George F. Russell, Secretary-Manager:

June 25th, 1918.—"Provide a penalty for idleness . . Common labor now works a few days and then loafs to spend the money earned . . Active prosecution of the I. W. W. and other radicals." 48

SEMINARY HILL

The union hall looks out on this hill, with Tower avenue and an alley betwen. It was admitted that Loren Roberts, Bert Bland and the missing Ole Hanson fired at the attacking mob from this position.

April 30th, 1919.—"Keep business out of the control of radicals and I. W. W. . . Overcome agitation . . .Closer co-operation between employers and employes . . Suppress the agitators . . Hang the Bolshevists."

May 31st, 1919.—"If the agitators were taken care of we would have very little trouble . . Propaganda to counteract radicals and overcome agitation . . Put the I. W. W. in jail."

June 30th, 1919.—"Make some of the Seattle papers print the truth . . . Get rid of the I. W. W.s."

July 2nd, 1919.—"Educate along the line of the three R's and the golden rule, economy and self denial . . Import Japanese labor . . . Import Chinese labor."

July 31st, 1919.—"Deport about ten Russians in this community."

August 31st, 1919.—"Personal contact between employer and employe, stringent treatment of the I. W. W."

October 15th, 1919.—"There are many I. W. W.s—mostly in the logging camps." . . .

October 31st, 1919.—(A little over a week before the Centralia raid.)—"Run your business or quit . . Business men and tax payers of Vancouver, Washington, have organized the Loyal Citizens' Protective League; opposed to Bolsheviki and the Soviet form of government and in favor of the open shop . . . Jail the radicals and deport them . . Since the Armistice these radicals have started in again. ONLY TWO COMMUNITIES IN WASHINGTON ALLOW I. W. W. HEADQUARTERS." (!!!)

December 31st, 1919.—"Get rid of all the I. W. W. and all other un-American organizations. . . Deport the radicals or use the rope as at Centralia. Until we get rid of the I. W. W. and radicals we don't expect to do much in this country . . Keep cleaning up on the I. W. W. . . . Don't let it die down . . Keep up public sentiment . ."

These few choice significant morsels of one hundred per cent (on the dollar) Americanism are quoted almost at random from the private bulletins of the officials of the Iron Heel in the state of Washington. Here you can read their sentiments in their own words; you can see how dupes and hirelings were coached to perpetrate the crime of Centralia, and as many other similar crimes as they could get away with. Needless to say these illuminating lines were not intended for the perusal of the working class. But now that we have obtained them and placed them before your eyes you can draw your own conclusion. There are many, many more records germane to this case that we would like to place before you, but the Oligarchy has closed its steel jaws upon them and they are at present inaccessible. Men are still afraid to tell the truth in Centralia. Some day the workers may learn the whole truth about the inside workings of the Centralia conspiracy. Be that as it may the business interests of the Northwest lumber country stand bloody handed and doubly damned, black with guilt and foul with crime; convicted before the bar of public opinion, by their own statements and their own acts.

FAILURE AND DESPERATION

Let us see for a moment how the conspiracy of the lumber barons operated to achieve the unlawful ends for which it was designed. Let us see how they were driven by their own failure at intrigue to adopt methods so brutal that they would have disgraced the head-hunter; how they tried to gain with murder-lust what they had failed to gain lawfully and with public approval.

The campaign of lies and slander inaugurated by their private newspapers failed to convince the workers of the undesirability of labor organization. In spite of the armies of editors and news-whelps assembled to its aid, it served only to lash to a murderous frenzy the low instincts of the anti-labor elements in the community. The campaign of legal repression, admittedly instituted by the Employers' Association, failed also in spite of the fact that all the machinery of the state from dog-catcher up to Governor was at its beck and call on all occasions and for all purposes.

Having made a mess of things with these methods the lumber barons threw all scruples to the winds—if they ever had any—threw aside all pretension of living within the law. They started out, mad-dog like, to rend, wreck and destroy the last vestige of labor organization from the woods of the Northwest, and furthermore, to hunt down union men and martyrize them with the club, the gun, the rope and the courthouse.

It was to cover up their own crimes that the heartless beasts of Big Business beat the tom-toms of the press in order to lash the "patriotism" of their dupes and hirelings into hysteria. It was to hide their own infamy that the loathsome war dance was started that developed perceptibly from uncomprehending belligerency into the lawless tumult of mobs, raids and lynchings! And it will be an everlasting blot upon the fair name of America that they were permitted to do so.

The Centralia tragedy was the culmination of a long series of unpunished atrocities against labor. What is expected of men who have been treated as these men were treated and who were denied redress or protection under the law? Every worker in the Northwest knows about the wrongs lumberworkers have endured—they are matters of common knowledge. It was common knowledge in Centralia and adjoining towns that the I. W. W. hall was to be raided on Armistice Day. Yet eight loggers have been sentenced from twenty-five to forty years in prison for the crime of defending themselves from the mob that set out to murder them! But let us see how the conspiracy was operating in Centralia to make the Armistice Day tragedy inevitable.

THE MAELSTROM—AND FOUR MEN

Centralia was fast becoming the vortex of the conspiracy that was rushing to its inevitable conclusion. Event followed event in rapid succession, straws indicating the main current of the flood tide of labor-hatred. The Commercial Club was seething with intrigue like the court of old France under Catherine de Medici; only this time it was industrial unionists instead of Huguenots who were being marked for a new night of St. Bartholomew. The heresy to be uprooted was industrial instead of religious protestantism; but the stake and the gibbet were awaiting the New Idea just as they had the old.

The actions of the lumber interests were now but thinly veiled and their evil purpose all too manifest. The connection between the Employers' Association of the state and its local representatives in Centralia had become unmistakably evident. And behind these loomed the gigantic silhouette of the Employers' Association of the nation—the colossal "invisible government"—more powerful at times than the Government itself. More and more stood out the naked brutal fact that the purpose of all this plotting was to drive the union loggers from the city and to destroy their hall. The names of the men actively interested in this movement came to light in spite of strenuous efforts to keep them obscured. Four of these stand out prominently in the light of the tragedy that followed: George F. Russell, F. B. Hubbard, William Scales and last, but not least, Warren O. Grimm.

The first named, George F. Russell, was a hired manager for the Washington Employers' Association, whose membership employed between 75,000 and 80,000 workers in the state. Russell is known to be a reactionary of the most pronounced type. He is an avowed union smasher and a staunch upholder of the open shop principle, which is widely advertised as the "American plan" in Washington. Incidentally he is an advocate of the scheme to import Chinese and Japanese coolie labor as a solution of the "high wage and arrogant unionism" problem.

F. B. Hubbard is a small-bore Russell, differing from his chief only in that his labor hatred is more fanatical and less discreet. Hubbard was hard hit by the strike of 1917 which fact has evidently won him the significant title of "a vicious anti-labor reptile." He is the man who helped to raid the 1918 union hall in Centralia and who appropriated for himself the stolen desk of the union secretary. His nephew Dale Hubbard was shot while trying to lynch Wesley Everest.

William Scales is a Centralia business man and a virulent sycophant. He is a parochial replica of the two persons mentioned above. Scales was in the Quartermaster's Department down on the border during the trouble with Mexico. Because he was making too much money out of Uncle Sam's groceries, he was relieved of his duties quite suddenly and discharged from the service. He was fortunate in making France instead of Fort Leavenworth, however, and upon his return, became an ardent proselyte of Russell and Hubbard and their worthy cause. Also he continued in the grocery business.

Warren O. Grimm came from a good family and was a small town aristocrat. His brother is city attorney at Centralia. Grimm was a lawyer, a college athlete and a social lion. He had been with the American forces in Siberia and his chief bid for distinction was a noisy dislike for the Workers' and Peasants' Republic of Russia, and the I. W. W. which h e termed the "A m e r i c a n Bolsheviki." During the 1918 raid on the Centralia hall Grimm is said to have been dancing around "like a whirling dervish" a n d waving t h e American flag while the work of destruction was going on. Afterwards he became prominent in the American L e g i o n and

AVALON HOTEL

From this point Elsie Hornbeck claimed she identified Eugene Barnett in the open window with a rifle. Afterwards she admitted that her identification was based only on a photograph shown her by the prosecution. This girl nearly fainted on the witness stand while trying to patch her absurd story together.

was the chief cat's paw for the lumber interests who were capitalizing the uniform to gain their own unholy ends. Personally he was a clean-cut modern young man.

SHADOWS CAST BEFORE

On June 26, 1919, the following notice appeared conspicuously on the first page of the Centralia Hub:

MEETING OF BUSINESS MEN CALLED FOR FRIDAY EVENING

"Business men and property owners of Centralia are urged to attend a meeting tomorrow in the Chamber of Commerce rooms to meet the officers of the Employers' Associaton of the state to discuss ways and means of bettering the conditions which now confront the business and property interests of the state. George F. Russell, Secretary-Manager, says in his note to business men: 'We need your advice and your co-operation in support of the movement for the defense of property and property rights. It is the most important question before the public today.' "

At this meeting Russell dwelt on the statement that the "radicals" were better organized than the property interests. Also he pointed out the need of a special organization to protect "rights of property" from the encroachment of all "foes of the government." The Non-Partisan League, the Triple Alliance and the A. F. of L. were duly condemned. The speaker then launched out into a long tirade against the Industrial Workers of the World which was characterized as the most dangerous organization in America and the one most necessary for "good citizens" to crush. Needless to state the address was chock full of 100% Americanism. It amply made up in forcefulness anything it lacked in logic.

So the "Citizens' Protective League" of Centralia was born. From the first it was a law unto itself—murder lust wearing the smirk of respectability—Judge Lynch dressed in a business suit. The advent of this infamous league marks the final ascendancy of terrorism over the Constitution in the city of Centralia. The only things still needed were a secret committee, a coil of rope and—an opportunity.

F. B. Hubbard was the man selected to pull off the "rough stuff" and at the same time keep the odium of crime from smirching the fair names of the conspirators. He was told to "perfect his own organiaztion." Hubbard was eminently fitted for his position by reason of his intense labor-hatred and his aptitude for intrigue.

The following day the Centralia Daily Chronicle carried the following significant news story:

Business Men of County Organize
Representatives from m a n y
communities attend meeting
in Chamber of Commerce,
presided over by Secretary of
Employers' Association.

"The labor situation was thoroughly discussed this afternoon at a meeting held in the local Chamber of Commerce which was attended by representative business men from various parts of Lewis County. George F. Russell, Secretary of the Employers' Association, of Washington, presided at the meeting.

BERT BLAND
Logger. American. (Brother of O. C. Bland.) One of the men who fired from Seminary Hill. Bland has worked all his life in the woods. He joined the Industrial Workers of the World during the great strike of 1917. Bert Bland took to the hills after the shooting and was captured a week later during the man-hunt.

"A temporary organization was effected with F. B. Hubbard, President of the Eastern Railway & Lumber Company, as chairman. He was empowered to **perfect his own organization.** A similar meeting will be held in Chehalis in connection with the noon luncheon of the Citizens' Club. . . . "

The city of Centralia became alive with gossip and speculation about this new move on the part of the employers. Everybody knew that the whole thing centered around the detested hall of the union loggers. Curiosity seekers began to come in from all parts of the county to have a peep at this hall before it was wrecked. Business men were known to drive their friends from the new to the old hall in order to show what the former would look like in a short time. People in Centralia generally knew for a certainty that the present hall would go the way of its predecessor. It was just a question now as to the time and circumstances of the event.

Warren O. Grimm had done his bit to work up sentiment against the union loggers and their hall. Only a month previously—on Labor Day, 1919,—he had delivered a "labor" speech that was received with great enthusiasm by a local clique of business men. Posing as an authority on Bolshevism on account of his Siberian service Grimm had elaborated on the dangers of this pernicious doctrine. With a great deal of dramatic emphasis he had urged his audience to beware of the sinister influence of "the American Bolsheviki—the Industrial Workers of the World."

A few days before the hall was raided Elmer Smith called at Grimm's office on legal business. Grimm asked him, by the way, what he thought of his Labor Day speech. Smith replied that he thought it was "rotten" and that he couldn't agree with Grimm's anti-labor conception of Americanism. Smith pointed to the deportation of Tom Lassiter as an example of the "Americanism" he considered disgraceful. He said also that he thought free speech was one of the fundamental rights of all citizens.

"I can't agree with you," replied Grimm. "That's the proper way to treat such a fellow."

THE NEW BLACK HUNDRED

On October 19 the Daily Hub published a news story headed "Employers Called to Discuss Handling of 'Wobbly' Problem." This story urged all employers to attend, stated that the meeting would be held in the Elks' Club and mentioned the wrecking of the union hall in 1918. On the following day, October 20, three weeks before the shooting, this meeting was held at the hall of the Benevolent and Protective Order of Elks—the now famous Elks' Club of Centralia. The avowed purpose of this meeting was to "deal with the I. W. W. problem." The chairman was William Scales, at that time Commander of the Centralia Post of the American Legion. The I. W. W. hall was the chief topic of discussion. F. B. Hubbard opened up by saying that the I. W. W. was a menace and should be driven out of town. Chief of Police Hughes, however, cautioned them against such a course. He is reported to have said that "the I. W. W. is doing nothing wrong in Centralia—is not violating any law— and you have no right to drive them out of town in this manner." The Chief of Police then proceeded to tell the audience that he had taken up the matter of legally evicting the industrialists with City Attorney C. E. Grimm, a brother of Warren O. Grimm, and the chief declared, "Gentlemen, there is no law by which you can drive the I. W. W. out of town." City Commissioner Saunders and County Attorney Allen spoke to the same effect. The latter, Allen, had gone over the literature of the organization with regard to violence and destruction and had voluntarily dismissed a "criminal syndicalist" case without trial for want of evidence.

Hubbard was furious at this turn of affairs and shouted to Chief of Police Hughes: "It's a damned outrage that these men should be permitted to remain in town! Law or no law, if I were Chief of Police they wouldn't stay here twenty-four hours."

"I'm not in favor of raiding the hall **myself**," said Scales. "But I'm certain that if anybody else wants to raid the I. W. W. Hall there is no jury in the land will ever convict them."

After considerable discussion the meeting started to elect a committee to deal with the situation. First of all an effort was made to get a workingman elected as a member to help camouflage its very evident character and make people believe that "honest labor" was also desirous of ridding the town of the hated I. W. W. Hall. A switchman named Henry, a member of the Railway Brotherhood, was nominated. When he indignantly declined, Hubbard, red in the face with rage, called him a "damned skunk."

THE INNER CIRCLE

Scales then proceeded to tell the audience in general and the city officials in particular that he would himself appoint a committee "whose inner workings will be secret," and see if he could not get around the matter that way. The officers of the League were then elected. The President was County Coroner David Livingstone, who made his money from union miners. William Scales was vice president and Hubbard was treasurer. The secret committee was then appointed by Hubbard. As its name implies it was an underground affair, similar to the Black Hundreds of Old Russia. No record of any of its proceedings has ever come to light, but according to best available knowledge Warren O. Grimm, Arthur McElfresh, B. S. Cormier and one or

two others who figured prominently in the raid, were members. At all events on November 6th, five days before the shooting, Grimm was elected Commander of the Centralia Post of the American Legion, taking the place of Scales, who resigned in his favor. Scales evidently was of the opinion that a Siberian veteran and athlete was better fitted to lead the "shock troops" than a mere counter-jumper like h i m s e l f . There is no doubt that the secret committee had its members well placed in positions of strategic importance for the coming event.

The following day the Tacoma News Tribune carried a significant editorial on the subject of the new organization:

"At Centralia a committee of citizens has been formed that takes the mind back to the old days of vigilance committees of the West, which did so much to force law-abiding citizenship upon certain lawless elements. It is called the Centralia Protective Association, and its object is to combat I. W. W. activities in that city and the surrounding country. It invites to membership all citizens who favor the enforcement

ELMER SMITH

Attorney at law. Old American stock—born on a homestead in North Dakota. By championing the cause of the "under-dog" in Centralia, Smith brought down on himself the wrath of the lumber trust. He defended many union men in the courts, and at one time sought to prosecute the kidnapers of Tom Lassiter. Smith is the man Warren O. Grimm told would get along all right, "if you come in with us." He bucked the lumber trust instead and landed in prison on a trumped-up murder charge. Smith was found "not guilty" by the jury, but was immediately re-arrested on practically the same charge. He is not related to Britt Smith.

57

of law and order. . . It is high time for the people who do believe in the lawful and orderly conduct of affairs to take the upper hand. . . Every city and town might, with profit, follow Centralia's example."

The reference to "lawful and orderly conduct of affairs" has taken a somewhat ironical twist, now that Centralia has shown the world what she considers such processes to be.

No less significant was an editorial appearing on the same date in the Centralia Hub:

"If the city is left open to this menace, we will soon find ourselves at the mercy of an organized band of outlaws bent on destruction. What are we going to do about it?" And, referring to the organization of the secret committee, the editorial stated: "It was decided that the inner workings of the organization were to be kept secret, to more effectively combat a body using similar tactics."

The editorial reeks with lies; but it was necessary that the mob spirit should be kept at white heat at all times. Newspaper incitation has never been punished by law, yet it is directly responsible for more murders, lynchings and raids than any other one force in America.

THE PLOT LEAKS OUT

By degrees the story of the infamous secret committee and its diabolical plan leaked out, adding positive confirmation to the many already credited rumors in circulation. Some of the newspapers quite openly hinted that the I. W. W. Hall was to be the object of the brewing storm. Chief of Police Hughes told a member of the Lewis County Trades Council, William T. Merriman by name, that the business men were organizing to raid the hall and drive its members out of town. Merriman, in turn carried the statement to many of his friends and brother unionists. Soon the prospective raid was the subject of open discussion,—over the breakfast toast, on the street corners, in the camps and mills—every place.

So common was the knowledge in fact that many of the craft organizations in Centralia began to discuss openly what they should do about it. They realized that the matter was one which concerned labor and many members wanted to protest and were urging their unions to try to do something. At the Lewis County Trades Council the subject was brought up for discussion by its president, L. F. Dickson. No way of helping the loggers was found, however, if they would stubbornly try to keep open their headquarters in the face of such opposition. Harry Smith, a brother of Elmer Smith, the attorney, was a delegate at this meeting and reported to his brother the discussion that took place.

Secretary Britt Smith and the loggers at the union hall were not by any means ignorant of the conspiracy being hatched against them. Day by day they had followed the development of the plot with breathless interest and not a little anxiety. They knew from bitter experience how union men were handled when they were trapped in their halls. But they would not entertain the idea of abandoning their principles and seeking personal safety. Every logging camp for miles around knew of the danger also. The loggers there had gone through the hell of the organization period and had felt the wrath of the lumber barons. Some of them felt that the statement of Secretary of Labor Wilson as to the attitude of the Industrial Workers of the World towards "overthrowing the government," and "violence and destruction" would discourage the terrorists from attempting such a flagrant and brutal injustice as the one contemplated.

Regarding the deportation of I. W. W.'s for belonging to an organization which advocates such things, Secretary of Labor Wilson had stated a short time previously: "An exhausitve study into the by-laws and practices of the I. W. W. has thus far failed to disclose anything that brings it within the class of organizations referred to."

Others of the loggers were buoyed up with the many victories won in the courts on "criminal syndicalism" charges and felt that the raid would be too raw a thing for the lumber interests even to consider. All were secure in the knowledge and assurance that they were violating no law in keeping open their hall. And they wanted that hall kept open.

Of course the question of what was to be done was discussed at their business meetings. When the news reached them on November 4th of the contemplated "parade" they decided to publish a leaflets telling the citizens of Centralia about the justice and legality of their position, the aims of their organization and the real reason for the intense hatred which the lumber trust harbored against them. Such a leaflet was drawn up by Secretary Britt Smith and approved by the membership. It was an honest, outspoken appeal for public sympathy and support. This leaflet—word for word as it was printed and circulated in Centralia —is reprinted below:

TO THE CITIZENS OF CENTRALIA WE MUST APPEAL:

"To the law-abiding citizens of Centralia and to the working

WESLEY EVEREST

Logger. American (old Washington pioneer stock). Joined the Industrial Workers of the World in 1917. A returned soldier. Earnest, sincere, quiet, he was the "Jimmy Higgins" of the Centralia branch of the Lumberworkers Union. Everest was mistaken for Britt Smith, the union secretary, whom the mob had started out to lynch. He was pursued by a gang of terrorists and unmercifully manhandled. Later—at night—he was taken from the city jail and hanged to a bridge. In the automobile, on the way to the lynching, he was unsexed by a human fiend—a well known Centralia business man—who used a razor on his helpless victim. Even the lynchers were forced to admit that Everest was the most "dead game" man they had ever seen.

class in general: We beg of you to read and carefully consider the following:

"The profiteering class of Centralia have of late been waving the flag of our country in an endeavor to incite the lawless element of our city to raid our hall and club us out of town. For this purpose they have inspired editorials in the Hub, falsely and viciously attacking the I. W. W., hoping to gain public approval for such revolting criminality. These profiteers are holding numerous secret meetings to that end, and covertly inviting returned service men to do their bidding. In this work they are ably assisted by the bankrupt lumber barons of southwest Washington who led the mob that looted and burned the I. W. W. hall a year ago.

"These criminal thugs call us a band of outlaws bent on destruction. This they do in an attempt to hide their own dastardly work in burning our hall and destroying our property. They say we are a menace; and we are a menace to all mobocrats and pilfering thieves. Never did the I. W. W. burn public or private halls, kidnap their fellow citizens, destroy their property, club their fellows out of town, bootleg or act in any way as lawbreakers. These patriotic profiteers throughout the country have falsely and without any foundation whatever charged the I. W. W. with every crime on the statute books. For these alleged crimes thousands of us have been jailed in foul and filthy cells throughout this country, often without charge, for months and in some cases, years, and when released re-arrested and again thrust in jail to await a trial that is never called. The only convictions

60

JUST BEFORE THE BOX WAS LOWERED

After the mob had worked its will upon the helpless body, the mortal remains of Wesley Everest were bundled into a rough box and dumped into a hole along the railroad tracks.

of the I. W. W. were those under the espionage law, where we were forced to trial before jurors, all of whom were at political and industrial enmity towards us, and in courts hostile to the working class. This same class of handpicked courts and juries also convicted many labor leaders, socialists, non-partisans, pacifists, guilty of no crime save that of loyalty to the working class.

"By such courts Jesus the Carpenter was slaughtered upon the charge that 'he stirreth up the people.' Only last month 25 I. W. W. were indicted in Seattle as strike leaders, belonging to an unlawful organization, attempting to overthrow the government and other vile things under the syndicalist law passed by the last legislature. To exterminate the 'wobbly' both the court and jury have to lie in every charge. The court held them a lawful organization and their literature was not disloyal nor inciting to violence, though the government had combed the country from Chicago to Seattle for witnesses, and used every pamphlet taken from their hall in government raids.

"In Spokane 13 members were indicted in the Superior Court for wearing the I. W. W. button and displaying their emblem. The jury unanimously acquitted them and the court held it no crime.

"In test cases last month both in the Seattle and Everett Superior Courts, the presiding judge declared the police had no

61

authority in law to close their halls and the padlocks were ordered off and the halls opened.

"Many I. W. W. in and around Centralia went to France and fought and bled for the democracy they never secured. They came home to be threatened with mob violence by the law and order outfit that pilfered every nickel possible from their mothers and fathers while they were fighting in the trenches in the thickest of the fray.

"Our only crime is solidarity, loyalty to the working class and justice to the oppressed."

"LET THE MEN IN UNIFORM DO IT"

On November 6th, the Centralia Post of the American Legion met with a committee from the Chamber of Commerce to arrange for a parade—another "patriotic" parade! The first anniversary of the signing of the armistice was now but a few days distant and Centralia felt it incumbent upon herself to celebrate. Of course the matter was brought up rather circumspectly, but knowing smiles greeted the suggestion. One business man made a motion that the brave boys wear their uniforms. This was agreed upon.

The line of march was also discussed. As the union hall was a little off the customary parade route, Scales suggested that their course lead past the hall "in order to show them how strong we are." It was intimated that a command "eyes right" would be given as the legionaires and business men passed the union headquarters. This was merely a poor excuse of the secret committeemen to get the parade where they needed it. But many innocent men were lured into a "lynching bee" without knowing that they were being led to death by a hidden gang of broadcloth conspirators who were plotting at murder. Lieutenant Cormier, who afterwards blew the whistle that was the signal for the raid, endorsed the proposal of Scales as did Grimm and McElfresh—all three of them secret committeemen.

Practically no other subject but the "parade" was discussed at this meeting. The success of the project was now assured for it had been placed into the hands of the men who alone could arrange to "have the men in uniform do it." The men in uniform had done it once before and people knew what to expect.

The day following this meeting the Centralia Hub published an announcement of the coming event stating that the legionaires had "voted to wear uniforms." The line of march was published for the first time. Any doubts about the real purpose of the parade vanished when people read that the procession was to march from the City Park to Third Street and Tower Avenue and return. The union hall was on Tower between Second and Third streets, practically at the end of the line of march and plainly the objective of the demonstrators.

"DECENT LABOR"—HANDS OFF!

A short time after the shooting a virulent leaflet was issued by the mayor's office stating that the "plot to kill had been laid two or three weeks before the tragedy," and that "the attack (of the loggers) was without justification or excuse." Both statements are bare faced lies. The meeting was held the 6th and the line of march made public on the 7th. The loggers could not possibly have planned a week and a half previously to shoot into a parade they knew nothing about and whose line of march had not yet been disclosed. It was proved in court that the union men armed themselves at the very last moment, after everything else had failed and they had been left helpless to face the alternative of being driven out of town or being lynched.

There is a report that about this time coils of rope were

LABOR'S SILENT JURY

W. J. Beard, Central Labor Council, Tacoma; Paul K. Mohr, Central Labor Council, Seattle; Theodore Meyer, Central Labor Council, Everett; E. W. Thrall, Brotherhood of Railway Trainmen, Centralia; John O. Craft, Metal Trades Council, Seattle.

purchased in a local hardware store. This rope is all cut up into little pieces now and most of it is dirty and stained. But many of Centralia's best families prize their souvenir highly. They say it brings good luck to a family.

A few days after the meeting just described William Dunning, vice president of the Lewis County Trades and Labor Assembly, met Warren Grimm on the street. Having fresh in his mind a recent talk about the raid in the Labor Council meetings, and being well aware of Grimm's standing and influence, Dunning broached the subject.

"We've been discussing the threatened raid on the I. W. W. hall," he said.

"Who are you, an I. W. W.?" asked Grimm.

Dunning replied stating that he was vice president of the Labor Assembly and proceeded to tell Grimm the feeling of his organization on the subject.

"Decent labor ought to keep its hands off," was Grimm's laconic reply.

The Sunday before the raid a public meeting was held in the union hall. About a hundred and fifty persons were in the audience, mostly working men and women of Centralia. Numerous loggers were present, dressed in the invariable mackinaw, stagged overalls and caulked shoes. John Foss, an I. W. W. shipbuilder from Seattle, was the speaker. Secretary Britt Smith was chairman. Walking up and down the aisle, selling the union's pamphlets and papers, was a muscular and sun-burned young man with a rough, honest face and a pair of clear hazel eyes in which a smile was always twinkling. He wore a khaki army coat above stagged overalls of a slightly darker shade,— Wesley Everest, the ex-soldier who was shortly to be mutilated and lynched by the mob.

"I HOPE TO JESUS NOTHING HAPPENS"

The atmosphere of the meeting was already tainted with the Terror. Nerves were on edge. Every time any newcomer would enter the door the audience would look over their shoulders with apprehensive glances. At the conclusion of the meeting the loggers gathered around the secretary and asked him the latest news about the contemplated raid. For reply Britt Smith handed them copies of the leaflet "We Must Appeal" and told of the efforts that had been made and were being made to obtain legal protection and to let the public know the real facts in the case.

"If they raid the hall again as they did in 1918 the boys

64

won't stand for it," said a logger, clenching his fists.

"If the law won't protect us we've got a right to protect ourselves," ventured another.

"I hope to Jesus nothing happens," replied the secretary.

Wesley Everest laid down his few unsold papers, rolled a brown paper cigarette and smiled enigmatically over the empty seats in the general direction of the new One Big Union label on the front window. His closest friends say he was never afraid of anything in all his life.

None of these men knew that the loggers from nearby camps, having heard of the plan to raid the hall, were watching the hall night and day to see that "nothing happens."

The next day, after talking things over with Britt Smith, Mrs. McAllister, wife of the proprietor of the Roderick hotel from whom the loggers rented the hall, went to see Chief of Police Hughes. This is how she told of the interview:

"I got worried and I went to the Chief. I says to him, 'Are you going to protect my property?' Hughes says, 'We'll do the best we can for you, but as far as the wobblies are concerned they wouldn't last fifteen minutes if the business men start after them. The business men don't want any wobblies in this town.' "

The day before the tragedy Elmer Smith dropped in at the union hall to warn his clients that nothing could now stop the raid. "Defend it if you choose to do so," he told them. "The law gives you that right."

It was on the strength of this remark, overheard by the stoolpigeon, Morgan, and afterwards reported to the prosecution, that Elmer Smith was hailed to prison charged with murder in the first degree. His enemies had been certain all along that his incomprehensible delusion about the law being the same for the poor man as the rich would bring its own punishment. It did; there can no longer be any doubt on the subject.

THE SCORPION'S STING

November 11th was a raw, gray day; the cold sunlight barely penetrating the mist that hung over the city and the distant tree-clad hills. The parade assembled at the City Park. Lieutenant Cormier was marshal. Warren Grimm was commander of the Centralia division . In a very short time he had the various bodies arranged to his satisfaction. At the head of the procession was the "two-fisted" Centralia bunch, followed by one from Chehalis, the county seat. Then came a few sailors and marines and a large body of Elks. The school children who were to have marched did not appear. At the very end were a couple of dozen boy scouts and an automobile carrying pretty girls dressed in Red Cross uniforms. Evidently this parade, unlike the one of 1918, did not, like a scorpion, carry its sting in the rear. But wait until you read how cleverly this part of it had been arranged!

The marchers were unduly silent and those who knew nothing of the lawless plan of the secret committee felt somehow that something must be wrong. City Postmaster Thomas H. McCleary and Ex-Mayor W. H. Thompson were seen carrying coils of rope. Thompson is a veteran of the Civil War and an ex-clergyman. On the witness stand he afterwards swore he picked up the rope from the street and was carrying it "as a joke." It turned out that the "joke" was on Wesley Everest.

"Be ready for the command 'eyes right' or 'eyes left' when we pass the 'reviewing stand,'" Grimm told the platoon commanders just as the parade started.

The procession covered most of the line of march without incident. When the union hall was reached there was some craning of necks but no outburst of any kind. A few of the out-of-town paraders looked at the place curiously and several business men were seen pointing the hall out to their friends. There were some dark glances and a few long noses but no demonstration.

"THERE AIN'T ANY REVIEWING STAND"

"When do we reach the reviewing stand?" asked a parader, named Joe Smith, of a man marching beside him.

"Hell, there ain't any reviewing stand," was the reply. "We're going to give the wobbly hall 'eyes right' on the way back."

The head of the column reached Third Avenue and halted. A command of 'about face' was given and the procession again started to march past the union hall going in the opposite direction. The loggers inside felt greatly relieved as they saw the crowd once more headed for the city. But the Centralia and Chehalis contingents, that had headed the parade, were now in the **rear**—just where the "scorpion sting" of the 1918 parade had been located! The danger was not yet over. Bad things might happen yet. The wobblies waited silently.

66

WHERE BARNETT'S RIFLE WAS SUPPOSED TO HAVE BEEN FOUND

Eugene Barnett was said to have left his rifle under this sign-board as he fled from the scene of the shooting. It would have been much easier to hide a gun in the tall brush in the foreground. In reality Barnett did not have a rifle on November 11th and was never within a mile of this place. Prosecutor Cunningham said he had "been looking all over for that rifle" when it was turned over to him by the "finder." Strangely enough Cunningham knew the number of the gun before he placed hands on it.

"LET'S GO! AT 'EM, BOYS!"

The Chehalis division had marched past the hall and the Centralia division was just in front of it when a sharp command was given. The latter stopped squarely in front of the hall but the former continued to march. Lieutenant Cormier of the secret committee was riding between the two contingents on a bay horse. Suddenly he placed his fingers to his mouth and gave a shrill whistle. Immediately there was a hoarse cry of "Let's go-o-o! At 'em, boys!" About sixty feet separated the two contingents at this time, the Chehalis men still continuing the march. Cormier spurred his horse and overtook them. "Aren't you boys in on this?" he shouted.

At the words "Let's go," the paraders from both ends and the middle of the Centralia contingent broke ranks and started on the run for the union headquarters. A crowd of soldiers surged against the door. There was a crashing of glass and a splintering of wood as the door gave way. A few of the marauders had actually forced their way into the hall. Then there was a shot, three more shots . . . and a small volley. From Seminary hill also rifles began to crack.

The mob stopped suddenly, astounded at the unexpected opposition. Out of hundreds of halls that had been raided during the past two years this was the first time the union men had attempted to defend themselves. It had evidently been planned to stampede the entire contingent into the attack by having

67

the secret committeemen take the lead from both ends and the middle. But before this could happen the crowd, frightened at the shots, started to scurry for cover. Two men were seen carrying the limp figure of a soldier from the door of the hall. When the volley started they dropped it and ran. The soldier was a handsome young man, named Arthur McElfresh. He was left lying in front of the hall with his feet on the curb and his head in the gutter. The whole thing had been a matter of seconds.

"I HAD NO BUSINESS BEING THERE"

Several men had been wounded. A pool of blood was widening in front of the doorway. A big man in officer's uniform was seen to stagger away bent almost double and holding his hands over his abdomen. "My God, I'm shot!" he had cried to the soldier beside him. This was Warren O. Grimm; the other was his friend, Frank Van Gilder. Grimm walked unassisted to the rear, of a nearby soft drink place, whence he was taken to a hospital. He died a short time afterwards. Van Gilder swore on the witness stand that Grimm and himself were standing at the head of the column of "unoffending paraders" when his friend was shot. He stated that Grimm had been his life-long friend but admitted that when his "life-long friend" received his mortal wound he (Van Gilder), instead of acting like a hero in No Man's Land, had deserted him in precipitate haste. Too many eye witnesses had seen Grimm stagger wounded from the doorway of the hall to suit the prosecution. Van Gilder knew at which place Grimm had been shot but it was necessary that he be placed at a convenient distance from the hall. It is reported on good authority that Grimm, just before he died in the hospital, confessed to a person at his bedside: "It served me right, I had no business being there."

A workingman, John Patterson, had come down town on Armistice Day with his three small children to watch the parade. He was standing thirty-five feet from the door of the hall when the raid started. On the witness stand Patterson told of being pushed out of the way by the rush before the shooting began. He saw a couple of soldiers shot and saw Grimm stagger away from the doorway wounded in the abdomen. The testimony of Dr. Bickford at the coroner's inquest under oath was as follows:

"I spoke up and said I would lead if enough would follow, but before I could take the lead there were many ahead of me. Someone next to me put his foot against the door and forced it open, after which a shower of bullets poured through the opening about us." Dr. Bickford is an A. E. F. man and one of the very few legionaires who dared to tell the truth about the shooting. The Centralia business element has since tried repeatedly to ruin him.

In trying to present the plea of the self-defense to the court, Defense Attorney Vanderveer stated:

"There was a rush, men reached the hall under the command of Grimm, and yet counsel asks to have shown a specific overt act of Grimm before we can present the plea of self-defense. Would he have had the men wait with their lives at stake? The fact is that Grimm was there and in defending themselves these men shot. Grimm was killed because he was there. They could not wait. Your honor, self-defense isn't much good after a man is dead."

The prosecution sought to make a point of the fact that the loggers had fired into a street in which there were innocent bystanders as well as paraders. But the fact remains that the only men hit by bullets were those who were in the forefront of the mob.

THROUGH THE HALL WINDOW

How the raid looked from the inside of the hall can best be described from the viewpoint of one of the occupants, Bert Faulkner, a union logger and ex-service man. Faulkner described how he had dropped in at the hall on Armistice Day and stood watching the parade from the window. In words all the more startling for their sheer artlessness he told of the events which followed: First the grimacing faces of the business men, then as the soldiers returned, a muffled order, the smashing of the window, with the splinters of glass falling against the curtain, the crashing open of the door . . . and the shots that "made his ears ring," and made him run for shelter to the rear of the hall, with the shoulder of his overcoat torn with a bullet. Then how he found himself on the back stairs covered with rifles and was commanded to come down with his hands in the air. Finally how he was frisked to the city jail in an automobile with a business man standing over him armed with a piece of gas pipe.

Eugene Barnett gave a graphic description of the raid as he saw it from the office of the adjoining Roderick hotel. Barnett said he saw the line go past the hotel. The business men were ahead of the soldiers and as this detachment passed the hotel returning the soldiers were going north. The business men were looking at the hall and pointing it out to the soldiers. Some of them had their thumbs to their noses and others were saying various things.

"When the soldiers turned and came past I saw a man on horseback ride past. He was giving orders which were repeated along the line by another. As the rider passed the hotel he gave a command and the second man said: 'Bunch up, men.'

"When this order came the men all rushed for the hall. I heard glass break. I heard a door slam. There was another sound and then shooting came. It started from inside the hall.

"As I saw these soldiers rush the hall I jumped up and threw off my coat. I thought there would be a fight and I was going to mix in. Then came the shooting, and I knew I had no business there."

Later Barnett went home and remained there until his arrest the next day.

In the union hall, besides Bert Faulkner, were Wesley Everest, Ray Becker, Britt Smith, Mike Sheehan, James McInerney and Tom Morgan. These, with the exception of Faulkner and Everest, remained in the hall until the authorities came to place them under arrest. They had, after the first furious rush of their assailants, taken refuge in a big and long disused ice box in the rear of the hall. Britt Smith was unarmed, his revolver being found afterwards, fully loaded, in his roll-top desk. After their arrest the loggers were taken to the city jail which was to be the scene of an inquisition unparalleled in the history of the United States. After this, as an additional punishment, they were compelled to face the farce of a "fair trial" in a capitalistic court.

WESLEY EVEREST

But Destiny had decided to spare one man the bitter irony of judicial murder. Wesley Everest still had a pocket full of cartridges and a forty-five automatic that could speak for itself. This soldier-lumberjack had done most of the shooting in the hall. He held off the mob until the very last moment, and, instead of seeking refuge in the refrigerator after the "paraders" had been dispersed, he ran out of the back door, reloading his pistol as he went. It is believed by many that Arthur McElfresh was killed inside the hall by a bullet fired by Everest.

In the yard at the rear of the hall the mob had already reorganized for an attack from that direction. Before anyone knew what had happened Everest had broken through their ranks and scaled the fence. "Don't follow me and I won't shoot," he called to the crowd, displaying the still smoking blue steel pistol in his hand.

"There goes the secretary!" yelled someone, as the logger started at top speed down the alley. The mob surged in pursuit, collapsing the board fence before them with sheer force of numbers. There was a rope in the crowd and the union secretary was the man they wanted. The chase that followed probably saved the life, not only of Britt Smith, but the remaining loggers in the hall as well.

Running pell-mell down the alley the mob gave a shout of exultation as Everest slowed his pace and turned to face them. They stopped cold, however, as several quick shots rang out and bullets whistled and zipped

HIS UNCLE PLANNED IT

Dale Hubbard, killed in self-defense by Wesley Everest on Armistice Day, 1919. F. B. Hubbard, lumber baron and uncle of the dead man, is held to have been the instigator of the plot in which his nephew was shot. Hubbard was martyrized by the lumber trust's determination "to let the men in uniform do it."

around them. Everest turned in his tracks and was off again like a flash, reloading his pistol as he ran. The mob again resumed the pursuit. The logger ran through an open gateway, paused to turn and again fire at his pursuers; then he ran between two frame dwellings to the open street. When the mob again caught the trail they were evidently under the impression that the logger's ammunition was exhausted. At all events they took up the chase with redoubled energy. Some men in the mob had rifles and now and then a pot-shot would be taken at the fleeing figure. The marksmanship of both sides seems to have been poor for no one appears to have been injured.

DALE HUBBARD

This kind of running fight was kept up until Everest reached the river. Having kept off his pursuers thus far the boy started boldly for the comparative security of the opposite shore, splashing the water violently as he waded out into the stream. The mob was getting closer all the time. Suddenly Everest seemed to

71

change his mind and began to retrace his steps to the shore. Here he stood dripping wet in the tangled grasses to await the arrival of the mob bent on his destruction. Everest had lost his hat and his wet hair stuck to his forehead. His ammunition was nearly gone. Eye witnesses declare his face still wore a quizzical half-bantering smile when the mob overtook him. With the pistol held loosely in his rough hand Everest stood at bay, ready to make a last stand for his life. Seeing him thus, and no doubt thinking his final bullet had been expended, the mob made a rush for its quarry.

"Stand back!" he shouted. "If there are 'bulls' in the crowd, I'll submit to arrest; otherwise lay off of me."

No attention was paid to his words. Everest shot from the hip four times,—then his gun stalled. A group of soldiers started to run in his direction. Everest was tugging at the gun with both hands. Raising it suddenly he took careful aim and fired. All the soldiers but one wavered and stopped. Everest fired twice, both bullets taking effect. But the soldier did not stop. Two more shots were fired almost point blank before the logger dropped his pursuer at his feet. Then he tossed away the empty gun and the mob surged upon him.

The legionaire who had been shot was Dale Hubbard, a nephew of F. B. Hubbard, the lumber baron. He was a strong, brave and misguided young man—worthy of a nobler death.

"LET'S FINISH THE JOB!"

Everest attempted to fight with his fists but was overpowered and severely beaten. Various men clamoured for immediate lynching, but saner counsel prevailed for the time and he was dragged through the streets towards the city jail. When the mob was half a block from this place the "hot heads" made another attempt to cheat the state executioner. A wave of fury seemed here to sweep the crowd. Men fought with one another for a chance to strike, kick or spit in the face of their victim. It was an orgy of hatred and blood-lust. Everest's arms were pinioned, blows, kicks and curses rained upon him from every side. One business man clawed strips of bleeding flesh from his face. A woman slapped his battered cheek with a well groomed hand. A soldier tried to lunge a hunting rifle at the helpless logger; the crowd was too thick. He bumped them aside with the butt of the gun to get room. Then he crashed the muzzle with full force into Everest's mouth. Teeth were broken and blood flowed profusely.

A rope appeared from somewhere. "Let's finish the job!" cried a voice. The rope was placed about the neck of the logger. "You haven't got guts enough to lynch a man in the daytime," was all he said.

At this juncture a woman brushed through the crowd and took the rope from Everest's neck. Looking into the distorted faces of the mob she cried indignantly, "You are curs and cowards to treat a man like that!"

There may be human beings in Centralia after all.

Wesley Everest was taken to the city jail and thrown without ceremony upon the cement floor of the "bull pen." In the surrounding cells were his comrades who had been arrested in the union hall. Here he lay in a wet heap, twitching with agony. A tiny bright stream of blood gathered at his side and trailed slowly along the floor. Only an occasional quivering moan escaped his torn lips as the hours slowly passed by.

"HERE IS YOUR MAN"

Later, at night, when it was quite dark, the lights of the jail were suddenly snapped off. At the same instant the entire city was plunged in darkness. A clamour of voices was heard beyond the walls. There was a hoarse shout as the panel of the outer door was smashed in. "Don't shoot, men," said the policeman on guard; "here is your man." It was night now, and the business men had no further reason for not lynching the supposed secretary. Everest heard their approaching footsteps in the dark. He arose drunkenly to meet them. "Tell the boys I died for my class," he whispered brokenly to the union men in the cells. These were the last words he uttered in the jail. There were sounds of a short struggle and of many blows. Then a door slammed and in a short time the lights were switched on. The darkened city was again illuminated at the same moment. Outside three luxurious automobiles were purring themselves out of sight in the darkness.

The only man who had protested the lynching at the last moment was William Scales. "Don't kill him, men," he is said to have begged of the mob. But it was too late. "If you don't go through with this you're an I. W. W. too," they told him. Scales could not calm the evil passions he had helped to arouse.

But how did it happen that the lights were turned out at such an opportune time? Could it be that city officials were working hand in glove with the lynch mob?

Defense Attorney Vanderveer offered to prove to the court

73

that such was the case. He offered to prove this was a part of the greater conspiracy against the union loggers and their hall, —offered to prove it point by point from the very beginning. Incidentally Vanderveer offered to prove that Earl Craft, electrician in charge of the city lighting plant, had left the station at seven o'clock on Armistice Day after securely locking the door; and that while Craft was away the lights of the city were turned off and Wesley Everest taken out and lynched. Furthermore, he offered to prove that when Craft returned, the lights were again turned on and the city electrician, his assistant and the Mayor of Centralia were in the building with the door again locked.

These offers were received by his honor with impassive judicial dignity, but the faces of the lumber trust attorneys were wreathed with smiles at the audacity of the suggestion. The corporation lawyers very politely registered their objections which the judge as politely sustained.

THE NIGHT OF HORRORS

After Everest had been taken away the jail became a nightmare—as full of horrors as a madman's dream. The mob howled around the walls until late in the night. Inside, a lumber trust lawyer and his official assistants were administering the "third degree" to the arrested loggers, to make them "confess." One at a time the men were taken to the torture chamber, and so terrible was the ordeal of this American Inquisition that some were almost broken—body and soul. Loren Roberts had the light in his brain snuffed out. Today he is a shuffling wreck. He is not interested in things any more. He is always looking around with horror-wide eyes, talking of "voices" and "wires" that no one but himself knows anything about. There is no telling what they did to the boy, but he signed the "confession."

When interviewed by Frank Walklin of the Seattle Union Record the loggers told the story in their own way:

"I have heard tales of cruelty," said James McInerney, "but I believe what we boys went through on those nights can never be equalled. I thought it was my last night in earth and had reconciled myself to an early death of some kind, perhaps hanging. I was taken out once by the mob, and a rope was placed around my neck and thrown over a cross-bar or something.

"I waited for them to pull the rope. But they didn't. I

heard voices in the mob say, 'That's not him,' and then I was put back into jail."

John Hill, Lamb, another defendant, related how several times a gun was poked through his cell window by someone who was aching to get a pot shot at him. Being ever watchful he hid under his bunk and close to the wall where the would-be murderer could not see him.

Britt Smith and Roy Becker told with bated breath about Everest as he lay half-dead in the corridor, in plain sight of the prisoners in the cells on both sides. The lights went out and Everest, unconscious and dying, was taken out. The men inside could hear the shouts of the mob diminishing as Everest was hurried to the Chehalis River bridge.

None of the prisoners was permitted to sleep that night; the

ARTHUR McELFRESH

A Centralia druggist. His wife warned him not to march to the union headquarters because "she knew he'd get hurt." McElfresh is the man said to have been shot inside the hall when the mob burst through the door.

fear of death was kept upon them constantly, the voices outside the cell windows telling of more lynchings to come.

"Every time I heard a footstep or the clanking of keys," said Britt Smith, "I thought the mob was coming after more of us. I didn't sleep, couldn't sleep; all I could do was strain my ears for the mob I felt sure was coming." Ray Becker, listening at Britt's side, said: "Yes, that was one hell of a night." And the strain of that night seems to linger in their faces; probably it always will remain—the expression of a memory that can never be blotted out.

When asked if they felt safer when the soldiers arrived to guard the Centralia jail, there was a long pause, and finally the answer was "Yes." "But you must remember," offered one, "that they took 'em out at Tulsa from a supposedly guarded jail; and we couldn't know from where we were what was going on outside."

"For ten days we had no blankets," said Mike Sheehan. "It was cold weather, and we had to sleep uncovered on concrete floors. In those days I had no more than three hours' sleep."

75

"The mob and those who came after the mob wouldn't let us sleep. They would come outside our windows and hurl curses at us, and tell each of us it would be our turn next. They brought in Wesley Everest and laid him on the corridor floor; he was bleeding from his ears and mouth and nose, was curled in a heap and groaning. And men outside and inside kept up the din. I tried to sleep; I was nearly mad; my temples kept pounding like sledge-hammers. I don't know how a man can go through all that and live—but we did."

All through the night the prisoners could hear the voices of the mob under their cell windows. "Well, we fixed that guy Everest all right," someone would say. "Now we'll get Roberts." Then the lights would snap off, there would be a shuffling, curses, a groan and the clanking of a steel door. All the while they were being urged to "come clean" with a statement that would clear the lumber trust of the crime and throw the blame onto its victims. McInerney's neck was scraped raw by the rope of the mob but he repeatedly told them to "go to hell!" Morgan, the stoolpigeon, escaped the torture by immediate acquiescence. Someone has since paid his fare to parts unknown. His "statement" didn't damage the defense.

THE HUMAN FIEND

But with the young logger who had been taken out into the night things were different. Wesley Everest was thrown, half unconscious, into the bottom of an automobile. The hands of the men who had dragged him there were sticky and red. Their pant legs were sodden from rubbing against the crumpled figure at their feet. Through the dark streets sped the three machines. The smooth asphalt became a rough road as the suburbs were reached. Then came a stretch of open country, with the Chehalis river bridge only a short distance ahead. The cars lurched over the uneven road with increasing speed, their headlights playing on each other or on the darkened highway.

Wesley Everest stirred uneasily. Raising himself slowly on one elbow he swung weakly with his free arm, strking one of his tormentors full in the face. The other occupants immediately seized him and bound his hands and feet with rope. It must have been the glancing blow from the fist of the logger that gave one of the gentlemen his fiendish inspiration. Reaching into his pocket he produced a razor. For a moment he fumbled over the now limp figure in the bottom of the car. His companions looked on with stolid acquiescence. Suddenly there was a piercing scream of pain. The figure gave a convulsive shudder of agony. After a moment Wesley Everest said in a weak v o i c e: "For Christ's sake, men; shoot me— don't let me suffer like this."

On the way back to Centralia, after the parade rope had done its deadly work, the gentleman of the razor alighted from the car in front of a little building. He asked leave to wash his hands. They were as red as a butcher's. Great clots of blood were adhering to his sleeves. "That's about the nastiest job I ever had to do," was his casual remark as he washed himself in the cool clear water of the Washington hills. The name of this man is known to nearly everybody in Centralia. He is still at large.

The headlight of the foremost car was now playing on the slender steel framework of the Chehalis river bridge. This machine crossed over and stopped, the second one reached the middle of the bridge and stopped while the third came to a halt when it had barely touched the plankwork on the near side. The well-dressed occupants of the first and last cars alighted and proceeded at once to patrol both approaches to the bridge.

WARREN O. GRIMM

Warren O. Grimm, killed at the beginning of the rush on the I. W. W. hall. At another raid on an I. W. W. hall in 1918 Grimm was said by a witness to have been in the mob, "waving two American flags and h o w l i n g like a dervish." Grimm's last words were reported to have been, "It served me right; I had no business there."

LYNCHING—AN AMERICAN INSTITUTION

Wesley Everest was dragged out of the middle machine. A rope was attached to a girder with the other end tied in a noose around his neck. His almost lifeless body was hauled to the side of the bridge. The headlights of two of the machines threw a white light over the horrible scene. Just as the lynchers let go of their victim the fingers of the half dead logger clung convulsively to the planking of the bridge. A business man stamped on them with a curse until the grip was broken. There was a swishing sound; then a sudden crunching jerk and the rope tied to the girder began to writhe and twist like a live thing. This lasted but a short time. The lynchers peered over the railing into the darkness. Then they slowly pulled up the dead body, attached a longer rope and repeated the performance. This did not seem to suit them either, so they again dragged the corpse through the railings and tied a still longer rope around the horribly broken neck of the dead logger. The business men were evidently enjoying their work, and besides, the more rope the more souvenirs for their friends, who would prize them highly.

This time the knot was tied by a young sailor. He knew how to tie a good knot and was proud of the fact. He boasted of the stunt afterwards to a man he thought as beastly as himself. In all probability he never dreamed he was talking for publication. But he was.

The rope had now been lengthened to about fifteen feet. The broken and gory body was kicked through the railing for the last time. The knot on the girder did not move any more. Then the lynchers returned to their luxurious cars and procured their rifles. A headlight flashed the dangling figure into ghastly relief. It was riddled with volley after volley. The man who fired the first shot boasted of the deed afterwards to a brother lodge member. He didn't know he was talking for publication either.

On the following morning the corpse was cut down by an unkrown hand. It drifted away with the current. A few hours later Frank Christiansen, a tool of the lumber trust from the Attorney General's office, arrived in Centralia. "We've got to get that body," this worthy official declared, "or the wobs will find it and raise hell over its condition."

The corpse was located after a search. It was not buried, however, but was carted back to the jail, there to be used as a terrible object lesson for the benefit of the incarcerated union men. The unrecognizable form was placed in a cell between two of the loggers who had loved the lynched boy as a comrade and a friend. Something must be done to make the union men admit that they, and not the lumber interests, had conspired to commit murder. This was the final act of ruthlessness. It was fruitful in results. One "confession," one Judas and one shattered mind were the result of their last deed of fiendish terrorism.

No undertaker could be found to bury Everest's body, so after two days it was dropped into a hole in the ground by four union loggers who had been arrested on suspicion and were released from jail for this purpose. The "burial" is supposed to have taken place in the new cemetery; the body being carried thither in an auto truck. The union loggers who really dug the grave declare, however, that the interment took place at a desolate spot "somewhere along the railroad track." Another body was seen, covered with ashes in a cart, being taken away for burial on the morning of the twelfth. There are persistent rumors that more than one man was lynched on the previous night. A guard of heavily armed soldiers had charge of the funeral. The grave has since been obliterated. Rumor has it that the body has since been removed to Camp Lewis. No one seems to know why or when.

"AS COMICAL AS A CORONER"

An informal inquest was held in the city jail. A man from Portland performed the autopsy; that is, he hung the body up by the heels and played a water hose on it. But the question of how Everest met death was never dealt with officially. The official inquest concerned itself only with the deaths of the four Legionaires. It was here that Dr. Bickford let slip the statement about the hall being raided before the shooting started. This was the first inkling of truth to reach the public. Coroner Livingstone, in a jocular mood, reported on Everest to a meeting of gentlemen at the Elks' Club. In explaining the death of the union logger, Dr. Livingstone stated that Wesley Everest had broken out of jail, gone to the Chehalis river bridge and jumped off with a rope around his neck. Finding the rope too short he climbed back and fastened on a longer one; jumped off again, broke his neck and then shot himself full of holes. Livingstone's audience, appreciative of his tact and levity, laughed long and heartily. Business men still chuckle over the joke in Centralia. "As funny as a funeral" is no longer the stock saying in this humorous little town; "as comical as a coroner" is now the approved form.

Acting on the theory that "a strong offensive is the best defense," the terrorists took immediate steps to conceal all traces of their crime and to shift the blame onto the shoulders of their victims. The capitalist press did yeoman service in this cause by deluging the nation with a veritable avalanche of lies.

For days the district around Centralia and the city itself were at the mercy of a mob. The homes of all workers suspected of being sympathetic to Labor were spied upon or surrounded and entered without warrant. Doors were battered down at times, and women and children abused and insulted. Many eyewitnesses of the tragedy were frightened into silence. Heavily

armed posses were sent out in all directions in search of "reds."
All roads were patrolled by armed business men in automobiles.
A strict mail and wire censorship was established. It was the
open season for "wobblies" and intimidation was the order of the
day. The White Terror was supreme.

So well organized was this Terror in Centralia that on the
evening of Armistice day appeals to informers had been posted
all over the city. The Citizens' Committee had already started
its campaign to obtain evidence against persons suspected of
being I. W. W.'s. Handbills and posters were plastered up ev-
erywhere calling on citizens to communicate with the chief of
police any information they might have regarding the shooting. The placards read:

"Have you any information of the whereabouts of an I. W.
W.? Any person having information no matter of how little importance concerning the whereabouts of a member of the I. W.
W. or any information whatever concerning the outrage committed Armistice day will confer a favor on the city officials if
they will call at once at the city
hall and give whatever data they
have to the chief of police. All
information will be treated strictly confidential. Office open at
8:30 a. m. Come at once."

All facts favoring the loggers
were suppressed. An Associated
Press reporter was compelled to
leave town hastily without bag or
baggage. Inadvertently he had
sent out Dr. Bickford's indiscreet
remark about the starting of the
trouble. Men and women did not
dare to think, much less think
aloud. Some of them in the district are still that way.

To Eugene Barnett's little
home came a posse armed to the
teeth. They asked for Barnett
and were told by his young wife
that he had gone up the hill with
his rifle. Placing a bayonet to her
breast they demanded entrance.
The brave woman refused to admit them until they had shown

TRIAL JUDGE

In his black robe, like a bird of prey,
he perched above the courtroom and ruled
always adversely to the cause of labor.
Appointed to try men accused of killing
other men whom he had previously eulog-
ized Judge John M. Wilson did not dis-
appoint those who appointed him. In open
court Vanderveer told this man: "There
was a time when I thought your rulings
were due to ignorance of the law. That
will no longer explain them."

80

a warrant. Barnett surrendered when he made sure he was to be arrested and not mobbed.

O. C. Bland, Bert Bland, John Lamb and Loren Roberts were also apprehended in due time. Two loggers, John Doe Davis and Ole Hanson, who were said to have also fired on the mob, have not yet been arrested. A vigorous search is still being made for them in all parts of the country. It is believed by many that one of these men was lynched like Everest on the night of November 11th.

HYPOCRISY AND TERROR

The reign of terror was extended to cover the entire West coast. Over a thousand men and women were arrested in the state of Washington alone. Union halls were closed and kept that way. Labor papers were suppressed and many men have been given sentences of from one to fourteen years for having in their possession copies of periodicals which contained little else but the truth about the Centralia tragedy. The Seattle Union Record was temporarily closed down and its stock confiscated for daring to hint that there were two sides to the story. During all this time the capitalist press was given full rein to spread its infamous poison. The general public, denied the true version of the affair, was shuddering over its morning coffee at the thought of I. W. W. desperadoes shooting down unoffending paraders from ambush. But the lumber interests were chortling with glee and winking a suggestive eye at their high priced lawyers who were making ready for the prosecution. Jurymen were shortly to be drawn and things were "sitting pretty," as they say in poker.

Adding a characteristic touch to the rotten hypocrisy of the situation came a letter from Supreme Court Judge McIntosh to George Dysart, whose son was in command of a posse during the manhunt. This notable document read as follows:

Kenneth McIntosh, Judge of the Supreme Court,
State of Washington.

George Dysart, Esq.,   Olympia, November 13, 1919.
Centralia, Washington.

My dear Dysart:

I want to express to you my appreciation of the high character of citizenship displayed by the people of Centralia in their agonizing calamity. We are all shocked by the manifestation of barbarity on the part of the outlaws, and are depressed by the

81

loss of lives of brave men, but at the same time we are proud
of the calm control and loyalty to American ideals demonstrated
by the returned soldiers and citizens. I am proud to be an in-
habitant of a state which contains a city with the record which
has been made for Centralia by its law-abiding citizens.

Sincerely,

(Signed)   KENNETH McINTOSH.

"PATRIOTIC" UNION SMASHING

Not to be outdone by this brazen example of judicial perver-
sion, Attorney General Thompson, after a secret conference of
prosecuting attorneys, issued a circular of advice to county prosecutors. In this document the suggestion was made that officers
and members of the Industrial Workers of the World in Washington be arrested by the wholesale under the "criminal syndicalism" law and brought to trial simultaneously so that they
might not be able to obtain legal defense. The astounding recommendation was also made that, owing to the fact that juries
had been "reluctant to convict," prosecutors and the State Bar
Association should co-operate in examining jury panels so that
"none but courageous and patriotic Americans" be given places
on the juries.

This effectual if somewhat arbitrary plan was put into opera-
tion at once. Since the tragedy at Centralia dozens of union
workers have been convicted by "courageous and patriotic" juries and sentenced to serve from one to fourteen years in the
state penitentiary. The verdict at Montesano is now widely
known. Truly the lives of the four Legion boys which were
sacrificed by the lumber interests in furtherance of their own
murderous designs, were well expended. The investment was
a profitable one and the results are no doubt highly gratifying.

But just the same the scheme of the Attorney General
was an obvious effort to defeat the purposes of the courts and
obtain unjust convictions by means of what is termed "jury
"fixing." There may be honor among thieves but there is plainly
none among the public servants they have working for them!

The only sane note sounded during these dark days, outside
of the startling statement of Dr. Bickford, came from Montana.
Edward Bassett, commander of the Butte Post of the American
Legion and an overseas veteran, issued a' public statement that
was truly remarkable:

"The I. W. W. in Centralia, Wash., who fired upon the men

that were attempting to raid the I. W. W. headquarters, were fully justified in their act.

"Mob rule in this country must be stopped, and when mobs attack the home of a millionaire, of a laborer, or of the I. W. W., it is not only the right but the duty of the occupants to resist with every means in their power. If the officers of the law can not stop these raids, perhaps the resistance of the raided may have that effect.

"Whether the I. W. W. is a meritorious organization or not, whether it is unpopular or otherwise, should have absolutely nothing to do with the case. The reports of the evidence at the coroner's jury show that the attack was made before the firing started. If that is true, I commend the boys inside for the action that they took.

"The fact that there were some American Legion men among the paraders who everlastingly disgraced themselves by taking part in the raid, does not affect my judgment in the least. Any one who becomes a party to a mob bent upon unlawful violence, cannot expect the truly patriotic men of the American Legion to condone his act."

PREPARATIONS FOR THE TRIAL

Defense Attorney George Vanderveer hurried across the continent from Chicago to take up the legal battle for the lives of the eleven men who had been arrested and charged with the murder of Warren O. Grimm. Vanderveer was at one time prosecutor for King County, Washington. He and two others were the only attorneys who dared to come to the defense of the persecuted I. W. W. Class feeling was keen all along the west coast. The Lewis County Bar Association pledged its members not to defend any I. W. W., no matter how slight the charge. Following the Centralia tragedy the Attorney General at Olympia had ordered the arrest of all I. W. W. members found anywhere within the boundaries of the state. It was under these conditions that the trial started, Vanderveer having but two days in which to prepare the legal defense for his clients.

The lumber interests had already selected six of their most trustworthy tools as prosecutors. Herman Allen, the prosecuting attorney for Lewis County, where the mob lawlessness took place, was discarded or at least shoved into the background as a lightweight. The real coup de force was directed and handled

by W. H. Abel and C. D. Cunningham—both lawyers for the lumber trust. Lewis county is reputed
to have paid them $5,000 each
for their services. Abel is Hubbard's man—serving the Eastern
Railway and Lumber Company;
Cunningham is attorney for
the West Coast Lumbermen's
Association. Hubbard is a lumber
baron and has the reputation of
being the most bitter anti-union
man on the Pacific Coast. He was
a leader in the 1917 drive to im-
pose low wages and mediæval
conditions upon the loggers in his
district. At this time he was president of the Employers' Association of the State of Washington.
Abel, who also has made himself
hated as a lumber baron, was
very active in opposing the union
loggers during the strike of 1917.
At this time he functioned as a
special deputy sheriff. These two
worthies and four others of similar
stripe had the full support, moral and financial, of the lumber
companies and the authorities in their efforts to break the necks
of the eleven loggers. For two and one-half months they had
been building up a case which they boasted would be "unbeat-
able." The White Terror ruled supreme in Washington. Back
of these prosecutors were the business interests with unlimited
funds. The subservient officials of the state were with them to
a man. Then, too, there were the lawless elements among the
American Legion.

THE JUDGE SOMERSAULTS

Centralia and adjoining towns were deluged with lumber
trust propaganda. Newspaper articles and leaflets appeared
every day vilifying the defendants, denouncing the defense
attorney and attacking the motives of anyone who had a good
word to say about the defense end of the case. One leaflet

went so far as to say that the juryman who did not vote 'guilty' was a 'traitor.' Open threats were made against the life of Vanderveer.

The defense attorney applied for a change of venue so that the case would not be tried in Lewis County, in which the tragedy occurred. Montesano, seat of Gray's Harbor County, was chosen; Montesano was not favorable to the I. W.W. by any means. A few years previously the business element had clubbed the union loggers from the city with pick handles. But Montesano, at this time, compared with other possible trial scenes, seemed preferable. However, in the weeks that preceded the trial, the lumber trust so infected the entire Gray's Harbor country that Montesano seemed to be as bad as the other cities from the standpoint of a fair and unprejudiced trial. Vanderveer again applied for a change of

LEWIS COUNTY'S LEGAL LIGHT THAT FAILED

Herman Allen, prosecuting attorney of Lewis County. He stood at the corner during the raid and received papers stolen from the hall. There is no record of his having protested against any illegal action. He turned over his office to the special prosecutors and acted as their tool throughout. During the entire trial he never appeared as an active participant.

venue. This was granted by Judge George Abel. Judge Wilson of Thurston County had a short time previously delivered a patriotic eulogy of the slain members of the Legion. This was on December 7, in the Elks' hall where the conspiracy was hatched. Judge Wilson was known to be strongly biased in favor of the prosecution. Judge Abel was then disqualified to hear the case for the reason that his brother W. H. Abel had been selected as one of the prosecutors. This left Judge Ben Sheeks of Gray's Harbor County as the logical man to preside. At the last moment Judge Wilson was foisted on the case over the head of Judge Sheeks, and Montesano, because of a peculiar chain of circumstances, was selected as the scene of the coming trial. The lumber interests had reason to rejoice. Attorney Vanderveer immediately asked for another change of venue. Tacoma or Olympia were indicated as possible cities in which a fair trial might be held. This was on January 3, 1920.

85

Judge Wilson at first seemed inclined to do the right thing, —but the ways of judges are incomprehensible. After listening to the argument for a change of venue he stated, "I have come to the conclusion that the defendants must not—could not—be tried in Montesano." A fair and obviously truthful statement. Things looked brighter for the defense.

Five days later Judge Wilson completely reversed his former position. He turned a complete somersault and stated that the case must be tried in Montesano. On the same day threats were made in Montesano that the defendants, if acquitted, would never get out of the county alive. Upon hearing the decision Vanderveer told the court, "No verdict can come out of Grays Harbor County for which the public can have any respect."

MONTESANO CLUTCHED BY REACTION

Montesano is a small and hostile lumber trust town located in the misty Gray's Harbor region forty miles northwest of Centralia, where the tragedy occurred. As a result of the vicious anti-labor propaganda of the lumber trust the atmosphere was tense and the town full of open hatred for the defendants. "Respectability" was in complete control. I. W. W. members were arrested on sight and sympathy for the loggers had long since been cowed into silence. The streets were full of Legionaires and gunmen. Black looks were directed at strangers from all directions. There were no hotel accomodations for defense witnesses, nor was it considered safe for them to be invited to come to Montesano. Attorney Vanderveer was ejected from a hotel when he attempted to engage a suite of rooms for a legal headquarters. Reporters for labor newspapers were given to understand their presence would not be tolerated. So the defense moved to Aberdeen, sixteen miles away, and made the trip to Montesano daily by means of auto stages.

In the meantime the forces of reaction elsewhere in the State of Washington had not been idle. Backed by all the forces of law and order the lumber trust Janizaries proceeded to hamper defense work in every way. Defense offices were raided and their fixtures destroyed or seized. Defense investigators and persons raising funds for defense purposes were intimidated or arrested and deported. Prospective defense witnesses were handled in a like manner. Attorney Ralph Pierce who had been sent from Seattle by the I. W. W. to safeguard the interests of the defendants was run out of town. The printing plants of the Seattle Union Record and the Industrial Worker of Seattle

STATE OF WASHINGTON   )
) ss.
COUNTY OF GRAYS HARBOR)

               E. E. TORPEN, being first duly sworn on
oath, deposes and says: That he was one of the jurors in the case
of the State of Washington, as plaintiff, vs. Britt Smith, et al,
as defendants, tried in the Superior Court of Washington, for
Grays Harbor County, during the first three months of the year
1920, as an outgrowth of the Armistice tragedy at Centralia,
Washington, November,11, 1919; that when the jury retired to the
jury room to deliberate upon their verdict, it was suggested by one
of the jurors, whose name I am now unable to recollect, that the
jury take a trial ballot to ascertain the sentiment of each juror
before any discussion was had; a ballot was then taken and it was
unanimous in favor of acquitting the defendants in the case.

       That the jury finally decided on the verdict as rendered be-
cause of the understanding the jurors had one with another that
they would recommend extreme leniency to the court in rendering
his sentence upon the defendants, and this was agreed to by all
of the jurors, and the verdict would not have been agreed to but
for that understanding.

       I verily believe, also, that if these men had not been affili-
ated with the I. W. W. organization they would never have been convicted of the crime as charged.AND MODIFIED BY THE VERDICT.

                         E. E. Torpen

Subscribed and sworn to before me this 17th day of May, 1922.

                                 Notary Public in and for
                                 the State of Washington,
                                 residing at Montesano.

were closed, the purpose evidently being to choke out all publicity that might reflect favorably upon the case of the loggers whose lives were at stake.

Many wage workers in Washington wished to contribute money to the defense fund, but all caught in the execution of this heinous crime were discharged. The lumber trust, on the other hand, by means of blackmail and intimidation, attempted to raise money for certain little expenses that could not stand a very close scrutiny. An incident at the Monarch coal mine near Centralia is an example in point.

The workers at this mine were given to understand they must either "kick in" for this purpose or lose their jobs. They contributed, but in order to protest the blackmailing process and to show which side they sympathized with they sent a bigger donation to the defense. When the fact became known every man in the mine was discharged. The prosecution even went so far as to enter the rooms of the defense attorney to rifle brief cases and desks there and to steal mail. A letter to Attorney Vanderveer from Rev. T. T. Edmunds was obtained in this manner and actually introduced as evidence in the trial.

BY ALL MEANS—UNIFORMS!

Even with the dice loaded against the defense the lumber trust head hunters were not satisfied. A touch of color was needed to give the hand of class persecution the proper aspect of patriotism and respectability. Special Prosecutor C. D. Cunningham telegraphed to Congressman Albert Johnson at Washington, D. C., as follows:

"Ex-service men desire to wear uniforms at I. W. W. trial at Montesano. Is there any federal law to prohibit?"

To which Congressman Johnson replied:

"The act of February 28, 1918, specifically permits the wearing of uniforms by honorably discharged soldiers, providing that a distinctive mark of indicating discharge be shown. War Department by regulations dated April 2, 1919, designated a red chevron as that mark. Therefore former soldiers have a clear legal right to wear uniform with red chevron at I. W. W. trial."

Nearly two weeks were consumed by the task of selecting a jury. One hundred talesmen were examined before the panel was completed. The prosecution, including the court, made every effort to see to it that men were excluded who showed any inclination to be fair. A man named Connors, for instance, was passed by the prosecution after admitting that one of the prosecutors was handling a law suit for him in which $14,000 was involved. Another man admitted saying that the defendants were guilty and should be hanged. The court refused to remove him for cause. This man and others who swore they hated the I. W. W. were passed by Judge Wilson, to be removed only by peremptory challenge.

The courtroom, in the early stages of the trial, was at all times crowded with men in uniform. Some of these were bold enough to intrude beyond the railing into the space reserved for the principals in the trial. As a result of Vanderveer's protest these were finally ordered to take seats with the spectators. Here they procured seats as much in prominence as possible and sat with folded arms, frowning and glowering at prospective jurors as the examination progressed. It is reported that five hundred of these legionaires were in Montesano during the trial. In the beginning fifty a day were detailed to the courtroom. All legionaires were paid four dollars per day out of the "slush fund" of the lumber interests to "stick around." Attorney Vanderveer protested vigorously but without result. They remained in decreasing numbers until the last day of the trial. Many of those who left early admitted that their manhood had been shocked upon discovering from the evidence of the trial, what dirty work they had been trapped into doing.

POINTS AT ISSUE

The two outstanding points at issue in the case were these: 1—Which side was the aggressor? 2—Did Eugene Barnett fire the shot which killed Warren O. Grimm? The defense claimed, and had testimony from both sides to prove, that the ex-service men precipitated the trouble by starting to attack the union hall; the prosecution claimed and offered their own kind of testimony to prove that the industrialists fired in cold blood and according to a premeditated plan upon the unoffending paraders. The prosecution offered no reason nor intent for the volley. The defense claimed the loggers fired simply in self-defense when attacked by superior numbers; that they had been warned of such an attack and that, under the law they had full right to prepare for such defense—with guns if necessary—if they had reason to fear their lives and property were about to be destroyed by a lawless mob. The defense claimed that Eugene Barnett was unarmed and in the Roderick Hotel, next door to the I. W. W. hall, at the time the raid took place; the prosecution, by means of an absurd chain of seemingly made-to-order evidence, sought to place Barnett in the Avalon Hotel, nearly three hundred feet away.

FACTS WITHHELD FROM JURY

Judge Wilson permitted the prosecution to introduce freely all evidence which tended to support the theory that the I. W. W. members had fired upon innocent passing soldiers; but he refused to permit the defense to introduce any evidence regarding the previous raid on the older hall or the conspiracy hatched in the Elks' Club to raid the new hall on Armistice Day. The defense was prohibited from presenting any of the following facts to the jury:

That 100 Centralia business men had met in the Elks' hall on the night of October 20, 1919, and laid plans to drive the I. W. W. out of town.

That the county prosecutor and the chief of police informed the meeting that the I. W. W. had committed no violation of law and could not lawfully be banished.

That F. B. Hubbard, lumber mill owner, then declared: "This is a damned outrage. If I were chief of police I would have the wobblies out of here within 24 hours."

That William Scales, local commander of the American Legion, who presided at the business men's meeting, said that while he did not favor raiding the I. W. W. hall, he was certain that no American jury would convict anyone who might raid it.

That there had been a previous attack upon an I. W. W. hall in Centralia on Memorial Day, 1918, this attack being made by the tail end of a Red Cross parade and being led by F. B. Hubbard, who appropriated a desk taken from that hall.

That on this occasion the raiders went through the I. W. W. quarters "like a swarm of rats," dragged industrial unionists outside, lifted them by the ears onto motor trucks, and transported them to the next county, warning them never to come back.

That Blind Tom Lassiter, a man who sold I. W. W. newspapers, suffered the loss of his news stand and all his possessions by burning at the hands of a mob; and that Lassiter subsequently was kidnaped by business men on the main street of Centralia in daylight, thrown into an automobile, and dumped into a ditch in the next county.

That the I. W. W. had been warned that their hall would be raided on Armistice Day, had asked for police protection, and were denied it.

That when this happened the local I. W. W. secretary issued 1000 handbills, appealing to the law-abiding citizens of Centralia for a square deal; and that these handbills were carried to practically every house in the town.

Judge Wilson took the peculiar position that the defense must first show an overt act on the part of Warren Grimm b e f o r e h e would permit the introduction of any evidence tending to show conspiracy by him and his fellow marchers. Nor would be admit any testimony concerning any utterance or action o f Warren Grimm in connection with the carrying out of the plan to raid the I. W. W. hall, on the ground that some special physical movement of the man must be shown before the shooting actually started. It was not sufficient to show that Grimm was close to the doorway of the hall and that he fell wounded in the front rank of the attacking party.

ANOTHER SPECIAL PROSECUTOR

W. H. Abel, sounded the gamut of rottenness in his efforts to convict the accused men without the semblance of a fair trial. Abel is notorious throughout Washington as the hireling of the lumber interests. In 1917 he prosecuted "without fee" all laboring men on strike and is attorney for a lumber company operating a camp known as the Cosmopolis "penitentiary," so-called on account of the brutality with which it treats employes. Located in Montesano, Abel has made a fortune prosecuting labor cases for the special interests.

A LITTLE INTIMIDATION

Two defense witnesses testified that Grimm was in the very doorway of the union hall just before the shots were fired from the inside. These were Guy Bray, 16, and Jay Cooke, 41. Bray testified that he was related by marriage to Lieut. Frank Van Gilder, second in command in the parade. Shortly before the procession started, Bray said, he saw Van Gilder walking with a large man in uniform. Bray asked Van Gilder who the man was, and Van Gilder said it was Warren Grimm. The witness described the parade in its essential points. As the ex-service men halted, he declared, he saw two men break from the rear ranks and rush toward the hall. They kicked in the door, he said, and then the shooting began. "Van Gilder and the large

91

man he had said was Grimm were then five or ten feet north of the hall door," Bray told the jury. "I saw the large man suddenly put both hands to his stomach, and double up."

Jay Cooke testified similarly with regard to Grimm's presence in the doorway of the hall. As they left the courtroom after testifying, both Cooke and Bray were arrested on charges of perjury, and efforts were made to break down Bray's testimony by means of the third degree. But obviously these arrests were made for their psychological effect, inasmuch as the two witnesses were never tried for perjury, the case against them being dropped after the I. W. W. trial had ended.

Frank Van Gilder, lifelong friend of Warren O. Grimm, testified that he stood beside Grimm while the latter was shot. "He hands over his abdomen and cried, 'Oh, God, I'm shot!'" "Something seemed to jar him,"

THE STATE'S CONTRIBUTION

Frank P. Christensen, who was the "fixer" for the prosecution. As Assistant Attorney General he used his office to intimidate witnesses and in the effort to cover up actions of the mob. He is reported to have been responsible for the recovery and burial of Everest's body, saying: "We've got to bring in that body and bury it. If the wobs ever find out what was done and get it they'll raise hell and make capital of it."

Van Gilder continued. "He turned very pale. I said, 'Are you hit?' and he said, 'Yes.' I told him to go to the hospital and he started across the street and when he had gone a few paces he bent over, his hands on his stomach, but went across."

According to Van Gilder's testimony this incident is supposed to have taken place a considerable distance from the hall. It was very necessary for the prosection that no one know definitely where Grimm went after being wounded. Van Gilder fell into the trap set for him by Attorney Vanderveer. He realized it too late. When asked where Grimm had gone, Van Gilder stammered, that he didn't know; he turned away and left him.

Lieutenant Van Gilder's testimony for the prosecution sought to place Grimm about half a block away from the union hall. Van Gilder explained Grimm's act of dropping out of the line of march by saying that Grimm had fallen back to remind the military sections to salute the old soldiers in the reviewing stand, and later rejoined him at the head of the ex-service men. He swore that Grimm was shot while facing southeast, and while his back was toward the hall. Attorney Vanderveer argued that Van Gilder's testimony was open to question on this point: That Van Gilder, a soldier, unhurt, did not even offer to help his mortally stricken comrade to safety. Any normal man under such circumstances would have aided his friend. In fact, in war time, soldiers are decorated for bravery for just such deeds. If Van Gilder is to be accepted as normal, Vanderveer continued, then one must conclude that Grimm wasn't at Van Gilder's side when the former was shot, but that he was where Bray and Cooke testified they saw him—in the doorway of the I. W. W. hall.

"EXCITEMENT—WHEN WE TURN BACK"

Van Gilder had said that Grimm had dropped back to remind the marchers to salute the old soldiers **in the reviewing stand.** Joseph Smith, of Chehalis, an overseas veteran and a participant in the march, gave vital testimony for the defense bearing on this point. While the parade was being formed, he said, the commander of the Chehalis division instructed his men to be ready, when they reached the reviewing stand, to give the "eyes right" salute—a quick turning of the head to the right.

They never came to any reviewing stand, Smith said, and evidently there wasn't any. Along the line of march, while going north, another marcher named Shields or Scales, turned to Smith and said, "You'll see lots of excitement after we turn to come back." Later a man who had been pointed out to Smith as Lieutenant Grimm came along the line, Smith declared, and one of the marchers called out, "How about that reviewing stand?" . . . "Will there be anything doing when we start back?" some other marcher asked Grimm. . . . "Sure there will," Grimm replied according to Smith.

THE STOOL PIGEON

Tom Morgan, who turned state's evidence. There is an historical precedent for Morgan. Judas acted similarly, but Judas later had the manhood to go out and hang himself. Morgan left for "parts unknown."

93

LT. FRANK VAN GILDER

Lifelong friend of Warren O. Grimm, who was killed near doorway of union hall. "I stood less than two feet from Grimm when he was shot," Van Gilder testified. "He doubled up, put his hands to his stomach and said to me, 'My God, I'm shot.' "What did you do then?" "I turned and left him."

"While coming back," Smith stated, "Herman Gibbons, another marcher, said to me: 'We are going to give the Wobbly hall eyes right as we go by.' At the Wobbly hall this command was given. Then I saw the men break ranks,' leap out and run toward the hall. I saw them kick in the door. Then the shots came."

The defense produced almost a hundred witnesses. These came from all walks of life. There were professional men, soldiers, workers, business men and even school children. Some came from the ranks of the marchers themselves. There is no reason to doubt the motives back of the statements made by these witnesses. It took courage to appear in court and speak in favor of men hated, as the defendants were by the predatory and respectable elements in the community. The mere fact that a hundred reputable citizens think enough of truth and fair dealing to tell the truth under such circumstances should convince even the most skeptical that there are two sides to the question.

DR. BICKFORD "SPILLS THE BEANS"

Not all the favorable evidence came from the side of the defense. Some of it was wrung from the reluctant lips of the prosecution witnesses—any amount, in fact, as the records will show. Dr. Frank Bickford, for instance, repeated his startling testimony given before the coroner's jury. Dr. Bickford, it will be remembered, was one of the marchers. He was immediately in front of the union hall at the time the trouble started. Dr. Bickford stated before the coroner's jury as follows: "I spoke up and said I would lead if enough would follow but before I could take the lead there were many ahead of me. Someone next to me put his foot against the door and forced it open, after which a shower of bullets poured through the opening about us."

Many others, ex-service men and paraders like Dr. Bickford,

testified that the union hall had been attacked before the shooting started. "There was a rush for the door, a crash of glass, then the shots from the interior of the hall." This is the invariable story. So evident was the truthfulness of this story that the prosecution, towards the end of the trial, simply gave up trying to rebut it, limiting their case to the fact that men had been killed on Armistice Day and relying upon the passion and prejudice of the moment to obtain their conviction.

The loggers were accused of conspiring to murder Warren O. Grimm. That is why the matter of Grimm's whereabouts is of such prime importance to both sides. If he were shot in cold blood while in the ranks of the paraders, as the prosecution claims, then the case of the defense is made hopeless and the men were guilty and justly convicted. If, on the other hand, Grimm was shot down while attempting to make illegal entry with an infuriated mob into a peaceful union hall, then Grimm alone is to blame for what happened.

WITNESSES SAW GRIMM IN DOORWAY OF HALL

Ten witnesses at least were unanimous in stating Grimm's location at the time he met his death. Grimm was a massively built man, over six feet in height. He was an officer, in officer's uniform, and the only one of the paraders to be shot in the abdomen. All of these witnesses have traced this conspicuous figure from the front of the union hall at the moment of the shooting, to the rear of a nearby soft drink stand. Two witnesses saw Grimm examine and display his wound at this place. All describe him as a big man running in a stooping posture, holding his hands over his abdomen. The following testimony is typical on this. point:

Mrs. A. Sherman, when questioned by Attorney Vanderveer stated that she was in front of the Roderick hotel when the parade was passing the. I.W.W. hall. She saw the soldiers in the parade make a break for the hall. About five men smashed in the door, she said, but she could not remember just how many came after. The crash of glass and the shooting were heard by her at about the same time. She also described a man who had evidently been shot in front of the hall as a large man wearing a soldier's overcoat. He was holding his arms across his stomach and went towards Second Street.

Walter Morell, a logger and Legion man, said he was marching in the parade and his platoon stopped in front of the union hall. He was talking to a marcher named Eubanks, who said something about raiding the hall. He heard someone in the rear say, "Let's go," which was followed by a crash of glass. He saw Grimm, doubled up and holding his stomach with his arms, nearly in front of the hall and some distance from where the prosecution said he was shot.

BRIDGE FROM WHICH EVEREST WAS HANGED

From this bridge, over the Chehalis River, Wesley Everest was left dangling by a mob of business men. Automobile parties visited this spot at different times during the night and played their headlights on the corpse in order better to enjoy the spectacle.

Vernon O'Reilly, high school boy, related clearly all that happened within his range of vision. He was just south of Second Street when the parade was opposite the I. W. W. hall. He said he saw the men break ranks and rush the hall. At first, he said, the men in the ranks seemed to be holding conference and soon after that they started for the hall. He heard the crash of glass and immediately afterwards, the shooting which he thought came from inside the hall. He located on the map which was in the courtroom about where he saw a large man who was holding his arms across his stomach. The location on the map was in front of the Roderick hotel. Later he saw the same man being loaded on an automobile at the corner of Second Street and Tower Avenue.

Guy Bray's testimony, which was touched upon before, was exceedingly damaging to the case of the prosecution. Bray stated that he was just north of the union hall at the time of the shooting. He saw the parade go by with Grimm and Van Gilder in the lead. He saw the lines halt in front of the hall on the return. "The soldiers bunched together," testified the boy, "two of them rushed toward the hall and smashed in the door. Two shots were fired, then more shots followed. There were quite a few soldiers there at that time. I saw Grimm and Van Gilder close together near the door of the hall and then in front of the Roderick. I saw Grimm grip his stomach with both hands and fall down."

Referring to the arrest of Bray and Jay Cooke for perjury, the Seattle Union Record commented editorially as follows:

"If this sort of tactics can be pursued by a prosecution in our state, what is law, what is trial by jury, what are witnesses? Prosecutor Abel has made a jest of these things. He deserves the contempt of all decent Americans."

The prosecution elaborated upon what it termed the "premeditated conspiracy" on the part of the loggers to fire into the parade. This is based in part upon the statement of the stoolpigeon Morgan and the "confession" of Loren Roberts and from admissions by the defense that shots were fired from Seminary hill and the Arnold and Avalon hotels after the hall had been attacked. As Warren Grimm was actually killed, the prosecution at first based its case upon the contention that the loggers had conspired beforehand to do this very thing. Afterwards they were glad to qualify this by stating that the loggers had done a legal act in an illegal manner. But until the very last when the props were knocked from under their made-to-order case the prosecution attempted to prove that the 38-55 bullet which killed Grimm was fired from the Avalon hotel. Some one of the defendants had to be placed in this hotel to fire the fatal shot. Eugene Barnett was selected from the other defendants for this purpose—one guess being as good as another.

THE PROSECUTION "IDENTIFIES"

Eugene Barnett was accused of firing from a window of the Avalon hotel, some 300 feet from the union hall. Elsie Hornbeck, bookkeeper in a garage across the street from the hotel told the jury that she saw a thin faced man in the hotel window on Armistice Day shortly before the shooting. This is the way Elsie deported herself on the witness stand:

"Could you identify him (Barnett) if you saw him now?" asked Special Prosecutor Abel.

"I might," the girl answered.

"Look at these defendants and then tell me."

Elsie scanned the defendants briefly, and after considerable hesitation, said: "It was the first one."

The 'first one' was Eugene Barnett, who the prosecution contended was at the window of the Avalon hotel, firing.

The tragedy had occurred three months previously and the witness had not been acquainted with Barnett. Vanderveer asked her if she had seen Barnett since the time she claimed to have seen him in the window. The witness said she had not. She admitted that she saw the man in the Avalon for only a fleeting instant.

CARTING AWAY WESLEY EVEREST'S BODY FOR BURIAL

After the mutilated body had been cut down it lay in the river for two days. Then it was taken back to the city jail where it remained for two days more—as an object lesson—in plain view of the comrades of the murdered boy. Everest was taken from this building to be lynched. During the first week after the tragedy this jail was the scene of torture and horror that equalled the worst days of the Spanish inquisition.

"How did you know he was in this line of men?" demanded Vanderveer. "How were you able to pick him out so quickly? You never looked at the other end of the line at all. How did you know that he was there at all?"

Vanderveer fired all this at her at once. The girl was nervous, hesitant in her replies, as indeed she was throughout the whole cross examination by the counsel for the defense.

Elsie Hornbeck looked hopelessly at Special Prosecutor Abel.

"He looks more like the man I saw in the window than any of the rest," she said in answer to Vanderveer's question.

"Knowing that it is a matter of a man's life or his death," said Vanderveer, "still you say under oath that Eugene Barnett is the man you saw in the Avalon window?"

Elsie Hornbeck lowered her eyes. She was breathing heavily and was a pitiful figure. Her eyes lifted and turned toward Abel.

"Look at me!" thundered Vanderveer. "Answer my question. Will you swear that Barnett is the man?"

"Yes."

Then Vanderveer by skillful questioning brought out the fact that she had been visited several times by persons in behalf of the prosecution; once it was an American Legion man.

"Were you ever shown a photograph of Barnett?" Vanderveer demanded.

"Yes." Presently she admitted she had seen two photographs.

"And when I asked you if you had ever seen Barnett since three months ago you answered no," said Vanderveer. "Look at

Barnett," he commanded. She obeyed. "Is he thin faced?"

"Well, his face isn't fat," she said.

Barnett's face is actually full; no one with good eyesight would ever describe him as thin faced. Eisie Hornbeck said that the first photograph of Barnett was brought to her by the American Legion man; the second, apparently a duplicate of the first, was shown her by Frank Christiansen from the state attorney general's office. Christiansen was one of the special prosecutors.

The girl left the stand in an almost fainting condition.

ANOTHER "IDENTIFICATION"

The thing that "identified" Barnett was not his physiognomy but his seat in the courtroom. Barnett was not thin faced, as Elsie Hornbeck had testified. His face is full and oval in shape as all photographs of him reveal, both on November 11th and during the trial. This is plain even in the picture taken of him after he had been in the hands of the mob for three days.

It is evident that the prosecution "schooled" this witness. But how was it done? The courtroom was connected with the corridor where the witnesses were held by means of a door with glass panels. Witnesses were seen to be observing the defendants on their straight backed bench frequently during the early days of the trial. Perhaps this fact throws some light on the subject.

Charles Briffett was a Port Angeles man. He claimed to have been in Centralia on Armistice Day. He said he had seen Barnett leave the alley at the rear of the Avalon hotel cramming cartridges into his rifle—a 38-55 calibre. Briffett was also very prompt in making the identification of Eugene Barnett, stating promptly that Barnett was the third defendant from the end of the row. Barnett was the third from the end. The marvel of it was how witnesses could identify him without hardly looking in his direction. Briffett did not know Barnett by sight. It had been months since he had seen the man with the rifle, and then only for a brief instant and during a moment of intense excitement. But Briffett was positive. Subsequently he was appointed by Governor Hart to the soft job of being superintendent of the Boys' Industrial School at Chehalis.

ELKS CLUB, CENTRALIA

It was here that the Centralia conspiracy was hatched and the "secret committee" appointed to arrange for the raid.

THE PROSECUTION FAILS TO IDENTIFY!

Two strikes on the defense! Attorney Vanderveer was "grooved," but he kept on smiling.

Leila Tripp was the third of these extraordinary witnesses. She mounted the witness chair with considerable assurance. The prosecutors were smiling broadly. Vanderveer's face went grim for a moment. Then he smiled again. Leila Tripp was telling the prosecutors about the man she had seen on Armistice Day. The usual "identification" was about to be asked for. It was 10:25—just a few minutes before the recess time. Vanderveer had been careful to stand between the witness and the defendants all the while Leila was on the stand. Now he asked the judge for a recess. It was granted. Grouping the defendants about him with their backs to Leila and the prosecutors, Vanderveer went into consultation. The faces of the group could not be seen by anyone excepting members of their own circle. Court reconvened and the defendants resumed their seats. Leila's face still beamed with self assurance but the faces of the prosecutors registered dismay. The defendants had changed places with one another!

Prosecutor Abel did not ask Leila Tripp to pick out the man she had seen. Instead he resorted to another trick.

"Eugene Barnett, stand up," he commanded sharply.

"Oh, no!" snapped Vanderveer, "I object to any more of this kind of stuff."

Judge Wilson sustained the objection. Leila didn't make her identification.

Then Vanderveer started a cross examination that was grilling. The girl admitted that she was excited when she saw the man in the alley and that she really didn't get a good look at him. She wasn't sure enough in her memory, she said, to be able to pick out the man from among the defendants. She also admitted that Prosecutor Frank Christiansen had discussed the case with her before she went on the witness stand.

100

SOLDIERS—HOW COME?

As day after day of such evidence was submitted, almost everyone around the courtroom became weary—some disgusted. The prosecutors seemed chagrined, the defendants jubilant, the judge slightly bored. The framework of the lumber trust's case seemed tottering. Then a really heroic move was made. Everyone was surprised one morning to find a troop of U. S. regulars encamped on the courthouse lawn. There had been no trouble in town and none was anticipated. But the soldiers were there. And oh, what a touch of stern and sinister color they added to the surroundings. And just at the time the prosecution had made itself ridiculous in the eyes of all.

Judge Wilson was as surprised as everybody else when he saw the white tents on the green lawn. Vanderveer asked his Honor if his Honor had sent for the soldiers. His Honor denied it and said there was no excuse for their being there. The commanding officer, Captain Carling, 35th Inf. U. S. A., was asked. "Orders from Governor Hart," was all he would say. Finally Prosecutor Allen admitted that he had sent for the soldiers. Just how the prosecutor got the authority to send for troops over the head of the trial judge and all the rest was never made plain. Nor did Allen ever give reasons, plausible or otherwise, for having taken this step. Judge Wilson, prodded by Attorney Vanderveer, weakly protested against the offensive move but finally gave in. In about two days he reversed himself again, saying the troops might remain and that they were needed. What the troops were needed for Judge Wilson didn't say. But everyone knew that the soldiers were needed for only one purpose; to create atmosphere that would induce the state of mind on the part of the jury to convict regardless of the evidence.

Coincidental with the arrival of the troops an alarming rumor—without foundation of any sort—was whispered about the courtroom by the agents of the lumber trust: "Thousands of I. W. W.'s are gathering in the hills about Montesano. A jail delivery is feared. The courthouse must be protected." Newspapermen laughed when they heard the rumor. But the jury also heard it. One of the jurors had gone to the window for a moment. He saw the soldiers and turned pale. "My God!" he cried to another at his side, "they are here to keep us from getting shot."

THE MYSTERY OF BARNETT'S "RIFLE"

James T. McAllister and his wife, proprietors of the Roderick hotel, swore that Eugene Barnett was in the office of their hotel when the raid took place. They also swore that he was unarmed. The prosecution claimed that Barnett had participated in the shooting and afterward had secreted a 38-55 rifle near a signboard and then went home. Prosecutor Cunningham and the man who owns the billboard rights for the city of Centralia are the joint creators of this fable. The billboard man was the prosecution witness. He claimed he had found a rifle near a bill board. It was just the kind of a gun the prosecution needed for its case. The prosecution lawyers attempted to prove that Barnett had thrown it there together with some shells in order to rid himself of incriminating evidence. The witness was describing quite dramatically how he had discovered the rifle and had just come to the place where he was telling how he walked along the street looking for someone in authority to turn it over. At this point Cunningham turned away from the witness and with Vanderveer was examining the gun, thus leaving the witness without a pilot to guide him over the dangerous sea of prevarication. The witness kept talking and told how he was going down the street in Centralia when he met Cunningham. This gentleman stopped him and said, "Why I have been looking all over for that gun, it is number so-and-so; where did you find it?" The witness was surprised that Cunningham should know the number of the gun, looked . . . and sure enough, the number was just as Cunningham had stated!

Vanderveer took advantage of this lead at once, driving home

CITY PARK, CENTRALIA

At this place the parade assembled that started out to raid the union hall and lynch its secretary.

in cross examination the point that Cunningham had planted the rifle a short time previously and was waiting for someone to come along and find it. The position of the bill board bears this out as it is situated only half a block from a school house where hundreds of children romp and play daily. The billboard is not secluded in any way and would be the last place in the world where a man would ditch a gun who wanted it to stay ditched. The gun is supposed to have been found two weeks after Barnett had placed it there. New bills had been posted in the meantime, but the prosecution did not see fit to bring on as witnesses the two billposters who stuck up the bills.

A great many witnesses testified as to the doings of Eugene Barnett on Armistice Day. In fact a perfect alibi was proved in court from the time he rode into town on his horse until he rode home again. The trial records prove that Barnett's alibi remained unshaken.

BARNETT'S UNSHAKEN ALIBI

Eugene Barnett's own statement as to his whereabouts on Armistice Day is significant in connection with his testimony given under oath by persons who saw him that day. The prosecution has yet to show that Eugene Barnett's story is anything but true. This is what Barnett actually did on the 11th of November: Barnett had taken up a little homestead on a hillside in Idaho. He had lived there for some time and had almost proved up on his claim. He left Idaho for Washington in order to make a little money with which to continue operations. A short time before Armistice Day he had received a letter from the Land Office in Idaho telling him it would be necessary for him to return to the homestead and live there another year. On Armistice Day, at eleven o'clock in the morning Barnett started for Centralia. He had written in reply to the letter from the Land Office and wished to make the necessary affidavit before a notary. Elmer Smith was the man he wished to see. He felt sure of finding him in. Mrs. Barnett had been asked to come along for the holiday but she felt disinclined. And so Bar-

RAY BECKER
From photograph taken after the night of horrors.

103

nett threw the saddle on his horse and started for Centralia. He took with him a pound candy box filled with geranium slips which Mrs. Barnett wished to send to her mother in Cottonwood, Idaho. He rode up to the City park between twelve and one o'clock.

He tied his horse and walked over to the postoffice but found it closed and so he proceeded at once to the law office of Elmer Smith. The attorney was at lunch but a notice said he would return shortly. He decided to go to the union hall to read a paper while waiting for Smith to return. Barnett was anxious to transact his business and start on the return. He had told his wife he would be home early.

Inside the hall were five or six men all but one of whom (the secretary) were unknown to him. There was some talk of the raid on the old union hall that took

BLIND TOM LASSITER

Tom Lassiter is the blind news dealer who was kidnaped and deported out of town in June, 1919, by a gang of business men. His stand was raided and the contents burned in the street. He had been selling The Seattle Union Record, The Industrial Worker and Solidarity. County Attorney Allen said he couldn't help to apprehend the criminals and would only charge them with third degree assault if they were found. The fine would be one dollar and costs! Lassiter was later thrown into jail in Chehalis charged with "criminal syndicalism."

place in 1918 and some talk of the possibility of a new raid. None of the speakers however expressed the belief that the raid would actually take place in broad daylight. Barnett shared this belief. He read his paper for a while and then started back to meet Attorney Smith at the law office. He had just left the door of the union hall when he saw Elmer Smith in front of the Roderick Hotel. Barnett spoke to him about fixing up the papers for the Land Office. Smith said he would be back at his office in about half an hour. Barnett agreed to meet him there at the specified time.

Just at this moment Barnett saw his old friend Mr. Mc-Allister, proprietor of the Roderick hotel. Barnett knew McAllister well, having once worked for him. They went indoors. Mrs. McAllister came in and started to prepare dinner. The hotel proprietor, Barnett, and another man sat there chatting until the parade started to pass. They discussed the raid on the old hall and the possibility of a new raid. Here, as in the union hall next door, the opinion prevailed that a mob would not be bold enough to raid a peaceable hall in the daytime.

As the parade passed the window Barnett stood up to watch the marching men. The line went north one block on the east side of the street, then about faced and returned, marching south on the west side of the street. The section of the parade composed of business men was now in front of the union hall. These gentlemen seemed to be calling the attention of the men in uniform to the men in the hall, some of them pointing; some putting their thumbs to their noses and making faces. The raid itself can best be described in Barnett's own words:

HOW THE RAID LOOKED

"There was an undercurrent of excitement among them that an onlooker could not fail to notice. By this time I had a feeling that something was going to happen. When the soldiers came back the east half of the parade stopped in front of the hall. A man on a brown horse gave the order: 'Bunch up, men!' Then he rode on towards the rear of the line. I could hear him still giving orders but could not understand them. I noticed one man in what I took to be the front line of the soldiers who had stopped. This fellow had turned around and stood facing the hall in a crouching position. His attitude reminded me of a ball player on second base waiting for a hit in order to start for the home plate. Every time the man on horseback gave an order he would make a false start. Then I heard a yell and they all appeared to be rushing for the hall door in a body. I pulled off my coat and started for the door determined to take my beating with the rest of the boys. But before I got to the door I heard windows being smashed and the door slamming against something. Then the shooting started from the interior of the hall. I walked back to the sewing machine where I had thrown my coat and

DEFENSE ATTORNEY,
GEORGE VANDERVEER
The "Fighting Lawyer" arrives from the east to take up the defense of the intended victims of the Armistice Day mob.

105

stood there. The stranger walked out the front door and I thought I had better be getting out too. I had my I. W. W. card in the pocket of my coat, so I put on my mackinaw and told Mr. McAllister to put coat, card and all back of his counter. I walked down to Second Street, crossed it, and walked west till I came to the alley. A crowd of people had assembled here. They seemed to be leading men down the alley from the direction of the hall. I walked to the southeast corner of Second and Tower and stood there watching the mob carry out

SHERIFF JOHN BARRY
Lewis County.

benches, etc., from the hall. These they piled on a fire in the street. Two men brought out a box of literature from the hall. A man met them on the street and took box, papers and all. I started up town to get my horse.

ON THE WAY HOME

"On the way I met a men named Hand. I had heard he didn't like wobblies so I wouldn't talk much with him. A little further on I met a coal miner, Charles Roy. He asked me what was going on and I said, 'Oh, the soldiers raided the hall and some of them got shot.' Some distance further I saw a mob around a man near a telegraph pole. I thought they were going to tie him to the pole and beat him.

"I went back to Tower Avenue and continued on south to Main Street. Here I met a man I knew, Alex Sigurdson, a miner. When I got to Main Street I thought about my land papers and remembered that they were in my coat pocket together with my union card. I stopped awhile at Gabel's store and got my package of geranium slips weighed and stamped. I took it to the postoffice. Then I went around the corner to where my horse was. I got on the horse and started for home. When I reached Third and Tower I noticed that the mob had gone, so I thought I would go in and get my coat. I was afraid the mob might return to burn down the building and I would lose my land papers.

"I found Mr. McAllister in the back room patching up a door

106

that had been smashed by the mob. He said: 'It was no use to say anything and get killed.' I got my coat, put the union card in my sock and went out. On the way back to my horse I heard a boy about twelve years old telling a bunch of kids how he had climbed a telegraph pole with the end of a rope to hang a wobbly. He said a woman had stopped him. I met an acquaintance named Arrowsmith. As I talked with him I led my horse to the middle of the street and put on my chaps. An automobile passed. A fellow on the running board shouted, 'We've got two more of the ————s.' In the car were John Lamb and his son, Dewey.

BY THIS TIME IT WAS DARK

"I walked my horse most of the way home. About three miles out a young fellow named Johnson caught up with me. He was on horseback. I told him about the trouble. Next I met a farmer named Jones. He was standing in front of his house. I told him about the trouble. He remarked that he had a nephew in the Legion. I learned since that it was this nephew who showed his fist to a coal miner after he had hit Wesley Everest in the face while three men were holding him with a rope around his neck. Jones afterwards got on the witness stand and swore point blank to lies.

"When I got home I turned my horse loose, thinking I would get someone to take me back to town in a car. I felt I should go back to try to help the boys in jail or to keep them from all being lynched. I asked my wife to get my rifle. I went to a neighbor to see if he would take me, but he was not at home. My wife begged me not to go. By this time it was dark."

MANY WITNESSES SAW BARNETT

Many witnesses testified as to the whereabouts of Eugene Barnett on Armistice Day. The truthfulness of his alibi was established beyond question. Because of Barnett's rather unusual appearance his actions were observed from the time he left his little home in Kopiah until his return. Barnett rode to town in chaps and cowboy hat and mackinaw which he had brought with him from his ranch in Idaho. These probably served him in lieu of a Sunday suit. Because of his custom of riding to town in his western outfit he was a familiar figure in the neighborhood. Then, too, there were many around Centralia who knew him personally.

107

C. E. Roy, for instance, a young fellow with whom Barnett had worked, testified as follows:

"I know 'Gene Barnett. I remember Armistice Day. I have known Barnett a little over three months. I met him at the Monarch mines. I saw him on November 11th just before he crossed the viaduct going into town. I was at the house. It is half a block from the main road, just half a block from the viaduct. He did not have any gun, packages, grips, suitcases or anything of that character in which a gun could be carried that I noticed. I saw him going out of town round about three or four o'clock. I was in front of the Pastime Pool Room right in the main part of town. He was going up the street on horseback, riding north."

This boy's mother, Alma Roy, also testified in behalf of the defense:

"I know 'Gene Barnett. I never was personally acquainted with him but knew him when I saw him. On the day of the Armistice Day parade I was sitting at my dining room window. He was going down the street at the next corner. He had come from towards Kopiah and rode over the viaduct, riding a horse. I believe the street is Marion Street. I watched him going over the viaduct. My son and I had a discussion about it. My son told me a little while before that that he was going to borrow some of Barnett's cowboy togs. He had on cowboy chaps, and what I call a cowboy hat. He didn't have any rifle that I saw. I didn't see any rifle—nothing at all."

John Mayhar, a schoolboy, also saw Barnett:

"I remember Armistice Day. I know 'Gene Barnett. I have known him since he lived up behind our place in the white house. He used to live up behind our place, about half a block away. I saw him on that day because I got out of school early. He was crossing the viaduct on his horse. He was coming from Centralia. He had a big felt hat on and chaps. He did not have any gun. I didn't see any packages. I watched him until he got to a couple of houses and didn't see him any more. The viaduct is on Marion Street. Then he started east on Marion Street. I did not see him until he passed the store. I watched him until he got up to the corner. He did not ride very fast. I have seen him ride on other days. He was riding kind of slow."

Edwin Ayers testified as follows:

"I remember Armistice Day. I saw Barnett that day. My uncle and I went hunting. It commenced to rain about two o'clock. When it rained we were up the Eastern track about two miles, so we came back. Saw Eugene Barnett by Puvis' store about half past three or a quarter after. He was riding up toward Kopiah. He was on horseback in black chaps. I think he had on a brown hat. He didn't have any gun. He did not have anything in which a gun could be carried. His horse was walking."

"HE DID NOT DO ANY SHOOTING"

J. T. McAllister, proprietor of the Roderick Hotel, had the following to say about the incident of the hotel office:

"I know 'Gene Barnett. He used to stop with me when I was in Chehalis. He boarded with me about two months. That was in 1912. I remember Armistice Day. I was in the office in the lobby of the hotel. My wife was there and Mr. Barnett sat there in a chair. There was another gentleman, a stranger that I didn't know. He was sitting there watching the parade. Mr. Barnett was in there at the time the parade passed. I suppose about an hour and a half. He remained there until they started

THE FUNERAL OF THE MOB LEADER
Main Street turned out en masse to honor its favorite son Warren O. Grimm, who fell while trying to give the Wobblies what was coming to them.

109

THE BURIAL OF THE MOB'S VICTIM

No undertaker would handle Everest's body. The autopsy was performed by a man from Portland, who hung the body up by the heels and played a hose on it. The men lowering the plank casket into the grave are union loggers who had been caught in the police dragnet and taken from jail for this purpose.

to tear the posts out from under the porch. He got out and he said: 'I had better get out of here or I can't get out.' Barnett didn't have any gun that I saw. He did not do any shooting. He sat there; he never moved."

McAllister had been browbeaten and intimidated by the prosecution until he was a nervous wreck before going on the witness stand. In re-direct examination by Attorney Vanderveer he stated about certain statements he had made before the inquisition:

"I told them I didn't want to be dragged into it, because I kept out of everything. I didn't tell them because I did not want to be mixed up in it. My wife was down in the jail. I was not in jail; they didn't put me there; they just took me down and let me go home. My place was all broken up. I didn't see anything going on outside the hall. I was not there long enough to see all of it when it started."

MRS. McALLISTER SPEAKS

Mrs. Mary McAllister, wife of the proprietor, and the real executive of the tiny hotel showed more nerve on the witness stand. She testified in part as follows:

"My name is Mary McAllister. I am nearly forty-nine. I

live at No. 805 North Tower, Centralia. That is the Roderick Hotel. My husband and I are the owners. Have owned and lived there nearly four years. Rented the hall known as the I. W. W. hall to Britt Smith. Gave him a written lease. The boys conducted themselves quietly and nicely. Was in the house all day of the parade. In the hotel office while the parade was passing were my husband and I and 'Gene Barnett, and another man. Have known him nearly eight years. He used to chum with one of my boarders. He was boarding with me part of the time. 'Gene went away before the porch was pulled down. He didn't have any gun. He didn't do any shooting. He was sitting behind the heating stove facing the other young man—sitting there and talking. Just before the porch was pulled down he came and stood behind me and said: 'I will have to be getting out of here for if this thing comes down I won't be able to get out at all.' Some Legion boys came in, maybe half a dozen. I said to the soldier boys: 'We all were here before the parade came up.' The soldier boys marched up to the corner and then came back, up to the corner of Third. The band kept on and the citizens kept on and the boy scouts and there was no one left except part of the soldiers. Part of them went on. A man on horseback blowed a whistle and then they all stopped and he told them to step out and close up ranks. They were all stretched out along a block or so. They stopped and talked among themselves and some laughed and some talked. Some of the men walked on our sidewalk and walked backwards and forwards, and I was looking for them to go on. And then somebody said something and the boys started to rush the hall. There were two men started to rush the I. W. W. hall. As near as I could tell there was only two of them got to the hall. I don't know exactly what they did but

MIKE SHEEHAN

Born in Ireland. 64 years old. Has been a union man for over fifty years, having joined his grandfather's union when he was only eight. Has been through many strikes and has been repeatedly blackhated, beaten and even exiled. He was a stoker in the Navy during the Spanish War. Mike Sheehan was arrested in the union hall, went through the horrible experience in the city jail and was found "not guilty" by the jury. Like Elmer Smith, he was re-arrested on another similar charge and thrown back to jail.

111

I heard a noise like a kick or a hit or something, and some glass shattered and then in a little while the shots rang out. The shots were from the hall. There were several men started for the I. W. W. hall but two men got there. I know two men got there because I heard a terrible crash. I seen them jump back."

COURT HOUSE AT MONTESANO—AND A LITTLE "ATMOSPHERE"

The trial was held on the third floor of the building as you look at the picture. The soldiers were sent for over the head of the judge by one of the lumber trust attorneys for the prosecution. Their only purpose was to create the proper "atmosphere" for an unjust conviction.

"NO SIR, NOT UNTIL THEY HIT THERE!"

The prosecution tried to trap Mrs. McAllister into admitting that the shooting started before the rush on the hall. This was a few days after her arrest on November 15th, during the time of the inquisition. The argument was about a statement Mrs. McAllister is alleged to have made to Prosecutor Cunningham to the effect that "the shooting started just as soon as they started to run for it." Prosecutor Abel was pressing the point, but Mrs. McAllister replied: "I didn't say it that way, that the shooting started just as soon as they started to run for it. There were so many in there crowding and they had me scared to death and I don't know what I put down. They may have understood it that way. The shooting did not start as soon as the persons started. No, sir, not until they hit there; then the shooting started."

Mrs. McAllister was an important witness. She knew where Barnett was on November 11th and was the kind of woman who could be relied upon to tell the truth. The prosecution didn't want Barnett in the Roderick hotel; they wanted him in the Avalon firing the 38-55 rifle which killed Warren O. Grimm. Mrs. McAllister was taken prisoner by some of the far-seeing members of the mob that wrecked the I. W. W. hall. She was spirited away to the county jail in Chehalis and held there incommunicado for 22 days. No charge was ever brought against

112

her. She was simply kept isolated in a rat-infested jail and
"questioned" repeatedly. But her spirit was not broken. She
still had the pluck and grit to get up on the witness stand and
tear to tatters the prosecution's absurd charge against Eugene
Barnett.

Barnett was seen less than fifteen minutes after he left the
Roderick hotel by a man named Hand who runs a second hand
store. Hand is a member of the Dunkard Church. He said:

"I have known 'Gene Barnett about a year; saw him that
afternoon when I went down to the bakery for my lunch, a little
after noon—I guess about ten or fifteen minutes after the shooting. We walked together about a block and a half, and then I
went into the bakery. I know the location of the viaduct which
leads over from the main part of Centralia. I do not know as
I ever saw a billboard about a quarter of a mile north of the
east end of the viaduct. I do not think Barnett could have
walked up there and walked to the point where I saw him after
the shooting. I saw part of the parade. Was out in front of
my store on the sidewalk. I saw the men break and rush back
down Tower Avenue. As near as I can recollect it was ten or
fifteen minutes after that Barnett came along. I went back into
the store and built a fire to put on my coffee. , I was crying
about the trouble."

MEN WHO SAW BARNETT

Alex Sigurdson, mentioned in Barnett's testimony, testified
on the witness stand as follows:

"I saw the parade passing down Tower Avenue and I stood
there until the parade came back, and just as the parade passed
there was an automobile coming up with two soldiers on and
they hollered that there was four soldiers shot at the I. W. W.
hall. The crowd got a little excited then. They started to go
north and I crossed the street from where I stood. While walking north I met 'Gene Barnett. It couldn't be more than five
minutes after the shooting. Where I met Barnett that day I
stood across the street from the Oliver Hardware Store, just
two buildings below the state bank."

Charles Fisher, a coal miner, saw Barnett on the way home.
This is what Fisher had to say:

"I saw Barnett on the 11th of last November. He was speaking to J. D. Jones as I came by, about three and one-half miles
out of town on the road to Kopiah. Jones is a farmer up there.
I knew him by sight. I was in an automobile driving from the

mine into town. I believe he (Barnett) was standing alongside his horse. I didn't notice that he had a gun, not carrying anything that I noticed. I didn't notice anything unusual about his horse. It was between four and five o'clock that I saw him talking to Jones."

"HE DIDN'T HAVE A GUN"

Aaron Johnson testified about Barnett's homeward trip:

"I know Eugene Barnett. I worked with him in the mine. I belong to the union. I saw him on Armistice Day between four and five o'clock, about three miles from town riding along on his horse going east toward Kopiah. I was going to get our mail. I rode alongside of Barnett for about a quarter of a mile. He didn't have a gun. He didn't have anything in his hands."

Graham Robinson testified about passing Barnett and noticing the condition of his horse:

"I didn't notice anything unusual about Barnett's appearance. He was going very slow where we were going because the road was bad. His horse was not overheated that I noticed. It was about five o'clock in the evening."

Even the testimony of Jones, the farmer who had a nephew in the Legion, was far from being damaging:

NEWSPAPER MEN AND WOMAN
Covering famous labor trial at Montesano for the press of the world.

114

"My name is Jones. I live four and one-half miles from Centralia. That is on the Kopiah road. I know Gene Barnett when I see him. Saw him on November 11th about four o'clock. He was riding horseback going towards Kopiah. Talked with him ten minutes, I guess. I never seen any rifle. He didn't have any package in which a rifle might have been concealed. Saw him approaching some distance before he stopped to talk to me. When he came up he was riding quite fast, and after he came around the turn he slowed up, and when he got by me his horse was walking. I never paid any attention to the condition of his horse."

"DID ELSIE HORNBECK LIE?"

The testimony of Cecil Arrowsmith was doubly valuable. This young man not only knew Barnett and saw him on Armistice Day, but he also saw the man whom Elsie Hornback, the garage bookkeeper, claimed was Barnett in the window of the Avalon hotel. This, in part, is what Arrowsmith said on the witness stand:

"I was in front of the North End garage; right in front of the main door on the sidewalk, pretty near up alongside of the building, and close to the building itself. I was in the garage about fifteen or twenty minutes and came out, stood at the front. At the time of the shooting I was right in front of the garage. I remained there for a short time. I saw Elsie Hornbeck come out of the garage. Previous to that time I had noticed a man in the Avalon hotel window. He was looking all around. I have good eyesight. I know Gene Barnett. I have known him five or six months. It was not Gene Barnett that I saw. From there I walked down past the Wobbly hall. I watched the fire there. They had a fire in front of the hall. They were burning up some benches and stuff. They were tearing the windows out, busting the front of it, burning it up, what they could get down. The porch came down. They let that down over the windows. From there I went down until I came to the Queen. There I met Barnett. He was getting on his horse. We spoke. He went down to his horse at the woodshed behind the Queen. He put his chaps on and got on his horse and went off home."

115

ORIGINAL ELEVEN CENTRALIA DEFENDANTS

This picture was taken during trial. Reading from left to right (top row): Loren Roberts, James McInerney, Britt Smith, O. C. Bland, Bert Faulkner, Ray Becker. Bottom row: Mike Sheehan, John Lamb, Eugene Barnett, Bert Bland, Elmer Smith. Faulkner was dropped from the case. Sheehan and Smith were found not guilty.

BARNETT'S WIFE TESTIFIES

Mrs. Eugene Barnett testified as to her husband's whereabouts. Her testimony, because of its obvious truthfulness, was extraordinarily impressive:

"I am the wife of the defendant Eugene Barnett. I live at Kopiah. I formerly lived in Cottonwood, Idaho. I recall November 11th, last. I don't know the exact time Gene left to go to town. It was perhaps nine or ten o'clock. He went down on horseback. He wanted to hitch up the rig—the buggy—and take me with him. He said he wanted me to go to town with him. I didn't have the baby's clothes ready. I sent some slips from geraniums to my mother, some that I had raised and cut myself. I put them in a candy box. He carried it in his pocket. He had on his soft hat and brown coat, a mackinaw over it, and his chaps. Gene had some land papers to see about that day in Centralia. I have had them attended to since then. When he returned I got them out of his coat pocket—his brown coat. Plaintiff's exhibit 'I' is Gene's rifle. He did not take that with

116

him on that day. It was in the bedroom. He hunts every idle day when he don't work. He had three hunting dogs. He did not take any weapon with him when he went to town that day, because that is the only weapon we have. I saw him return that evening right after I lit the lamp, possibly six or somewhere around there. I did not know anything about the trouble that had occurred. 'Gene said they raided the hall and four of them was shot. He said he was in the Roderick hotel. He told me he wanted to go back to town to see they didn't hang those men they had in jail. He wanted to take his rifle with him. I would-n't let him. He said he came out to get his gun to go back and protect those fellows. There was no use to go back. He wanted to go right back to town. He was not afraid to go. He came ten miles to get his gun and go back. I persuaded him not to go to town. I think he needed persuasion. The next morning he wanted to go to town again and I again persuaded him not to go. I did not know that the authorities wanted him; he did not. He took to the woods just because they were getting every-body that had a red card. At the time some people came to arrest him Gene was feeding his dogs in the back yard. He saw them coming. He and I had talked about what he should do when he saw these people coming. He left, took his rifle, went back of the house on the hill. I saw him until he crossed the creek. He was in the brush after that. Don't know what point he went to on the hill. The timber is just close."

SMOKE AND FLAME?

The prosecution was not content to try to prove that a rifle was fired by Eugene Barnett from the window of the Avalon; they also sought to prove that flame and smoke burst from the barrel of the rifle when it was fired. This was the realistic touch, born of a perfervid imagination which was manufactured to convince the unwary. Unfortunately for its case the pros-ecution overdid it. Tests were made on different occasions and with different rifles, but never did the gun belch flame and smoke. Altogether six witnesses, some of them experts, all with good eyesight, testified after these tests. Robert Hudson, Basil Carmichael, Walter Blanchard, Joseph Smith, Frank Nehring, Sheriff Bartell and J. F. Emigh were the men who made the ex-periments. The latter's testimony gives an idea of the result:

"My name is J. F. Emigh. I was in the United States army during the war. I am a member of the American Legion. I was present at a test made this noon. State's Exhibit 'N' was used.

117

The shells were taken by the clerk and given to me, taken from a box which belonged to the exhibits here. When the test was made I was standing about sixty-five feet from the gun. I had a background building painted dark red, the darkest background I could find for the man who fired the gun. The other people were standing on the opposite side about the same distance from the gun. The other people were Mr. Smith and the sheriff of this county, Mr. Bartell. I could see no flame at all shoot out."

The evidence submitted above was substantiated by another actual test made on the scene at the hotel Avalon. Mr. F. H. Fisher visited this spot with a cameraman. The photographs were in evidence as was Mr. Fisher's testimony:

"My eyesight is very good. Been in railway service about nine years. There is in that service a very strict examination of eyes. There were two men inside the North End garage. One of these had a man take a designated position in the south window of Hotel Avalon, the second story. You could see the fellow that had hold of the rifle. I knew the boy. It was Tommy Hughes. Had known him and seen him pretty nearly every day for about two months. I stood in the North End garage—about six feet from the door. I could not recognize him in that window from where I stood. I could not tell whether the gun barrel was r o u n d or octagonal. I also assumed a position somewhere near Ax Billy's corner. We could just see the gun and the face of the man who had hold of it. But I couldn't tell that I knew exactly who it was. It was a nice bright day."

G. E. Thurber, who was also present when the tests were made, testified similarly. This straight-from-the-shoulder testimony hurt the evidence of Leila Tripp, Elsie Hornbeck and the other prosecution witnesses tremendously. The absurdity of the charge against Eugene Barnett was patent to everyone in the courtroom—even to the capitalist newspaper reporters.

CAPTAIN CARLING
35th Infantry, U. S. A. at Montesano.

JAMES McINERNEY

Logger. Born in County Clare, Ireland. Joined the Industrial Workers of the World in 1916. Was wounded on the steamer "Verona" when the lumber trust tried to exterminate the union lumberworkers with bullets at Everett, Washington. McInerney was one of those trapped in the Centralia hall. While in the jail his neck was worn raw with a hangman's rope in an effort to make him "confess" that the loggers and not the mob had started the trouble. McInerney told them to "go to hell." He is Irish and an I. W. W. and proud of being both.

A CONVENIENT SIGNBOARD

The signboard where Barnett is supposed to have hidden the rifle suffered even worse. The man who was sawing wood near the signboard on Armistice Day gave the coup de grace to this fine little piece of imaginative fiction. He said:

"My name is C. W. Green. I am sixty-two. I know where the signboard is. It is on our place. On the afternoon of Armistice Day I was sawing wood, back next to the railroad near this sign, forty feet from it. I was there about four hours, leaving at 4:30. The character of the ground—there is very little brush—short brush. There was no brush at the place the rifle was found. There was no woods or growing brush, none four feet high or anything between me and the signboard to obstruct my view of the signboard. While I was at work there I didn't see anybody go near the signboard to hide a rifle. I saw quite a few men walk up the railroad track that afternoon. While I was sawing wood I don't think anyone slipped that gun under the signboard. They could not have done it without me seeing them."

"THEY CARRIED ROPES"

The prosecution had a dreadfully hard time trying to cover up the fact that ropes were carried in the parade. The evidence was all against them. Prosecutor Abel finally conceded that rope was carried and offered the feeble plea that it was to be used for the purpose of "leading a calf." This is about as profound a remark as Abel made during the trial. Everyone in Centralia now knows the truth. This is what a few of the witnesses had to say about the ropes being carried in the parade:

Mrs. T. W. Siddle testified as follows: "I was on Tower

119

JAMES McINERNEY
(After he had undergone the "third degree.")

McInerney had a rope around his neck nearly all night before this picture was taken. One end of the rope had been pulled taut over a beam by the tormentors. McInerney had told them to "go to hell." "It's no use trying to get anything out of a man like that," was the final decision of the inquisitors.

avenue. The parade passed me twice. I saw T. H. McCleary and Reverend Thompson c a rr y i n g ropes. It was in the business men's section."

Mrs. Nelson Hiatt said: "I was standing right in front of Mr. Crossit's dry goods store. Saw people in the parade carrying ropes. I saw T. H. McCleary."

Serena N. Armengrout also saw a rope carried: "I have lived in Centralia on and off for the last fourteen years. I saw the parade. T. H. McCleary was carrying a rope."

Mrs. Maggie Stockdale and several others saw the ropes. Mrs. Nettie Pierce declared that others besides Postmaster McCleary and the Reverend Thompson carried "wobbly neckties":

"I was on the corner of Main and Tower. I saw persons carrying ropes, two men. They were in the rear of the parade. The men who carried the ropes were in uniform. They had them coiled in their hands. I suppose they were about a half-inch rope. I wouldn't swear to one. The other was Mr. McCleary. There was possibly twelve feet or more of rope."

Wesley Everest, it will be recalled, was murdered with ropes that answer to the above description. McCleary testified that he picked up "an old piece of rope" and used it in a playful tug-of-war with other paraders.

AT THE DOOR OF THE HALL

The door of the I. W. W. hall was for a long time the storm center of the legal battle at Montesano. The question: "Who was the aggressor?" could only be settled at this point. The prosecution sought to keep the legionaires as far away from this door as possible. They endeavored by all means fair and foul to keep Grimm and McElfresh away from that door. But it was a hard job. This is what some of the eyewitnesses stated on the subject:

Mrs. May Sherman stated on the witness stand, "I heard they were going to raid the I. W. W. hall. That is why I was there."

This is what Mrs. Sherman saw:

"I was right by the office of the Roderick hotel. I seen them make a break for the hall. I would judge about five of them. They smashed in the door. I saw the door smashed in and the glass fly. I heard shooting. I saw somebody that had been shot. I saw a tall heavy-set fellow weighing 200 to 220 pounds. He threw his hands across his stomach. He passed me going down the corner. At the time he passed me he already had his hands doubled over his stomach."

Tom Meaden, a tailor, stated as follows: "Then we heard louder talking—several voices: 'Let's go! Come on, let's get them.' Then some of the parade started towards the side of the street that the hall was on. They went at a sort of a pace. About fifteen or twenty started in that direction, followed by a movement by the rest of the parade. They went toward the I. W. W. hall. I saw them run into the doorway. I heard a noise that sounded like a crash of glass and the breaking of the casing. I saw men who had been wounded."

Walter Morrow was one of the ex-service men and members of the Legion who testified for the defense. After describing the attack on the hall he stated as follows: "When I heard the crash and the shots I turned around and looked towards the hall. I saw several men up there in uniform, and one was by the door. I seen one fellow down by the edge or under the window. Looked to me like he was stooping over there, crouching down there. I saw one soldier with a gun. He was in the

O. C. BLAND

Logger. American. Resident of Centralia for several years. Has worked in woods and mills practically all his life. Has a wife and seven children. Bland was in the Arnold hotel at the time of the raid. He was armed but had cut his hand on broken glass before he had a chance to shoot. Since his arrest and conviction his family has undergone severe hardships. Friends came to their rescue when the Lewis county supervisors refused to give them the aid to which they were legally entitled.

121

rear of the Elks' parade. He was one of the Chehalis soldiers."

Vernon O'Reilly, a high school lad, testified as follows: "I saw several of the men in the platoons sort of draw together and talk to one another confidentially. I saw several men go towards the street. They approached as nearly as I could locate the I. W. W. hall. I saw about three to begin with. There were several followed them after that—about half a dozen. Some of the men seemed in a hurry, others walked to the sidewalk. I heard the sound of breaking glass and shots immediately followed that. I noticed the breaking glass first. I saw a man apparently wounded in the vicinity of the I. W. W. hall. He appeared to be a large man. I didn't notice about his height, for he was rather doubled up and I could not tell. He had his hands over his stomach and appeared to be reeling forward. He was a heavy-set, broad shouldered man. He was not fat but he was big all over."

"I SAW ONE MAN WOUNDED"

Jay Cooke's testimony is significant on this point also: "They ran up there and they kicked and I heard the glass fall and the wood crack. I heard shooting. I saw one man wounded coming down right next to the curb, thirty-five or forty feet from where I stood. He was coming down this way with both hands over his abdomen."

The effect of John Patterson's testimony on the prosecution was fairly smashing. This is in part what Patterson said:

"The people that I saw rush the hall came out of the parade. I couldn't tell what part of it because I had three children with me. The first thing I knew the glass was flying from the window. I heard the crash of the door. The men were rushing the hall—right in the door—at the time of the crash. There had not been any shots before the door crashed. I knew two was wounded. I saw one man with blood on his arm. He was dressed in a soldier's uniform. When I saw him he was on the sidewalk. The fellow who had the blood was straight in front of the doorway. I should judge about the middle of the sidewalk. I saw them carry one out of the door. He was there in front of the hall. He went down the street south. He was quite a large fellow. He appeared to be wounded in the side. He said, 'Oh God, Oh God!' One of the boys said: 'Are you hit?' and he said, 'Yes, I am shot.' He said: 'You'd better beat it.' I saw two wounded men in front of the hall. One was wounded and one was supposed to be dead. They said he was dead and his

122

JOHN LAMB

Logger. American. Joined the Industrial Workers of the World in 1917. Lamb was in the Arnold Hotel with O. C. Bland during the raid on the hall. Neither of them did any shooting. John Lamb has lived for years in Centralia. He is married and has five children who are left dependent since the conviction.

name was McElfresh. He was carried out of the doorway."

WHERE WAS McELFRESH?

Further evidence about the whereabouts of McElfresh at the moment of the raid was given by a young man by the name of Forrest Campbell, who viewed the attack from a point directly opposite the I. W. W. hall. Campbell said in part:

"The segment of the parade remained halted there a very short time. Then they broke ranks and ran towards the I. W. W. hall. There was a kind of group seemed to break ranks. There was about two or three close to the door and the rest were after them. They rushed towards the I. W. W. hall running. They ran into the door. I heard the crash of glass. I heard the shots from the hall. There wasn't much of an interval between the crash and the shots. The crash was first. I saw McElfresh near the door. I didn't know at that time who it was. I know now, of course. He was near the I. W. W. door. I think he was one of the first to smash into it, if I remember. I don't know any of the other men who smashed in the door."

ABEL FAILS TO SHAKE WITNESS

Prosecutor Abel tried frantically to break down the damaging testimony of this boy, but without avail. The young man stuck to his point stubbornly. "McElfresh was lying on the ground," Campbell told Abel, "just the way I said it. All I remember is that a man dropped there. I didn't see him drop. I knew he was there. It was general talk that McElfresh was shot at the door. I say the man dropped there. Well, he was lying there. What caused the crash was when they hit the door. . . " Altogether Prosecutor Abel had an uncomfortable time with this witness.

"OUT DAMNED SPOT!"

BRITT SMITH

American. Logger. 38 years old. Had followed the woods for twenty years. Smith made his home in the hall that was raided and was secretary of the union. When the mob broke into the jail and seized Wesley Everest to torture and lynch him they cried, "We've got Britt Smith!" Smith was the man they wanted and it was to break his neck that ropes were carried in the "parade." Not until Everest's body was brought back to the city jail was it discovered that the mob had lynched the wrong man.

Luma Moss, a twelve-year-old girl, added to the discomfiture of the prosecution by testifying about a pool of blood, right near the doorway of the union hall and over half a block from where the lumber trust lawyers wanted Grimm or McElfresh to fall. This is the statement of Luma Moss: "I noticed something on the sidewalk in the vicinity of the I. W. W. hall. I thought it was blood. It was a few feet from the entrance, south—a few feet away from the building. It was perhaps a foot and a half square on the pavement there."

T. W. Siddle, a railway brakeman, saw the blood also. This is what Siddle says about it: "It was about five minutes after we learned of the trouble down there. I saw blood on the sidewalk. There was some blood by the hall right where I stood. Saw a kind of splotch or patch of blood somewhere around ten or twelve inches in diameter."

W. C. Hawkins also testified about blood spots on the sidewalk: "There were splotches of blood around there in different places in front of the I. W. W. hall. The trail of blood started close to the door. It ended about a rod or so from the corner. This line was just a kind of regular drizzle."

After the I. W. W. hall had been properly wrecked, all stains were removed, obviously in order to cover up trace of the crime committed by the mobsters. But it was too late. All they could do was to try to explain it away.

The defendants themselves were on the witness stand for hours. They were grilled and questioned and cross examined unmercifully. The prosecution used its power and prestige lavishly to discredit the unfortunate men and to create further pre-

124

judice against them. Legal traps without number were laid for them, and all the courtroom tricks of cheap lawyers were used to get the loggers to incriminate themselves. In the face of the hideous charge placed against them and the network of lies and insinuations in which they were entangled by means of manufactured "evidence," it is surprising that they bore up as well as they did. Their testimony would fill a good sized book. Here we can only touch upon it briefly. The testimony of Eugene Barnett, who was charged with having killed Warren O. Grimm, is given elsewhere. James McInerney testified in part as follows:

McINERNEY TESTIFIES

"When the parade went by I was away in the back part of the hall. I didn't watch the first part of the parade. I stood up on a bench when the band was passing and stepped down again to see the parade when it was coming back. I came back and talked with Britt Smith then. He was in the back of the hall about twelve feet from the desk. I told him I didn't think they were going to bother us, because they were coming back. I was talking there to him. I had my back turned for a few seconds and I heard a command from outside, and they made for the hall, and smashed the glass and broke the doors in. Then the shooting started. I turned around and saw the soldiers moving on towards the hall and all the doors were smashing in. I went through the back door to the ice box. I took it off (the gun). I left it in the ice box. I did not shoot it. The shells are in the gun and in the belt as they were when I received it. I had no other shells. When I was taken out of the ice box there was a soldier there who said that I was the man that shot somebody and he wanted to burn me at the stake. He took me out of the jail,

GEORGE VANDERVEER

This man single handed opposed six high-priced lumber trust prosecutors in the famous trial at Montesano. Vanderveer is a man of wide experience and deep social vision. He was at one time prosecuting attorney for King County, Washington. The lumber trust has made countless threats to "get him." "A lawyer with a heart is as dangerous as a workingman with brains."

125

COURT ROOM IN WHICH THE FARCICAL "TRIAL" TOOK PLACE

This garish room in the court house at Montesano was the scene of the attempted "judicial murder" that followed the lynching. The judge always entered his chambers through the door under the word "Transgression"; the jury always left through the door over which "Instruction" appears. In this room the lumber trust attorneys attempted to build a gallows of perjured testimony on which to break the necks of innocent men.

wanted me to make a statement. Had a rope and took me outside of the jail, and the mob had me, and finally came to a conclusion and took me back in again. I didn't know any of the men in the parade. Had no feeling against them for any reason. I never at any time entered into any conspiracy to injure any of those men or any members of the Legion."

O. C. BLAND TESTIFIES

O. C. (Commodore) Bland told his story in part as follows: "I heard the threatened raid mentioned in conversations about the hall quite a few times. It was general conversation. It was at home that I heard the particulars—my neighbor at home. Henry is the only name I know him by. He lives right adjoining my place on the corner. He told me about it the fourth Sunday before. I had heard it spoken of in general discussion, but this was a real definite word I was depending on. It was the first time I had ever met the man, and it was in the way he told it and the honesty he displayed in telling it I depended on.

"I left the hall on the afternoon of the 11th about forty minutes before the parade came along. I went straight to the Arnold. Lamb went with me. I went up there and emptied the rifle cartridges out on the bureau, set the gun down in the corner and sat down on the bed. The gun was loaded. We were conversing about casual matters until the parade came along. Saw it go down out of sight and come back pretty soon. All at once this bunch of soldiers got even with the hall. They stopped there and commenced marking time. We had decided there would be no raid on the hall until we saw the soldiers stop there. They had been there possibly three minutes. I heard a loud voice but could not distinguish what was said. The window was closed. I went to the window. I seen two men break and rush for the door and the third followed almost immediately. The lead man hit the door with a rush with his foot, a soldier at the same time. Both doors flew open and the glass fell from the doors. He hadn't any more than hit the door until I had my rifle in my hand, shoved the muzzle of it through the window light. I was down on one knee. I had my hand up near the muzzle of the rifle and run my hand, rifle barrel and all through the window; broke the light with my hand instead of the rifle barrel. I did not shoot.

"When I left the hotel I went straight home. I changed the towel on my hand and tried to get Lamb to pull this flesh back on my hand and he started to faint.

"My haste in getting away was, I couldn't do nothing. Why should I stay and be beat up? I could not do anything because my hand was numb to my side. It was to keep from being beat up and me helpless. I had reason to believe they were after me at my house or wherever I would be. I was threatened in this meeting that was talked of—I in person was threatened. I did not figure that I would be safer down town in a room than in my own home; I figured that my children would be safer—my wife and children. I had no ill will against any of them, and there was no reason I should want to hurt them."

JOHN LAMB TESTIFIES

The following excerpts will give an idea of John Lamb's testimony:

"We went over to get a room, both registered our right names. I would judge it was about one o'clock when we went into the room. Bland took some shells out of his pocket. I hadn't seen his gun until that time. I did not have a gun of any kind. When the parade came along I was sitting in a position where I could see it. I was sitting on the bed near the window. I just watched the parade go by. I watched it until the tail end of the parade got out of sight. I went out in the back room then. Commodore said: 'They are going to raid the hall,' and at that I heard a crash across the street; sounded like two or three had

127

jammed the door. Then I heard the breaking of glass and the report of shots.

"I don't know how Commodore got the glass out. I know he broke out a glass of the front window and when he turned he said: 'I have hurt my hand.' I saw his hand. It was badly cut. No shots were fired in the room. After he cut his hand he went out the back way. I think he went straight back to the railroad, passing the south side of the shed. I saw that other man with a rifle. He was right close to us when he came out to the railroad. I didn't know him. Don't know now who he was. When I went to that room I was just the same as Commodore. I had been threatened before and was trying to look out for myself—to keep out of the way when the trouble would start up. I didn't know just where it would start up and where it wouldn't. I was there in order to be out of the way. I had no intention of using the rifle or revolver. I was in that room to keep clear from mobs."

BERT BLAND TAKES THE STAND

Bert Bland was one of the men who fired from Seminary hill. Loren Roberts and the missing John Doe Davis were also on the hill. This is a part of what Bert Bland said on the witness stand:

"I was in the hall Tuesday. I heard discussion there about a threatened raid on the hall that day. Most everybody present was discussing the raid. I heard it on the streets, I heard it in the hall and I heard some of it out in the logging camp.

"We only figured on defending our hall. Was wondering whether to stay in the hall or get on the outside of the hall, and we decided that on the outside would be safest. I myself figured that the soldiers would be armed. We first decided to go to the Queen rooming house. We went to the Queen in Wesley Everest's room. He was not with us. We looked out of the window and sized up the situation. It would be very easy to surround us there. Was in Everest's room possibly five minutes. When we left we were going up on the hill. I believe it is known as Seminary hill. After about forty-five minutes saw the parade coming on. It came north and went as far north as Third street, and it turned to go back. I heard a command and I did not understand it, but it consisted of about four or five words. I saw the soldiers break ranks into a group. Three or four of them rushed the hall, with about twenty of the soldiers twenty feet behind them. They were in a hurry. We heard the glass fall from the windows and the door glass broke in. Just as soon as the shots started

128

County of Multnomah) ss

I, P.V.Johnson, being first duly sworn, do depose and
say:

That I was one of the jurors in the case of the state of
Washington as plaintiff, versus Britt Smith, et al, as
defendants, tried in the superior court of Washington,
for Grays Harbor county, during the first three months
of the year 1920 as an outgrowth of the Armistice Day tragedy
at Centralia, Wash., November 11, 1919.

That I have been a resident of said Grays Harbor
county, Wash., for twelve years immediately preceding
my jury duty in this case and that this residence
had been continuous on my part.

That I have read the affidavit signed by E.E.Torpin,
one of the jurors in the trial, which affidavit was
subscribed and sworn before O.M.Nelson, a notary public
in and for the state of Washington, residing at Montesano,
Washington, upon the 17th day of May ,1922. That the
facts as stated in said affidavit are true to my own personal
knowledge and belief.

That if the jury had been permitted to consider what I
have since learned was a premeditated attack upon the
hall, the jury would never have returned a verdict of guilty.
It is my firm belief that the men are not guilty of murder
in any degree.

That Warren Grimm was killed while advancing upon and
engaged in an attack upon the I.W.W.hall in Centralia, Wash.

That one of the most determining elements in securing conviction of the seven defendants was the bringing in of a large
number of soldiers a few days before the conclusion of the
trial ; that these men were camped close to the court house
and the jury was paraded in sight of them ; that these soldiers
were brought in to protect the jury and as the jury was led to
believe ; that it was were informed that a thousand or more I.W
.W. were in hiding in the woods near the town. That this tended
to create a feeling in the minds of the jurors that the I.W.W.
organization was composed of outlaws and that therefore the
organization was as much on trial as the individuals.

That I have read the affidavits of Torpen as above stated
and know the contents of the affidavits of E.E.Sweitzer and
W.E.Inman, former jurors and agree with the statements therein
made.

That I am making this affidavit because I want to
see justice done and it is my firm belief that justice is not
obtained through lawless attacks upon peaceful citizens.

P V Johnson

Subscribed and sworn to before me, this 99th day of May,1922.

R L Jun

BERYL A. GREEN
Notary Public for Oregon.
My commission expires 11/23/24

129

from the inside of the hall we all of us started shooting. We were shooting at the people that were rushing the door. I was shooting at people that rushed the door and when that stopped all of us stopped.

"On the 11th a person who has been called John Doe Davis around here said he had a 38 special revolver, and he said in looking it over he accidentally shot a hole through the mirror in Room 10 of the Avalon hotel, which is the room I had myself; had paid for. I immediately went up with him to the hotel. He and I were in the room possibly twenty minutes. He asked me if I had any objections to his staying in my room. That occurred, I believe, in the hall. When I was in the room with him he had a 38-55. I can identify it. I was arrested seven days later."

THE SECRETARY SPEAKS

This is what Britt Smith, the secretary of the Centralia branch of the I. W. W. had to say: "I heard lots of talk of further violence. It got to be common talk. They were going to come and raid us—clean us out on the 11th. When the parade passed I was about twelve feet from the back part of the hall—about twenty-eight feet from the front part of the hall. Morgan, Mike Sheehan, Bert Faulkner, Wesley Everest, Ray Becker, McInerney and myself were in the hall at the time. The first thing I saw was soldiers coming from out on the street. I saw Wesley Everest about two minutes before the shooting started. He was standing pretty near the center of the hall. I knew he had a gun but didn't see it. It's a big automatic . I was looking towards the door just about a second before the shooting started in the hall. There was shooting there. It was from where Everest was standing—three or four standing close together. I couldn't swear for sure if there was anything broken in the hall. I was back getting my gun and my mind was occupied with that. I went out the back upstairs on the porch. I dropped the gun behind the toilet. I was afterwards questioned about the gun. I didn't tell them nothing. I told Chief of Police Hughes the next day where the gun was. He told me he got it. The gun never was shot. Not to my knowledge was there any discussion of any plan to start any trouble or to murder anybody. I have always advocated staying away from violence. I just want the jury to know that we were going to defend our hall if they raided it."

The trial had been in progress from January 25th to March 13th, 1920. When the prosecution had concluded the presentation of its evidence, Judge Wilson ordered Bert Faulkner released, finding that no case had been made against him. March 12th was just like the preceding days of the trial. The attendance was considerably larger and the interest perhaps keener than at any other time. Automobiles started to line up around the court house in the early morning hours. All day they waited there in the drenching rain, their numbers being hourly augmented. Long before court convened the garish little courtroom on the third floor was filled to capacity. Standing room was at a premium. Reporters were compelled to climb over chairs and tables to make their exit to the press room and telegraph.

A LITTLE DRAMA OF REAL LIFE

The audience was distinctively respectable: business men, legionaires, with here and there a soldier in uniform. Occasionally could be seen a logger in stag shirt and overalls who had braved the danger of "arrest on suspicion" to see how the Majesty of the Law was dealing with his kind in a court of justice.

Many women were present, neat and smug in appearance; busy with bits of sewing or crocheting; laughing and chatting as though the affair were a church social instead of a grim lawsuit in which life and death, justice and judicial outrage hung in the balance. The relatives and friends of the defendants, dressed in their pitiful Sunday best, were huddled into a corner of the crowded room. The men on trial sat stiffly in a straight row, glancing about the room now and then, or looking soberly through the dripping window panes to the familiar gray hills, fringed with a lace work of pointed trees.

The widow of Warren Grimm was present with her baby daughter. The pretty youngster had to be restrained from playing with the tots across the way whose fathers were accused of having killed her papa. Eugene Barnett's sweet little baby boy was sitting beside his mother. He was fondling a red-headed celluloid doll and casting childish looks of unspeakable affection at his boyish father on the prisoner's bench.

After the usual colorless "Hear ye! hear ye! hear ye!" of the court clerk, the judge, in his usual black robes but with unusual uneasiness, started to read his now infamous instructions to the jury. As his nasal voice droned out the words, "And, gentlemen of the jury, if from a fair consideration of the testimony of the case you arrive at a conclusion of the guilt of these defendants, you are instructed to specify your charges . . murder in the first degree the penalty of which is hanging . . ."

Just at this moment Barnett's baby boy, his eyes big with a

131

strange fear, looked from the vulture-like judge and stern faced prosecutors to his mother beside him and sobbed out in heart-breaking baby notes:

"Daddy! daddy! Mama, what those men do to my daddy?"

For a moment there was a hushed silence. Even the church women dropped their sewing. Everyone looked over the heads of the crowd in the direction of the "Rebel Madonna" and her child. For a second the majesty of the law was vanquished by a baby's voice. A great warm wave of life welled up against the cold dead walls of the courtroom. The majesty of the law came back to its own again. But a sob remained in the throats of more than one.

THE LUMBER TRUST WINS THE JURY

On Saturday evening, March 13th, the jury brought in its final verdict of guilty. In the face of the very evident ability of the lumber interests to satisfy its vengeance at will, any other verdict would have been suicidal—for the jury.

The prosecution was out for blood and nothing less than blood. Day by day they had built the structure of the gallows there in the courtroom. They built a scaffolding on which to hang ten loggers—built it of lies and threats and perjury. Dozens of witnesses from the Chamber of Commerce and the American Legion took the stand to braid a hangman's rope of untruthful testimony. Some of these were members of the mob; on their white hands the blood of Wesley Everest was hardly dry. And they were not satisfied with sending their victims to prison for terms of from 25 to 40 years, they wanted the pleasure of seeing their necks broken. But they failed. Two verdicts were returned; his honor refused to accept the first; no intelligent man can accept the second.

Here is the way the two verdicts compare with each other: Elmer Smith and Mike Sheehan were declared not guilty and Loren Roberts insane, in both the first and the second verdicts. Britt Smith, O. C. Bland, James McInerney, Bert Bland and Ray Becker were found guilty of murder in the second degree in both instances, but Eugene Barnett and John Lamb were declared guilty of manslaughter, or murder "in the third degree" in the jury's first findings, and guilty of second degree murder in the second.

The significant point is that the state made its strongest argument against the four men whom the jury practically exonerated of the charge of conspiring to murder. More significant is

State of Washington)
County of Lewis   ) SS

    W.E.Inmon and E.E.Sweitzer of Grays Harbor
County,Washington,each for himself upon his oath says;
That he was one of the Jurors in the Case of the State
of Washington vs Britt Smith et al,tried in Grays Harbo
County,at Montesano,Washington during the first three
months of the year 1920,as an outgrowth of the Armistic
day tragedy at Centralia,Washington,Nov.11th,1919;
That during the consideration of said case by the jury,
one Harry Sellers,one of said Jurors,stated in the
Jury Room in substance," Every one of them is guilty
and ought to be hung no matter what the evidence shows;
That the evidence showed,as affiants verily believe,
that all the defendants were innocent and not guilty
and that not one of said defendants Loren Roberts,Bert
Bland,O.C.Bland,Eugene Barnett, John Lamb,James
McInerny,Ray Becker and Britt Smith,killed,injured,
wounded or harmed anyone;That these affiants,and each
of them,believed that in the event of a hung jury,a new
jury would have been called and in the face of the
hysteria that then existed,innocent men might have been
hung;That rather than have this happen these affiants
believed that it was better to have a second degree
verdict against seven defendants and acquit two,thus
leaving the two free to work for the release of the
others and leaving an opportunity to spread the truth;
That in the event of another trial and these affiants
were to sit as jurors in this case,and were permitted
to receive in evidence what they now know, their verdit
for each and all said defendants would be" Not Guilty"
and no power or influence could induce them to return
a verdict of Guilty in any degree.

_____

_____

Subscribed and sworn to before me this 15th day of
May,1922.

_____

Notary Public in and for the State of Washington
residing at Centralia,Washington.

the fact that the whole verdict completely upsets the charge of conspiracy to murder under which the men were tried. The difference between first and second degree murder is that the former, first degree, implies premeditation, while the other, second degree, means murder that is not premeditated. Now, how in the world can men be found guilty of conspiring to murder without previous premeditation? The verdict, brutal and stupid as it is, shows the weakness and falsity of the state's charge more eloquently than anything the defense has ever said about it.

BUT LABOR SAYS, "NOT GUILTY!"

But another jury had been watching the trial. Its verdict came as a surprise to those who read the newspaper version of the case. No sooner had the twelve bewildered and frightened men in the jury box paid tribute to the power of the Lumber Trust with a ludicrous and tragic verdict than the six workingmen of the Labor Jury returned their verdict also. Those six men represented as many labor organizations in the Pacific Northwest with a combined membership of many thousands of wage earners.

The last echoes of the prolonged legal battle had hardly died away when these six men sojourned to Tacoma to ballot, deliberate and to reach their decision about the disputed facts of the case. At the very moment when the trust-controlled newspapers, frantic with disappointment, were again raising the blood-cry of their pack, the frank and positive statement of these six workers came like a thunderclap out of a clear sky,—"Not Guilty!"

The Labor Jury had studied the development of the case with earnest attention from the beginning. Day by day it had watched with increasing astonishment the efforts of the defense to present, and of the prosecution and the judge to exclude, from the consideration of the trial jury, the things everybody knew to be true about the Centralia tragedy. The Labor Jury comprised men of long experience in the labor movement. They could see through a maze of red tape and legal mummery to the simple truth that was being hidden or obscured. The Lumber Trust did not fool these men and it could not intimidate them.

It cannot be said that the Labor Jury was biased in favor of the defendants or of the I. W. W. If anything, they were predisposed to believe the defendants guilty and their union an outlaw organization. It must be remembered that all the Labor Jury knew of the case was what it had read in the capitalist newspapers prior to its arrival at the scene of the trial. These men were not radicals but representative workingmen—members of conservative unions—who had been instructed by their organizations to observe impartially the progress of the trial and to report to their unions what they observed. Read their report:

LABOR'S VERDICT

"Labor Temple, Tacoma, March 15, 1920.

"The Labor Jury met in the rooms of the Labor Temple and organized, electing P. K. Mohr as foreman.

"1. Were the defendants guilty or not guilty? Verdict, 'Not guilty.'

"2. Shall we give our report to the press? Verdict, 'Yes.'

"3. Was there a conspiracy to raid the I. W. W. on the part of the business interests of Centralia? Verdict, 'Yes.'

"There was evidence offered by the defense to show that the business interests held a meeting at the Elks' Club on October 20, 1919, at which ways and means to deal with the I. W. W. situation were discussed. F. B. Hubbard, Chief of Police Hughes and William Scales, commander of the American Legion at Centralia, were present. Prosecuting Attorney Allen was quoted as having said, 'There is no law that would let you run the I. W. W. out of town.' Chief of Police Hughes said, 'You cannot run the I. W. W. out of town; they have violated no law.' F. B. Hubbard said, 'It's a damn shame; if I was chief I would have them out of town in 24 hours.' William Scales, presiding at the meeting, said that although he was not in favor of a raid, there was no American jury that would convict them if they did, or words to that effect. He then announced that he would appoint a secret committee to deal with the I. W. W. situation.

"4.**Was the I. W. W. hall unlawfully raided? Verdict, 'Yes.' The evidence introduced convinces us that an attack was made before a shot was fired.**

"5. Had the defendants a right to defend their hall? Verdict, 'Yes.' On a former occasion the I. W. W. hall was raided, furniture destroyed and stolen, ropes placed around their necks and they were otherwise abused and driven out of town by citizens, armed with pick handles.

"6. **Was Warren O. Grimm a party to the conspiracy of raiding the I. W. W. hall? Verdict, 'Yes.' The evidence introduced convinces us that Warren O. Grimm participated in the raid of the I. W. W. hall.**

"7. To our minds the most convincing evidence that Grimm was in front of and raiding the I. W. W. hall with others, is the evidence of State Witness Van Gilder, who testified that he stood

135

at the side of Grimm at the intersection of Second street and Tower avenue, where, according to his testimony, Grimm was shot. This testimony was refuted by five witnesses who testified that they saw Grimm coming wounded from the direction of the I. W. W. hall. It is not credible that Van Gilder, a personal and intimate friend of Grimm, would leave him when he was mortally wounded, to walk half a block alone and unaided.

"**8. Did the defendants get a fair and impartial trial? Verdict, 'No.' The most damaging evidence of a conspiracy by the business men of Centralia, of a raid on the I. W. W. hall, was ruled out by the court and not permitted to go to the jury. This was one of the principal issues that the defense sought to establish.**

"Also the calling of the federal troops by Prosecuting Attorney Allen was for no other reason than to create atmosphere. On interviewing the judge, sheriff and prosecuting attorney, the judge and sheriff informed us that in their opinion the troops were not needed and that they were brought there without their consent or knowledge. In the interview Mr. Allen promised to furnish the substance of the evidence which in his opinion necessitated the presence of the troops the next morning, but on the following day he declined the information. He, however, did say that he did not fear the I. W. W., but was afraid of violence by the American Legion. This confession came after he was shown by us the fallacy of the I. W. W. coming armed to interfere with the verdict. Also the presence of the American Legion in large numbers in court."

This report was signed by the whole Labor Jury:

Theodore Meyer, Everett Central Labor Council; John O. Craft, Seattle Metal Trades Council; E. W. Thrall, Brotherhood of Railway Trainmen, Centralia; W. J. Beard, Tacoma Central Labor Council; Otto Newman, Portland Central Labor Council; P. K. Mohr, Seattle Central Labor Council.

The prosecution, in order to cover up the crime of the real culprits, sought to press the absurd charge in court that the loggers had fired into the ranks of peaceful paraders. The evidence was all against them. Thanks to the capitalist papers however, the legend existed. It was a valuable asset to the prosecution—bought and paid for with lumber trust gold. And this legend was used to the limit to produce the passion and prejudice that would assure the unjust conviction. Only two deductions were possible: either the loggers fired in self-defense or they fired with the intention of committing wanton murder. It happened that the loggers were members of the I. W. W. This fact, in connection with the gravity of the charge and

State of Washington   )
)
County of Grays Harbor) SS

    Carl O. Hulten being first duely sworn upon his oath
deposes and says, that I was one of the jurors in the case of
the State of Washington as plaintiff, versus Britt Smith et al
as defendents, tried in the superior court of the State of
Washington for Grays Harbor County during the first three
months of the year 1920, as an outgrowth of the Armistice
Day tragedy at Centralia, Washington, November 11th 19
                                                 19.
    That I knew the contents of the affidavits of E.E.
Switzer,W.E.Immen, E.E.Terpen and P.V.Johnson also jurors in
the above stated cases as these statments appeared in the public
public press during the month of May,1922. That their said
affidavits coincedd with my view of said trial. That I verily
believe the defendents in said action did not have a fair
and impartial trial and there is not now in my mind an abiding
conviction of their guilt of the murder of Warren O.Grimm.

    That the said trial was conducted under extreme excitment
and pressure which made it impossible to conduct a trial in
a normal manner and leave the jury free and unhampered in
their deliberations.

                               Carl O. Hulten

    Subscribed and sworn to before me this First day of June
A.D.1922

                         J.M. Phillips
        Notary Public in and for the State of
        Washington ,residing at Aberdeen, Wash.

the atmosphere of hysteria that surrounded the courtroom, made a fair trial impossible. If the "evidence" of the prosecution would not convince, the admitted shooting and the admitted membership in the I. W. W. of the men who did the shooting would be sure to convince. Then there was the terror to be considered, the obvious and determined bias of the judge and the machinations of the prosecution lawyers who "framed" the trial.

JUDGE BARS VITAL EVIDENCE

The defense admitted that there was shooting on Armistice Day in Centralia, that legionaires were killed and that the union loggers were armed. But the defense claimed—what everyone knew to be a fact—that the loggers had armed themselves as a measure of self-protection against a certain number of men who were bent upon murder and destruction. All things considered, in view of the attacks upon both union halls, there should have been a verdict of "justifiable homicide in self-defense." But the trouble is, all things were not considered—in fact, were not permitted to be considered in court. The judge, subservient to the will of the lumber trust, ruled out, as inadmissible, all evidence that the union hall had been raided in 1918 and that the intention of the leaders of the Armistice Day parade was to raid it again. The judge sought religiously to keep from the jury all evidence of the conspiracy to raid the hall and of the complicity of Warren O. Grimm and others in this conspiracy.

The reason the prosecution wanted the case confined to facts of the shooting, instead of the conspiracy of the associated industries' officials that precipitated the shooting, is easy to be seen. But how did they manage to drill their witnesses so that the story would sound plausible? What kind of "machine" did they use to "frame" their case and "make" witnesses in order to put their version of the shooting across? How could they best manage to keep the defense from reaching the jury with the real facts, or as many of the real facts as possible? The real story of this machiavellian plot to defeat the ends of justice has leaked out since the trial. A special investigator for the defense has given his findings to the world. It reads like a page from fiction—but it is the gospel truth.

American Legion men had gathered together in considerable numbers in Montesano to attend the trial. The prosecution saw to this detail which, like the camping of regular troops on the courthouse lawn, was intended to create the proper "atmosphere." Tacoma, Centralia, Chehalis, Bellingham, Port Angeles,

Aberdeen, Hoquiam, Mt. Vernon, Anacortes and Bremerton—
each of these towns and cities supplied its quota of delegates,
all of them O. K.'d by the prosecution before they came. These
men were sent to Montesano with the understanding that they
were to submit to the orders of their commander, a Mr. Schant,
a former army captain who was in charge of the Montesano
American Legion. These men were paid four dollars a day by
the lumber interests. In addition to this stipend they were given
sleeping accommodations in the fire department section of the
City Hall and in a garage nearby. This latter place was a veritable fortress, well supplied with high power rifles and ammunition of all kinds. A certain Lieut. Crawford of Mount Vernon
was in charge of this little lumber trust army. The legionaires
did guard duty twenty-four hours each day in their fortress.

AN ARMED CAMP

It must be remembered that the legionaires were private
citizens, living in an armed camp of their own in the midst of
a community that had ample protection from the customary
law-enforcing machinery. Who armed them and gave them permission to camp in the heart of the city? Why had they been
gathered together and for what purpose? Can it be that the
lumber interests were waiting, as was openly intimated, for an
opportunity to wreak vengeance upon the defendants in case
the jury did not do its "duty?"

Lieut. Balcon was in charge of the secret service work for
the prosecution. Under him were several legionaires dressed
like loggers and workingmen. It was the duty of these lumber
trust spies to gain the confidence of defense witnesses, learn
in advance of the testimony they intended to give and, wherever
possible, influence it to suit the programme of the prosecution.
As soon as a defense witness had been interrogated by these
sleuths, the findings were transmitted to Chief Balcon who was
privileged to enter that part of the courtroom occupied by the
attorneys. Balcon would then pass his information over to
Prosecuting Attorney Christiansen, who would in turn give it
to Prosecutors Cunningham or Abel.

Christiansen was the most active of all the detectives for
the prosecution. His position as Assistant State's Attorney afforded him absolute freedom of action. He had access to everything that went on at the courthouse and the American Legion
fortress and headquarters. By examination of the subpoenas
issued for defense witnesses, it was simple for him to keep the
prosecution informed about all witnesses likely to be called.

Lieut. Frank Van Gilder was one of the chief members of this Intelligence Department. Whenever possible this officious person visited prospective defense witnesses before their arrival at Montesano and learned, or tried to learn, their testimony. Van Gilder's method of approach was suave but forceful. He always boasted that he "knew his stuff." And it was the smooth stuff that Van Gilder was supposed to put over. When this method failed to make the right kind of an impression on the witness other agents would follow him up with a different line. Threats and intimidation were indulged in and the witnesses would be informed in unmistakable language as to what their future in the community would be like and what would happen to them in case the testimony they were about to give was found to be objectionable by the prosecution.

LEGIONAIRES DISGUISED AS LOGGERS

Upon the arrival of the defense witnesses at Montesano, Lieut. Balcon's forces began work at once and made persistent efforts to interview those who had escaped Van Gilder's attentions. These men, in various attires intended to make them look as much like workers as possible, tried by confidential means to learn prospective testimony. Some defense witnesses were openly threatened in the courtroom immediately following their testimony. The arrest of two defense witnesses for perjury was part of the plan to intimidate other witnesses waiting their turn to go on the stand for the loggers.

As the defendant's attorney, George Vanderveer, neared the conclusion of his case the espionage machinery of the prosecution was already operating at high speed to manufacture the rebuttal witnesses to impeach all of the important testimony of the defense. Assistant State's Attorney Christiansen was the man selected to put the polish on these "made" witnesses. The testimony itself was "framed" by Lieut. Van Gilder or his associates, before the witness was brought to Montesano. The finishing touch was put on by Attorney Christiansen. Then each witness was taken before the special prosecutors for approval.

Two years passed by. The Centralia loggers were locked up securely behind the walls of the State prison at Walla Walla. The war hysteria had died down to a great degree. A new I. W. W. hall had been opened in Centralia. Some of the old wounds were beginning to heal over. Ordinarily the tragedy and conviction would have been a closed incident—a black page

WIVES AND CHILDREN OF CENTRALIA PRISONERS
At Prison Gate, Walla Walla, Washington.

of history turned down forever. But no one was satisfied with
the outcome of the trial. The lumber trust was out for blood;
it had been disappointed. The defense wanted an acquittal and
was disappointed also. Even the Legion was dissatisfied with
the inconclusive verdict.

Rumors began to spread up and down the Pacific Coast that
the trial jurors were saying they were sorry for what they had
done. And so it happened that almost two years after the verdict affidavits were made by six of the jurors which gave a new
angle to the case. Facsimile reproductions of sworn statements
of five of these jurors are printed elsewhere in this book.

JURORS REVEAL TERROR INFLUENCE

Juror E. E. Torpen, in addition to making the affidavit,
talked freely about the case. Torpen's most striking remark perhaps is the one in which he tells about the first trial
ballot taken by the jury when they retired from the courtroom
with the evidence fresh in their minds. This trial ballot resulted in a unanimous verdict of NOT GUILTY. Both Torpen's affidavit and the subsequent statements of other jurors
lead one to believe that the jury felt confident that its recommendation for leniency would be binding on the judge.
Torpen's affidavit shows clearly that it was prejudice against

141

the I. W. W. rather than actual evidence that induced the verdict of guilty. Juror Torpen, in an interview with a press representative, made the following statement:

"There are a lot of things I have learned about the trial both in the jury room and after I got out of it that I am not going to tell now. There were peculiar goings-on. If I am ever on the witness stand again I will tell them exactly as I remember them."

Torpen says he is convinced that the trial was unfair— that it was an injustice prompted by hysteria; that the evidence of guilt was inadequate; that important witnesses were prevented from testifying; that some of the jurors were determined to convict from the beginning regardless of the evidence; that other jurors were intimidated by the public opinion that prevailed at the time of the trial, and that one juror was "afraid of his life." He declared also that the jury had been instructed that 11 out of 12 could convict without the concurrence of the 12th juror. "In a way," stated Torpen, "I felt that I ought to have voted for an acquittal. On the other hand, I was afraid that a hung jury would mean a new trial with a worse jury, and the innocent men would be put to death. So I voted for a second degree verdict against seven and acquittal for two. It seemed better that way, with two of the men free to work for the release of the others."

"I remember," continued Torpen, "when we went to the window and got first sight of the soldiers. 'My God!' one of the jurors remarked to me, 'they are here to keep us from being shot.' I couldn't see why we should worry. But some of them did. A man had to be plain ornery to do any thinking. Some, I'll always figure, had their thinking all done and out of the way when they took their seats on the jury."

"I did not believe that any of the men convicted were guilty. The men that did the shooting never came to trial."

TWO MORE JURORS TELL THE TRUTH

The minds of Jurors Inmon and Sweitzer were far from being at ease also. Often they met and talked together about the trial and the injustice they had helped to work upon seven men whom they now felt were innocent. Walter Bland, brother of two of the convicted men, hearing of their attitude, had visited Inmon and asked him to help right the wrong that he had done.

One day Jurors Inmon and Sweitzer were dining together

and talking on the subject uppermost in their minds. They decided to swear out a joint affidavit. This affidavit states that "not one of the said defendants killed, wounded or harmed anyone." The remark about the statement made by Juror Sellers is still undisputed although Sellers has recourse to the libel laws if he thinks the two men lied about him. Sellers is alleged to have said, "Every one of them is guilty and ought to be hung no matter what the evidence shows."

Juror P. V. Johnson also made out an affidavit stating that he agrees with the statements made in the affidavits of Torpen, Inmon and Sweitzer. Johnson is perturbed because he was not permitted to learn of the facts about the premeditated raid on the union hall by the business interests. He is of the opinion that the presence of troops on the courthouse grounds coupled with the statement that "a thousand or more I. W. W.'s were hiding in the woods around Montesano created a feeling in the minds of the jurors that the I. W. W. organization was composed of outlaws and that therefore the organization was as much on trial as the individuals."

Juror Carl O. Hulten yielded to the promptings of his conscience and offered a sworn statement also. Hulten says that "the defendants . . . did not have a fair and impartial trial." He states that there is not now in his mind "an abiding conviction of their guilt of the murder of Warren O. Grimm."

U. G. Robinson, foreman of the jury, took oath as follows: "During the trial. . . a squad of soldiers was brought into Montesano and camped diagonally across the street from . . . our jury quarters. Nearly always while we were out for exercise . . . we could see these soldiers either marching around the streets or at their camp. A number of the jurors believed that these soldiers had been brought in to protect the jury against some threatened assault by the I. W. W., and there were three or four jurors, as I now remember . . . who so feared such an assault that they wanted guns for their protection. It is my recollection also that these same jurors were the ones who voted to find the defendants guilty of murder in the first degree."

FOUR OTHER JURORS MAKE ADMISSIONS

Four other jurors were approached by friends of the defendants. All expressed themselves as surprised at the severity of the sentences, having expected sentences of from 2 to 5 years, at the utmost 10 years, would be imposed. All declared emphatically that they would not care to be tried under circumstances similar to those at the trial. One uttered the belief that if the men were to be tried now they would be acquitted.

One of the jurors declared that, neither at the trial nor at the rendering of the verdict, was there an abiding conviction in his mind of the guilt of the defendants, and that as time goes on he is still less sure of the justice of the verdict. This man, like some of the other jurors, is in a position where the lumber trust can bring pressure to bear upon him. If such a thing as a grand jury investigation were possible, he would join the majority of the jurors in adopting a course similar to that of the men who have made sworn affidavits.

The union men convicted at Montesano are still buried alive at Walla Walla. Their sentences are from 25 to 40 years. Unless the country is aroused to a realization of the great injustice that has been done, these men will probably stay in prison until they die. It is up to you who read these lines, if still in doubt, to investigate further the facts of this case. And it is up to you, once convinced, to do all in your power to see that justice is done. What are you going to do?

Mourn Not the Dead

Mourn not the dead that in the cool earth lie—
Dust unto dust—
The calm, sweet earth that mothers all who die
As all men must;

Mourn not your captive comrades who must dwell—
Too strong to strive—
Each in his steel-bound coffin of a cell,
Buried alive;

But rather mourn the apathetic throng—
The cowed and meek—
Who see the world's great anguish and its wrong
And dare not speak!

R. C.

Wesley Everest

Torn and defiant as a wind-lashed reed,
Wounded, he faced you as he stood at bay;
You dared not lynch him in the light of day,
But on your dungeon stones you let him bleed;
Night came . . . and you black vigilants of Greed, . . .
Like human wolves, seized hard upon your prey,
Tortured and killed . . . and, silent, slunk away
Without one qualm of horror at the deed.

Once . . . long ago . . . do you remember how
You hailed Him king for soldiers to deride—
You placed a scroll above His bleeding brow
And spat upon Him, scourged Him, crucified . . .?
A rebel unto Caesar—then as now—
Alone, thorn-crowned, a spear wound in His side!

R. C.

Centralia: Tragedy and Trial

By Ben Hur Lampman

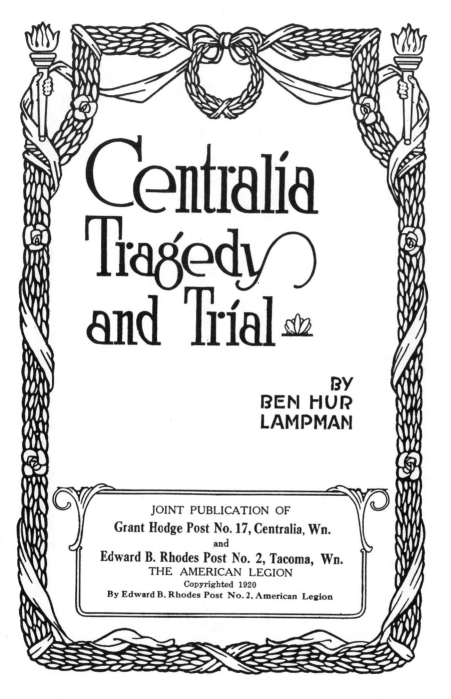

Centralia Tragedy and Trial

BY
BEN HUR
LAMPMAN

JOINT PUBLICATION OF
Grant Hodge Post No. 17, Centralia, Wn.
and
Edward B. Rhodes Post No. 2, Tacoma, Wn.
THE AMERICAN LEGION

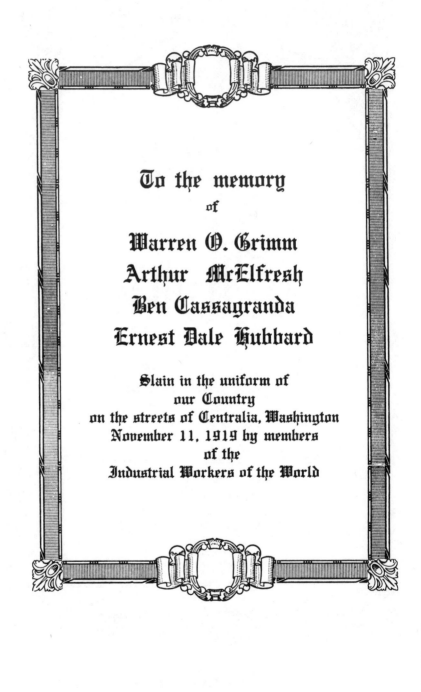

To the memory
of

Warren O. Grimm
Arthur McElfresh
Ben Cassagranda
Ernest Dale Hubbard

Slain in the uniform of
our Country
on the streets of Centralia, Washington
November 11, 1919 by members
of the
Industrial Workers of the World

Foreword

BY F. W. GALBRAITH, JR.,

National Commander, The American Legion

The name "Centralia" has been emblazoned in letters of blood before the American people. And this fact is of particular significance to us of the American Legion, because it is with the blood of martyrs that it was written there—the blood of four murdered comrades, stricken down unawares by the cowardly hand of anarchy.

It is fitting that the details of this shocking crime against the Republic should be set forth accurately and fairly and so preserved that all may read; and that the vivid lesson Centralia holds may strike home to every American heart.

You will read with horror and amazement this tale of peaceful paraders shot down by organized and vicious exponents of lawlessness. You will read with pride how Legion men curbed their natural human impulses of revenge and waited on law to take its course against the criminals.

That the Legion must always do. I. W. W.-ism, radicalism, and all other isms which seek to overthrow our government deserve no quarter from the American Legion and should receive none. But let us always proceed fairly and in accordance with the forms of government under which this nation has grown great, and which we are sworn under all circumstances to protect.

Centralia will serve to keep alive a sense of the danger that is with us. And thus will be fostered, I hope, a keener sense of obligation to the flag. I commend the story of Centralia to all Americans.

Introduction

By Major General Leonard Wood, U. S. A.

The Government of the United States is one of Law and not of Men, and must ever remain so if the Republic is to be maintained. Respect for the Law, for the constituted authorities, for the rights of property and the rights of others lies at the very foundation of our national structure, as does the obligation to serve the country in peace and to defend it in war. This obligation rests equally upon all.

If men are dissatisfied with the law or its application the Constitution provides in the Ballot, the means to make changes and correct abuses, and it is upon this that we must depend if we are to have a sound and orderly government and maintain those principles for which and on which our Government stands.

There is no force in the country which stands more strongly for these basic principles than does the American Legion. Its membership is made up of the best type American,—the man who has offered everything in the service of his country in time of war and whose actions in time of peace embody respect for Law and the constituted authorities.

The American Legion has adopted a constitution which breathes patriotism and good citizenship, respect for Law and obligation for service in peace and war to the limit of our physical and mental ability. The Legion stands squarely against those elements which are trying to break down our form of government, forces which stop at nothing to accomplish their purpose, menacing all who stand in their way, intimidating and often terrorizing timid officials. These enemies of government are dangerous only because of our own indifference. The forces of disorder are comparatively small in numbers. They are effective and dangerous in part because of their organization and intensity of purpose but principally because of the indifference of that great, sane, sound mass of the American people who only wake up to take drastic action when conditions become absolutely intolerable, and then go to sleep again. We want that constant interest which acts as a preventative. Eternal vigilance is the price of Liberty.

We Americans must be more keenly alive to the danger of failing to discharge our citizenship obligations in peace as well as in war.

If the sane, sound public opinion of the country will only arouse itself sufficiently to act, these lawless organizations which are striving to overthrow government through discrediting the Courts, through terrorism, through creating lack of confidence in our form of government and those dangerous political elements which strive to and often succeed in setting aside the will of the people, thus destroying confidence in the Ballot, will disappear like snow before the sun.

Government under our Constitutional Democracy can only attain a full measure of efficiency when the citizens discharge the obligations of citizenship in Peace and War.

That experience and training in the Army makes for good citizenship, respect for Law and Order, was clearly demonstrated by the action of the American Legionnaires on the occasion of the murderous attack by a band of cowardly assassins representing the Red element, upon the first Armistice Day Parade at Centralia, Washington.

There is no finer illustration of self-control and respect for law than was given by these ex-soldiers, men who had served the country devotedly and fearlessly at home and abroad, and who were assembled to celebrate the first anniversary of the signing of the Armistice. They wore the uniform of many fighting divisions, organizations which had been overseas and of less fortunate organizations which served in the homeland. Their purpose was a purely patriotic one. They had the force and the power to destroy those who murdered their fellows, but instead of taking the law into their own hands and meting out summary vengeance on the spot they were the principal force in the capture and arrest of the murderers and turned them over to the Courts for trial.

Never was there a more unprovoked and cowardly attack than this, and it required the highest degree of self-restraint and the highest respect for Law and Order on the part of the Legionnaires to turn these wilfull assassins, who were caught red-handed, over to the Courts for an orderly and fair trial.

The Legion men did well to do as they did. They ran true to form. They stood for the law. They showed conclusively that the country can have absolute confidence in them as a great force for national stability, for the maintenance of Law for the upholding of our Constitution and our institutions. The story of the trial brings out clearly the character of the assassins and their hatred of any force which stands for Law and Order, for government under the Constitution, for America First. The American Legion stands for all these.

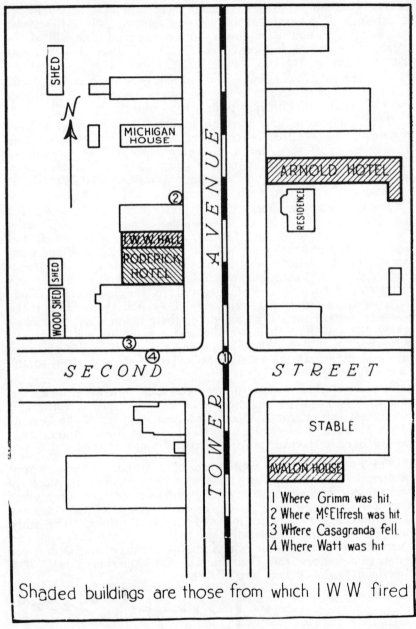

Map of section of Centralia, Washington, where the Armistice Day parade was ambushed by members of the I. W. W.

Brief Outline of Centralia's Tragedy

ON NOVEMBER 11, 1919, an Armistice Day parade was held in Centralia, Washington.

CENTRALIA has a population of approximately 10,000. The principal street, Tower Avenue, runs north and south, and most of the business houses are on this street.

THE I. W. W. HALL was situated on Tower Avenue, between 2nd and 3rd Streets. It was rented by the I. W. W.'s early in September, 1919.

GRANT HODGE POST of the American Legion of Centralia, about four weeks prior to Armistice Day, decided to hold a parade in celebration of the signing of the Armistice, and invited all ex-service men, whether Legionnaires or not, to march with them. The Loren Fiscus Post of Chehalis, four miles distant, decided to march in the parade as a unit.

THE PARADE began at 2 o'clock, was scheduled to march north on Tower Avenue to 3rd Street, counter-march, going south on Tower Avenue to Main Street, pass the reviewing stand and assemble in the auditorium for patriotic addresses.

DR. DAVID LIVINGSTONE, mounted, was Marshal of the parade. All the ex-service men in the parade were in uniform and unarmed. The following units participated in the order named: Elk's band; Boy Scouts; Canadian Veterans; Ex-Sailors of the War; Chehalis Lodge of Elks; Centralia Lodge of Elks; Chehalis Post of the American Legion, led by J. E. Murray; Centralia Post of the American Legion, led by Warren O. Grimm; Red Cross nurses in automobiles.

THE EX-SERVICE MEN were formed into platoons of eight or nine men, each led by a platoon commander. In making the turn at 3rd Street to counter-march, the parading soldiers had not kept their proper distances, and when the head of the Centralia contingent had reached the intersection of 2nd Street and Tower Avenue, the command "Halt, Close Up" was given by the commander, Warren O. Grimm. Frank Van Gilder, commanding the first platoon was standing at Grimm's side. Some of the platoons were closing up, others were marking time, and some had halted. When the

Centralia contingent had practically closed its ranks to the proper distances, and was ready to move—

A SHOT WAS FIRED from the I. W. W. hall. A moment later, two more were fired from the same place. Taken by surprise, and not understanding the meaning of the shots (for most of the ex-service men did not even know of the existence of an I. W. W. hall in Centralia), the parade broke formation. Some sought cover down the side-streets or in the store entrances, others ran towards the I. W. W. hall from which the shots had come.

THEN CAME A VOLLEY of shots from the Hall, and a fusilade from the upper rooms of buildings on all sides of the parade, the Arnold Hotel, the Avalon Hotel, and from Seminary Hill —a vantage point a quarter-mile distant which commanded the street intersection and the front and north of the I. W. W. hall. The parade of unarmed ex-service men had been ambushed, caught in a pocket. Members of the I. W. W. had taken their positions in pursuance of an agreement and understanding to shoot when the signal was given from the I. W. W. hall.

WARREN O. GRIMM was mortally wounded as he stood at the head of the parade at the intersection of 2nd Street and Tower Avenue. He was shot by a 38-55 Winchester rifle fired from the Avalon Hotel. He was assisted into an automobile and taken to a hospital where he died an hour later.

ARTHUR McELFRESH was instantly killed as he ran across Tower Avenue to seek cover. He was hit in the head by a bullet fired from a 22 high-power Savage rifle by Loren Roberts from Seminary Hill. One of the Red Cross nurses braved the shots and hurried over to him, but found him already dead.

BEN CASSAGRANDA was shot down as he ran west on 2nd Street. He was shot by some member of the I. W. W. who ran out of the rear of the hall and down the alley to 2nd Street. Cassagranda was taken to the hospital where he died a few hours later.

EARL WATTS was shot down within a few feet of where Cassagranda fell. Watts was shot thru the body, but recovered.

EUGENE PFITZER was shot in the left arm while he was in front of the I. W. W. hall. The shot was fired from the hall, but the wound was not serious.

BERNARD EUBANKS *was shot in the left leg as he was standing on the curb just north of 2nd Street.*

DALE HUBBARD *was killed in the pursuit of Wesley Everest, the ringleader of the I. W. W. conspirators. Everest ran out of the rear of the hall, around buildings, over fences, hotly pursued by ex-service men. He would empty his gun at his pursuers, and re-load as he ran. He evidently was attempting to get into the woods which skirt the Skookumchuck River, about one mile distant from the I. W. W. hall. In the chase he wounded Alva Coleman, shooting him in the leg. Coleman had a revolver obtained from the occupant of a house along the line of chase. He gave it to Dale Hubbard as he passed him. Hubbard outstripped his comrades in the chase, being a powerful athlete.*

WHEN EVEREST *reached the Skookumchuck River, he attempted to ford it, but, the water being too deep, he turned back and retraced his steps. When he reached the edge of the wood, he was met by Dale Hubbard who jumped out from behind a stump and ordered him to put down his gun. In answer, Everest opened fire and Hubbard went down. Everest then emptied his gun into Hubbard's prostrate body, before he was overwhelmed by other ex-service men. Hubbard died shortly after.*

THE I. W. W. CONSPIRATORS *were captured in the following way. Britt Smith and Bert Faulkner were captured in the I. W. W. hall. Ray Becker, Mike Sheehan, James McInerney, and Tom Morgan were captured in the ice-box at the rear of the I. W. W. hall. John Lamb and O. C. Bland, who fired from the Arnold Hotel, were captured at their homes by citizens and civil authorities. Of the three who fired from Seminary Hill, Loren Roberts gave himself up two days later, Bert Bland was captured a week later near Independence by deputy sheriffs, and Ole Hanson was never apprehended. Eugene Barnett, who fired from the Avalon Hotel, was taken by a posse at his home, two days after the shooting. Jack Davis, who was with him in the Avalon, has never been taken. Elmer Smith, Centralia I. W. W. attorney, was arrested in his office immediately after the shooting. All were charged with the crime of first degree murder except Elmer Smith who was charged with being an accessory.*

Where the Trial Was Held

Grays Harbor County Courthouse, at Montesano, Washington. Due to the intense feeling naturally existing in Lewis County (in which Centralia is situated) following the firing from ambush into an unarmed Legion, civilian, and Red Cross parade, the judge granted a change of venue to Grays Harbor County. Montesano, the county seat, has a population of only 2,500, and its facilities for handling the crowd of several hundred witnesses and additional hundreds of interested spectators were naturally inadequate. Hotels being overcrowded, the large rooms of the City Hall were pressed into service, private citizens opened their homes for the visitors, and, for the ex-service men in attendance, the upper floors of garages were fitted into barracks. When the restaurants were overcrowded, mess-halls were provided by the ex-service men.

Insets: Right, W. H. Abel, Prosecuting Attorney for Grays Harbor County; Left, Herman Allen, Prosecuting Attorney for Lewis County. These two. with Special Prosecutor C. D. Cunningham of Centralia, were the "Big Three" representing the state.

Centralia---Tragedy and Trial

GREAT many folk are forgetting the war. With Germany defeated they no longer have selfish cause to calculate what price America might have paid had the tide of battle been unturned. And, quite as casually, they are prone to shelve with liberty loans and Red Cross crusades all recollection of those valiant and high-hearted boys who crossed the submarine lanes to fight and suffer and die gloriously in France—that certain American ideals and institutions might remain intact for the salvation of the world.

To the American who does remember, and who most fortunately constitutes the majority, the perils of the present are not less than those of the past—and are trebly hazardous in that they besiege us at home. For he has seen, amid the disorder that rides in the wake of the world conflict, certain elements as utterly foreign as Prussianism gather to the attack on the free institutions of his land. Spurred forward by alien radicals, who seek to sever the bonds of nationalism and establish soviet rule in the United States, the wild horses of unrest threaten to trample their way through law and order toward the chimera of revolution and the overthrow of a government that is democratic in the fullest degree, and which today represents the complete expression of personal liberty, power of the popular voice, and human freedom.

It is the common-sense of the average citizen which will defeat the purpose of the radical—for here in America is no dream of actual brotherhood, but the fact itself. And the land of Washington and Lincoln needs no tutors risen from unhappy Europe to teach it a new doctrine of democracy, no prophets of revolution to point toward a halcyon day when, after such ruin as Russia knows, America shall be privileged to attempt another social and industrial disorder. Near at hand, whenever we choose, and when occasion requires, is the weapon of revolution more effectual than rifle and bomb—the ballot. There are times when we take it up, as for a righteous cause, and correct summarily such evils as may have fastened themselves upon the body of the land. It is tried and sufficient.

Far different is the revolutionary concept of the soviet, of the communist, of the I. W. W.—of all the kindred clans that seek chaotic disruption. To them the economic contest resolves itself into "the class war," calling for measures as keen and sanguinary as ever the barricades of Paris saw when tyranny departed from France, as ever Russia beheld when her bewildered peasantry kindled to the flame of revolt and obliterated the house of Romanoff. To those who love their homeland, let this be said: In the mutterings of the alien radical and the fatuous throng who follow him, bides a danger that is real, lurid with death and devastation, having for its sole object the attainment of American destruction by whatsoever means.

A Couplet of Soviet Signs

Permitting no soft words to cozen him, no specious argument to distract his logic, the genuine American may turn for examples of the revolutionary purpose to two ill-timed but viciously sincere expressions of direct action in radicalism. Both were of recent date and neither should fade from his memory. They were the Seattle general strike, so-called, and the Armistice Day assassinations at Centralia, Washington. The one, under the guise of attaining an industrial objective, throttled a great city in the attempt to inaugurate the first instance of communistic municipal control in the United States; the other, fruitage of the desperate seeds of class hatred as sown by the I. W. W., comprised an ambuscade of parading American veterans in uniform and took four youthful, loyal lives as its toll. Of both these manifestations the revolutionary orator and the radical press have fashioned a propaganda of falsehood and renewed intrigue—piling lie upon lie until Munchausen himself has been brought to envy and Judas and Arnold outshone as traitors.

The Seattle revolution was a flare-back, reacting upon the evil purposes that conceived it. With it we are no longer concerned—save to remember and hold its lesson fast for future guidance. But of the Centralia murders, and the trial of the assassins, so multitudinous and prevalent are the falsehoods of the red propagandist that citizens are yet within the danger zone of conversion to opinions unrelated to the facts and discreditable to their citizenship.

I. W. W. Murderers on Trial

It is for the purpose of portraying, clearly, in conformity with the records, the Centralia tragedy and ensuing events, that herewith is undertaken a comprehensive review of the trial at Montesano, Washington. It was there that ten members of the

I. W. W., together with the renegade legal adviser who counseled their crime, were arraigned for the murder of Lieutenant Warren O. Grimm, one of the four victims in the Armistice Day attack, and were found guilty of naught save murder in the second degree, or were freed.

"A cowardly verdict," was the consensus of legal and public opinion when that verdict was returned — unsatisfactory alike both to prosecution and defense, and eloquent of the fear-haunted minds that conceived it. For but few of those who heard the evidence and followed the course of the trial hold other belief than that the jurors cowered beneath dread of the vengeance of the I. W. W., and returned a finding through which they hoped to escape both the retaliation of the reds and the too scathing censure of an outraged citizenry.

WARREN O. GRIMM
30 years old. Graduate of University of Washington. Great football player. Centralia's favorite son. Practicing law when war broke out. Commissioned 1st Lieutenant July, 1917, and served in Siberia. As Commander of Grant Hodge Post, Grimm led the Centralia section of the parade. He had just given the command to mark time when the I. W. W. suddenly opened fire. Mortally wounded by one of the first shots, Grimm died within an hour. He left a wife and year old child.

In the abstract it matters little that Judge John M. Wilson, presiding, gave to the seven convicted murderers one of the sternest sentences possible under second degree conviction, decreeing terms of twenty-five to forty years in the penitentiary— though his determined and courageous action must receive the endorsement and commendation of all right-thinking members of society. This terrible truth remains—that the assassination of American veterans of the world war, the needless blotting out of lives once freely offered on the nation's battle fields, was held by a jury of their fellow citizens to be one of the lighter, lesser forms of murder.

Centralia's Ghastly Holiday

The story of Centralia's tragic holiday has been told repeatedly—but men forget. They forget that on the holiday streets of Lewis county's little metropolis, on the afternoon of Armistice

Day, November 11, 1919, while members of the American Legion laughed and jested, in parade line, the zestful autumn air suddenly was rife with whistling lead. Back from France and Siberia they were, those boys, with the fancy in their hearts that peril was past. Yet four of them died on the streets of their own home town, while others, who had gone scathless through the fields of Flanders, and the deadly oaken thickets of the Argonne, felt the stab of wounds or saw their comrades stagger to the impact of hostile bullets.

The shots that broke that parade formation, that plunged spitefully through the throngs of women and children on the gala streets, came from the haggard windows of the I. W. W. hall, on Centralia's main thoroughfare, Tower Avenue, from the blistered old rooming houses that flanked the avenue, and from the distant vantage point of Seminary Hill. As each hidden rifle cracked it spoke the welcome of radicalism to men who had returned from peril overseas.

The dead were Warren O. Grimm, favorite son of Centralia, Arthur McElfresh, Ernest Dale Hubbard and Ben Cassagranda—slain in the same uniform they wore when America called them home again. Through their deaths, as by a renewed votive offering, their country was privileged to see how sharp the fangs of discord are, how ruthless and how terrible are the eventual strokes of the red adder of radicalism. America sensed the horror of that illustration—but Centralia, above the bodies of her sons, vowed vengeance. Are you among the critical? Had you been in Centralia that day yours would have been the first among the voices lifted for retributive justice.

Red-handed they took them, the men who had compassed this thing—took them with rifles and pistols yet hot from the discharge, eyeballs yet dilated by the zest of killing. In the turmoil of Centralia's streets, through the ramshackle warrens of the I. W. W. hall and the ragged old rooming houses, in the timbered wilderness of Lewis County, citizens and Legionnaires sought out the murderers and brought them back to trial. Dale Hubbard, Legionnaire, took his death wound as he closed to the capture of Wesley Everest, fleeing gunman. Fighting desperately, and firing to the last, Everest pistoled Hubbard an instant before other ex-service men had made the capture; and shot him twice after he had fallen to the ground.

How One Gunman Died

Everest 'died that night. From among his fellow prisoners in Centralia jail, when the lights of the city were turned out, unknown avengers took him forth to the outskirts of the town and hanged him from a river-bridge, sending a rifle bullet through his dangling body. The lynching of Everest was an unlawful error. Not only did it afford additional propaganda for the radicals, but—and in this was the greater harm—it removed from trial one of the ringleaders of the Centralia reds, against whom evidence was damningly complete and conclusive. In cartoon the lynched "wobbly" has been depicted as an ex-service man, executed by his "buddies." He wore the uniform by compulsion, after nimble draft dodging, as the records attest—and died the violent death of one who preached and advocated violence.

This, and this only may be said of the I. W. W. who participated in the Centralia Armistice Day attack: They *believed* their hall was to be raided during the progress of the parade. Misled by their renegade counsel—now the feted darling of the reds though under indictment for

ARTHUR McELFRESH

26 years old. A Centralia druggist. Served in France with the 91st Division. The parading Legionnaires broke ranks when the I. W. W. without warning commenced firing into the parade from four sides. McElfresh was seeking cover when instantly killed by a shot thru the head from a 22 high power rifle fired by Loren Roberts from Seminary Hill. McElfresh was unmarried.

the murder of Arthur McElfresh—they planned and prepared the ambuscade. But in all the course of the long bitterly contested trial which ensued there was adduced no evidence, of conclusive or admissable nature, that such a raid was to be held, and none that should have warranted the jury in concluding that the I. W. W. hall was attacked by the paraders before the fussillade opened. The record will speak for itself, and in proper sequence this review will treat of the testimony.

These were the men who were brought to trial for the murder of Warren O. Grimm — the prosecution centering its efforts upon the evidence directly relating to the murder of the ex-lieutenant who led the Centralia contingent of the American Legion in the Armistice Day parade: Elmer Smith, radical attorney, charged with equal guilt as an accessory; Britt Smith, secretary of the Centralia I. W. W., Ray Becker, Bert Faulkner,

DALE HUBBARD
26 years old. Attended University of Washington for a time. Hubbard was a logger, and served in France with the Forestry Engineers. A splendid athlete, Dale Hubbard outstripped his comrades in the pursuit of Wesley Everest, who was loading and firing as he ran. Everest, finally cornered, turned and shot Hubbard at a distance of only a few feet, and then shot him twice more as he lay helpless. Hubbard left a bride of only a month.

James McInerney, Bert Bland, Mike Sheehan, Eugene Barnett, Loren Roberts, John Lamb, and O. C. (Commodore) Bland. Of the eleven original defendants, the charge against Bert Faulkner was dismissed by the court at the conclusion of the state's case midway in the trial, while Elmer Smith and Mike Sheehan were freed by the final verdict, to be re-arrested immediately for the murder of Arthur McElfresh. The remaining seven were convicted of murder in the second degree.

Opening of the Montesano Trial

The Centralia Armistice Day murder case, after change of venue from Lewis county, opened in Montesano, county seat of Grays Harbor County, Washington, on January 26, 1920, with the examination of veniremen as prospective jurors. Eleven days were consumed in the selection of the jury, comprising twelve members of the regular panel and two alternates, and approximately one hundred talesmen had been interrogated before the trial was ready to proceed.

In the middle of the trial one of the jurors became so ill that his place was taken by an alternate.

Appearing as leading counsel for the prosecution were C. D. Cunningham, of Centralia, Washington, assistant prosecutor for Lewis county; W. H. Abel, of Montesano, Washington, assistant prosecutor; and Herman Allen, prosecuting attorney of Lewis county. For the defense appeared George F. Vanderveer, widely known as a defender in cases where radicals have come to trial and reputed to be held in $50,000 annual retainer to the national organization of I. W. W., as chief legal adviser. Additional members of the legal staff of the prosecution were

Frank P. Christensen, assistant attorney general of Washington; John Dunbar, assistant in the office of the attorney general, and J. H. Jahnke, of Centralia.

Every phase of the case was fraught with the elements of drama. A courtroom dotted with the uniforms of men who fought overseas. A row of silent prisoners on a single oaken bench. Judge Wilson in black silken robes, gravely moody, speaking his rulings, with the deliberation of finality. Every seating space held by an occupant. Deputy sheriffs, young chaps, seated near the accused, with a bulge at their hips and the gleam of brass cartridge cases at their waists.

And against this setting the verbal fencing of the attorneys —Vanderveer, cynical, persuasive, tense, with a smile that turned at times to comradeship and again to a fighting sneer; Abel, suave, dignified, gifted with quiet sarcasm, master of the law, slow of speech and quick of thought; Cunningham, contemplative, with incisive flashes of speech, excelling in argument, resourceful, square-chinned, grim-mouthed at times, with a pleasant voice that could turn on the instant to the slither of steel.

BEN CASSAGRANDA
25 years old. Centralia boot-black. Served in France with the 91st Division and returned safely, only to be shot from ambush in the streets of his home town. Cassagranda was seeking cover down 2nd St. when shot and killed. It is not known definitely who fired the shot that killed Cassagranda. Unknowingly, he was seeking shelter down the street that was being most swept by bullets. Cassagranda also left a bride of but a few months.

Prosecutor Allen's Opening Statement

The choosing of the jury, to which was entrusted the decision in a case of utmost importance not only to Americans, but to the designs of the revolutionists, may well be said to have illustrated the chief weakness of the existing system of jury selection —in that examinations of so rigid and searching a character automatically dispose of all save such as confess to no opinion whatsoever, and who maintain this pitiful protestation, or who by successful knavery are enabled to win their way through utter falsehood to seats on the panel. It is an open secret that the Montesano jury harbored not less than two avowed reds, while another of the twelve was of sympathetic trend toward the doctrines of unrest.

Moreover, as the press of evidence and the instruction of the court at the conclusion of the trial left no possible verdicts save acquittal or conviction in the first degree—the jurors are open to the charge of false stewardship in their return of second degree murder. And not one of them, in the examinations, but had declared lack of real objection to the infliction of the death penalty in proper cases. In Washington, it should be understood, the extreme retributive function rests with the jury and not the court.

A so-called labor "jury", entirely unofficial, also sat at the trial, in seats reserved for its members, delegated to attend from various labor councils of Washington and Oregon. One of the "jurors" was to admit, on the stand, that his "disinterested" attitude had not prevented him from hunting witnesses for the defense. The majority of the "jury" did not consider it worth their while to arrive in Montesano until the defense had opened its case. In every instance these men were the representatives of the most drastically radical element of organized labor. The verdict of exoneration later returned by the "labor jurors" was wholly in keeping with the intent which dispatched them to the Grays Harbor capital.

Prosecutor Allen's Opening Statement

In a crowded courtroom, sprinkled with the uniforms of the ex-service men attending the trial, and with a plentiful representation from the radical labor element, the case opened on February 7 when Prosecuting Attorney Allen delivered the opening statement for the state. Charging the eleven defendants with vicious and premeditated murder, the prosecutor outlined the structure of the state's case, delineating the role of each of the accused in the Centralia tragedy.

Vanderveer, caustic counsel for the defendants, interrupted to inquire whether the prosecution would "stand or fall" upon the contention that no attack was made upon the I. W. W. hall before the firing began, precipitating by this inquiry the first skirmish of the many that were to follow.

"Our position is that the boys were standing in the street in military formation," replied Prosecutor Allen, "under the charge of their commander, paying close attention to him when he gave the command to halt and close up ranks, and that they were marking time when they were fired upon."

"In other words," pursued Vanderveer, "it is equivalent to a statement that there was no attack on the hall, and the doors were not smashed in before there was any shooting, and you will be judged by it hereafter?"

"We surely will" flashed Abel, rising to his feet.

The opening statement of the prosecution placed the head of the Centralia contingent almost at the intersection of Tower Avenue and Second Street, two hundred feet south of the I. W. W. hall, where it rested when the attack began.

"It was while the men were in this position," said the prosecutor, "that they were fired upon. Four or five shots rang out. There was a distinct pause of a few seconds. The boys began to break ranks and seek shelter. When the ranks broke and the boys began scattering, several volleys came from the I. W. W. hall. A great number of shots were fired, ranging from 50 to 150.

HERMAN ALLEN

Prosecuting Attorney of Lewis County. He delivered the opening statement for the prosecution, and outlined the case. "Our position is that the boys were standing in the street in military formation, under the charge of their commander, paying close attention to him when he gave the command to halt and close up ranks, and that they were marking time when they were fired upon."

"The evidence will show that all the defendants participated in a conspiracy to kill ex-service men; that while some of them did not actually shoot and kill, they were present, aiding, abetting and encouraging; and that all the defendants were present with the exception of Elmer Smith, their lawyer, who, though not present, did advise, encourage, counsel and abet the defendants in their unlawful conspiracy which resulted in murder."

In outlining its case the state did not resort to forensics—contenting itself with a calmly dispassionate statement of the evidence and testimony in prospect. It was asserted that the prosecution would show—as it did—that plans for the ambuscade were perfected some days prior to the parade, that the defendants were cognizant of such plans, and that Elmer Smith, as their legal adviser, consulted with them regarding their preparedness on the day of the parade. The records of the trial will

C. D. CUNNINGHAM
Special Prosecutor in charge of the case against the I. W. W. Member of the Grant Hodge post of the American Legion. Mr. Cunningham was in the parade in Centralia when it was fired upon, and was one of the men who captured Wesley Everest. He had been Lewis County's Prosecuting Attorney for two terms before he enlisted in the army. As leading prosecutor in the Montesano trial, Cunningham was able to use his first-hand knowledge of the tragedy to telling effect.

demonstrate that the state kept its promise almost to the letter —to be partially cheated by a verdict utterly unanticipated.

Vanderveer's Promise

As for the defense, requesting leave to make its opening statement in immediate succession to that of the state, Vanderveer pledged himself and his witnesses to proof which never was achieved. He declared that the men on trial would be known, within a decade, as "true Americans." Later his claims regarding the strategy of the reds were to return and plague him, as when the state proved beyond dispute that shots were fired from the Avalon Hotel—a charge which Vanderveer denied categorically in his opening statement. This charge he was to admit, as he was to admit others, when the structure of the defense crumbled before the state's unimpeachable witnesses.

The plea was self-defense. Upon the assertion that the I. W. W.'s fired only in protection of their hall, and that their armed preparation was made at the rumor of an impending raid, the defendants and their counsel staked the wager of freedom or punishment.

Almost upon the echo of his assertions, the I. W. W. counsel, who maintained that the I. W. W. hall alone was defended, that it was in a state of siege, and that no shots were fired from ambush elsewhere, was buffeted by the testimony of Edward C. Dohm, state field engineer of Washington, a member of General Pershing's overseas staff.

One of the first witnesses summoned by the state, Mr. Dohm testified that he had examined bullet marks in buildings adjoining the I. W. W. hall, on the west side of Tower Avenue, and that the angle of their entrance proved conclusively that they had been fired from three points —the Avalon Hotel, the Arnold Hotel and Seminary Hill.

"Do you contend," queried Vanderveer, "that you can establish the degree of incidence of bullets that came from the hill, within four or five degrees?"

"I can," was the reply. "Within one or two degrees."

Similar was the testimony of Sidney Gallagher, city engineer of Centralia, who testified convincingly that bullet holes on the opposite side of the street pointed, with scientific infallibility, to the upper windows of the Avalon Hotel, whence the defense had declared no shots were fired.

At the outset of its testimony the prosecution had demolished two main and important contentions of the defense—namely, that no shots were fired from the Avalon or the Arnold Hotel, and had proved the essential truth of the declaration that the Armistice Day attack was not a defense, but an ambuscade.

W. H. ABEL

Special Prosecutor. Mr. Abel was Prosecuting Attorney for Grays Harbor County, of which Montesano is the county seat, and was called in to assist Mr. Cunningham and Mr. Allen in the conduct of the state's case. His clashes with Vanderveer throughout the trial provided a dramatic setting in keeping with the nature of the case.

Plans of the Ambuscade

The strategy of the defense, as testimony was to develop beyond dispute—casting down the early denial of the defendants' counsel—was to station armed men in the hall itself, in the Arnold and Avalon Hotels, and on Seminary Hill. Britt Smith, witnesses testified, pointed to these locations, while in conversation with Elmer Smith, I. W. W. legal adviser, only an hour before the assassination occurred. The testimony of the defendants themselves was to disclose that there existed a general and cohesive understanding of the part each was to play and the ambush to be taken.

The testimony of all Legionnaires who marched in the parade was that the men in the ranks were unarmed, that none of them had heard of any plan to raid the hall, and that many of them did not even know there existed such an institution in Centralia.

Within the hall when the firing began were Britt Smith, James McInerney, Mike Sheehan, Ray Becker, Bert Faulkner, and Wesley Everest. Elmer Smith, having assured himself that preparations were complete and deadly at the hall, returned to his own office to arm and resist any violence that might be directed toward him, if a raid were held. On Seminary Hill were Loren Roberts, Bert Bland, and Ole Hanson, the latter yet uncaptured. In the Arnold Hotel were O. C. (Commodore) Bland and John Lamb. In the Avalon Hotel were John Doe Davis, who escaped, and Eugene Barnett, according to the contention of the state.

During the entire case the defense sought to cast the burden of blame for rifle-fire, upon the dead radical, Wesley Everest, and upon Loren Roberts, alleged to be insane. Toward the close of the trial, with the certainty that the cards were all on the table, the defense admitted that Bert Bland had fired upon the parade. But no one of all the defendants, upon their sworn testimony, knew who among them had fired from the hall— though they conveniently admitted that Everest had. And Everest was dead.

Attempts to Force the Labor Issue

The special line of defensive policy, presented in Vanderveer's opening statement, was an attempt to inject into the case the elements of class strife—labor versus capital—with the I. W. W. depicted as peaceful propagandists who do not countenance violence and who were driven to resistance in Centralia by threats of a raid upon their hall. Against the I. W. W., he charged, were arrayed the commercial interests of Centralia, who had held meetings in the Elks' Club of that city, for the perfection of plans to oust the radicals. So confident was Vanderveer that he would be able to show the existence of this alleged commercial conspiracy, that he was led— by expediency and the desire for dramatic effectiveness—to absolve the American Legion from all blame. Later he recanted, and made venomous attack upon the organization and upon individual Legionnaires, and when the court had ruled against the admission of any testimony relative to the alleged conspiracy, unless it first be shown that Warren O. Grimm, for whose murder the defendants were on trial, was either an actual aggressor or a party to the purported plot, the defense made the attempt —even through perjury—to involve Grimm, to blacken the name of the slain Legionnaire, but failed at every point.

"I exonerate, now and forever after, the American Legion, as an organization, from
any responsibility!" was Vanderveer's pledge in his opening
statement.

That first day of the trial,
with heads curiously thrust forward, the spectators saw the
weapons with which the Centralia attack was made — the
rifles, revolvers, and automatic
pistols that spat death into the
peace pageant. The defendants,
for the first time since their
capture, looked upon the familiar weapons that they plied
with such deadly effect on Armistice Day. Even when a cause
is righteous, he who has killed
might be expected to gaze with
some degree of gravity upon
the tool with which he took life.
These men, on trial for murder,
laughed as the unskilled hands
of counsel fumbled with the
mechanisms, and gave no sign
of perturbation.

GEORGE VANDERVEER

The "High Priest" of the I. W. W.
whose eloquent and combative forensic ability and knowledge of legal technicalities is relied upon by the I. W. W.
to extricate them, however revolting
their crime. He achieved high rank in
the I. W. W. Hall of Fame by his successful defence of the I. W. W. in the
Everett Massacre Trial. Reported to
be held in $50,000 retainer fee by the
national I. W. W. organization. He
conducted Haywood's defense in Chicago, and lost. His was a hopeless case
at Montesano; the array of facts was
too much for him.

Proof of the Seminary Hill Ambush

In its opening statement the defense had made no reference
to the charge that riflemen were stationed on distant Seminary
hill, one-quarter mile to the east and overlooking the route of
parade. Here, according to the state, and to the confessions of
Loren Roberts, were posted Bert Bland, Roberts, and a third
marksman, Ole Hanson, who is yet uncaptured. Roberts and
Bland, it seemed certain, were to constitute the propitiatory
offerings of the defense, though for the former a plea of insanity
was to be entered.

Whether the defense concurred in the fact of the Seminary
hill rifle pit, or whether it denied, made but slight difference
when several witnesses testified to visiting the ridge after the
firing and there discovering more than a score of empty cart-

LOREN ROBERTS

I. W. W. Age 21. Roberts came in and surrendered himself two days after the shooting. His full and voluntary confessions laid bare the entire plot of stationing armed men in various buildings along Tower Avenue. Roberts was one of the three men stationed on Seminary Hill, and is believed to have been the one who killed McElfresh. It was to get rid of his damaging confessions that inspired the defense to enter a plea of "insanity." Curiously enough, his "symptoms" of insanity dated from the arrival of Vanderveer to handle the case. The jury ordered his confinement in an insane asylum.

ridges — plain and irrefutable proof of the heavy firing that was directed from the safety of that shrewdly chosen vantage point. The shells were of 25-30, 32-20 and 22 high-power calibers, and were placed in evidence. Arthur McElfresh was slain by a missile from a 22 high-power rifle. Roberts used such a weapon—the only one of its caliber concerned in the attack.

It was further shown by the state that Bert Bland and James McInerney had registered frequently, prior to November 11, at the Avalon Hotel, and that on that specific day Room 10 had been assigned to Bland. It was from Room 10, though the state did not assert that Bland was stationed there, whence came the bullet that killed Grimm, a split-nosed 38-55 caliber slug. And this rifle, which was to figure with tragic prominence in the trial, had been denied by the defense when the murder weapons were introduced. It had been found, a fortnight after the attack, beneath a bill-board at the edge of the city. Despite the denial of the defense that any such rifle had been used, the testimony of Bert G. Clark, of Seattle, an expert on ballistics, proved that the bullet which killed Grimm was of 38-55 caliber.

Confessions of Loren Roberts

On the third day of the state's case there were introduced in evidence two documents which offered conclusive proof of the premeditated nature of the attack and cast light upon the principals involved. They were the confessions of Loren Roberts, defendant, and in reply the defense could advance naught save the plea of lunacy for the pensive, lanky stripling who had uttered them. Objections to the introduction of the confessions were vigorous, but the court ruled their admissibility,

SEMINARY HILL
Across the railroad track from the I. W. W. hall. This picture taken from the I. W. W. hall. Loren Roberts, Ole Hanson and Bert Bland fired from Seminary Hill into the parade at this point. Their location was just to the right of the water-tank. Loren Roberts and Bert Bland both admit firing into the parade, and Ole Hanson was never captured.

after counseling the jurors that the damaging declarations made therein should apply only to their author, Loren Roberts. The defense failed equally in an endeavor to show that the confessions, dated November 17 and 24, were obtained under duress.

In the two confessions, one supplementary, Roberts revealed discussions and plans of the Centralia radicals prior to Armistice Day, related their resolve to arm themselves and resist any raid upon their hall, and told of their subsequent strategical move of stationing riflemen in the hall, the Avalon Hotel and other buildings on Tower avenue, and on Seminary Hill. These plans were carried out.

Three Riflemen at Work

With Bert Bland and Ole Hanson, Roberts took his post in a grassy swale on the summit of Seminary Hill. They were to fire, so ran their orders, when they heard shots. Far below them the parade moved up Tower Avenue, turned and retraced its course. Bert Bland, cuddling his rifle, observed: "I hope to Jesus no trouble starts." Almost on the words they heard shots, declared the confession, and they in turn began firing at random into the parade—where marched many of the former schoolmates of Bland and Roberts. Observe this well: Roberts, with every reason to shield himself and seek extenuation, and with a perfect recollection of the Armistice Day parade as he lay and anxiously watched it before he loosed the shot that killed Arthur McElfresh, saw no rush toward the hall before the shooting began.

"I'll tell the truth now and what I saw," he confessed. "It may be used against me, but I can't help it. I saw the soldiers run for the building when the shooting started."

There stands the confession of Loren Roberts, unimpeached, said by every examining alienist to have been sane when he uttered it—yet who was commended to the court for incarceration in the state institution for insane, by the verdict of the jury. It speaks in direct contradiction to the propagandist pretense that the I. W. W. hall was raided and that lives were taken only in its defense.

Tom Morgan on the Stand

Let it be followed, as it was at the Montesano trial, blow upon blow, by the testimony of cool-eyed young Tom Morgan, who was in the hall when the firing began, who was arrested and detained by the state, and who took the stand as a witness for the prosecution. For Morgan said, looking the I. W. W. counsel fairly in the eye, that the shots from ambush preceded any rush of Legionnaires toward the radical headquarters.

It is the plaint of the propagandist that Morgan proved renegade to his fellows and the truth, and that he "turned state's evidence," upon promise of immunity. Admittedly the state had no case against Tom Morgan, after investigation— and quite obviously the value of the witness, as well as his own personal safety, demanded that he be kept aloof from the machinations of the I. W. W. Morgan had little or nothing to fear from the state—yet his soul might well have been possessed by terror when he appeared against the reds. But the witness did not flinch or shift his gaze as he testified, and at a taunt from the I. W. W. attorney he bent upon that gentleman a look so hostile and direct that in the clash of glances it was Vanderveer who turned away.

"Where were the soldiers at the time the shots were fired?" asked Special Prosecutor Abel, when Morgan took the stand.

"Some were closing up and others were keeping time," answered the 19-year-old timber worker. "Some shots were fired from across the street."

Morgan testified that he came to Centralia with Ray Becker, defendant, alias "Rough-Ground Shorty," and that he was in the I. W. W. hall at the time of the parade. He named the defendants known by him to be present — Mike Sheehan, Ray Becker, Britt Smith, and James McInerney. Elmer Smith, he testified, entered the hall and held conference with Britt Smith, secretary, just before the parade was due, remarking, "They are going to raid the hall, are you ready?" "We are always ready," answered Britt.

Then, walking to the back of the hall, they held a whispered conversation together, Britt pointing in the direction of the Arnold, Avalon, and Queens' Hotels, where the men had been told to station themselves.

"When he turned to go out," testified Morgan, speaking of Elmer Smith, "he asked Britt Smith if he had plenty of men. Britt said he had. Elmer said he was going up to his own office to protect it."

BERT BLAND
I. W. W. Age about 29 years. Has been an I. W. W. agitator for some time. With Roberts and Ole Hanson, he was stationed on Seminary Hill, where, according to his own testimony, "We commenced shooting. I shot between four and eight shots. I shot with one knee on the ground." Bert Bland, unmarried, was found guilty of second degree murder and given 25 to 40 years in the state penitentiary.

"Did anyone speak to you?" queried Prosecutor Abel.

"Britt Smith asked me if I had a gun, and I told him I didn't want one."

"It was only when shots had been fired that the Legionnaires broke ranks," asserted Morgan, remaining unshaken throughout cross examination. He had seen the man known as "John Doe" Davis, yet uncaptured, attempt to hide a rifle down his trouser-leg, with such comic results in walking that all laughed at him. Davis then wrapped the rifle in an overcoat and went out, turning in the direction of the Avalon Hotel.

"Where were the soldiers when the first shots were fired?" asked Prosecutor Abel.

"They were keeping time," answered Morgan.

Under cross-examination Morgan told Vanderveer flatly that he had refused to see him while in jail at Chehalis, though he had talked with him at a later time. He had heard the first shots from across the street. Efforts of the defense to entrap him into statements that would lend color to the supposition that the raid preceded the firing were futile. Vanderveer played his last card, more for effect on the jury than to disconcert the cool, straightforward witness.

"Did anyone ever promise not to prosecute the case against you, or that if you'd tell what they wanted you to, they'd let you go?" insinuated the defense.

"They did not."

BARNETT AND THE HOTEL AVALON

It was the contention of the state that Eugene Barnett, coal miner, of Kopiah, known to Centralia I. W. W. as "the nervy guy," had been the rifleman who fired the 38-55 caliber Winchester from an upper window of the Avalon hotel, giving Warren O. Grimm his death wound. Against this contention, and the evidence submitted, the defense later introduced an attempted alibi. In the minds of the jury the case against Barnett must have been conclusive—for had his alibi been true he was guiltless. But if the testimony and claims of the state were correct, as the jurors signified, then Barnett was the man who slew Grimm, or at least was present in the room from which the shot was fired, as identification witnesses declared.

Two state witnesses made positive identification of Barnett as one of the Avalon riflemen, while additional testimony was given to show that he carried a rifle of the type of the 38-55 caliber when he fled from the old hotel. These witnesses were Elsie Hornbeck, bookkeeper in a garage just opposite the Avalon, and Charles Briffett, superintendent of Port Angeles (Wash.) schools, who was in Centralia on business at the time of the assassinations.

Thou Art the Man

Miss Hornbeck testified that she saw a man lean from an upper window of the Avalon just before the firing started. She identified this man, in the prisoners' dock, as Eugene Barnett.

"Will you, knowing that this is a life or death proposition, say on your oath that you think this is the man?" insisted the defense.

"Yes," said the witness, after a reflective pause.

Equally unhesitating was the identification by Briffett, who pointed out Barnett as the rifleman he saw leaving the alley at the rear of the Avalon Hotel, cramming fresh cartridges into his weapon. Briffett, who for many years was the proprietor of a gun store and whose hobby is firearms, also testified that the rifle was of the type and appearance of the 38-55 caliber rifle introduced by the state.

"Would you know the man you saw leaving the alley?" asked Prosecutor Abel.

"I would."

"Is he among these defendants?"

"The third from the end," replied Briffett, pointing out Barnett.

The testimony of Leila Tripp, of Everett, Washington, corroborated that of Briffett respecting the gunman who emerged from the alley at the rear of the Avalon. Briffett had said that he saw, at the same moment, a young woman peering from the fence corner at the

EUGENE BARNETT

I. W. W. Coal miner and timber worker. Arrested for seditious utterances in Idaho during the war. Known as "the nervy guy." Was stationed in the Avalon Hotel with a 38-55 caliber rifle. Barnett was charged with firing the shot that killed Warren Grimm. Found guilty of murder in the second degree, and given 25 to 40 years in the state penitentiary.

opposite side of the alley. In Miss Tripp the state produced this witness. She had seen the rifleman emerge and walk hastily away, reloading his weapon, but was unable to identify this man as Barnett, other than to say that there was a general resemblance.

Mrs. Warren O. Grimm, widow of the murdered Legionnaire, testified briefly in identification of the garments worn by her husband on the day of the parade, and of their appointment to meet when he should have completed his duties as leader of the Centralia contingent.

Firing Upon the Flag

That the American colors were under fire with especial vengeance, and that bullets from hidden riflemen sped between his body and the staff as he raced for shelter, was the testimony of Clarence Watkins, color bearer of the Centralia contingent in the parade. Watkins also identified Barnett as the rifleman whom he saw lean from a window of the Avalon.

John Earl Watt, of the Centralia contingent, testified that his platoon was marking time before the I. W. W. hall when the first shots were fired. He ran for shelter toward the intersection of Tower Avenue and Second Street and was hit in the right side just as he gained fancied safety. Nearby Ben Cassagranda had been shot down. Both Watt and Watkins place the location of Warren O. Grimm at the head of the column, near the street intersection, when the attack was made. The latter saw the Centralia leader stricken, and watched him reel across the street for succor.

Grimm and Where He Stood

More than a score of witnesses were called by the state to fix definitely and beyond dispute the fact that the head of the Centralia contingent was halted at the street intersection, 200 feet beyond the I. W. W. hall, with Grimm as leader, and that the ranks were in formation and marking time when bullets spat among the marchers. This point proved of superior importance later in the trial, when the I. W. W. counsel, by witnesses who were met with perjury charges, attempted to disprove the location of the head of the column and to establish that Warren O. Grimm was actually in front of the I. W. W. hall when struck—an endeavor so manifestly at variance with the established facts that one felt its own crudeness must defeat it, as transpired.

Commodore Bland's Slashed Hand

In the Arnold hotel, each with weapons, were stationed two Centralia radicals, O. C. (Commodore) Bland and John Lamb, the latter far-famed for his indisposition to toil and his loudness of voice in economic debate. Though admitting that these men were armed, the defense denied that they had fired from their room in the hotel—explaining the ragged gash in Bland's left hand as an accidental injury received when his enthusiasm for the parade caused him to lose balance and plunge the member through the window-pane. The theory of the state was that Bland came by his injury when he thrust his rifle through the glass and joined in the firing. The state brought forward witnesses who testified that they saw the glass break, and that at the same instant smoke belched from the shattered window.

By promise and threat, the I. W. W. attorney had created an impression that the appearance of Lieutenant Frank R. Van Gilder on the witness stand would be the signal for forensic fireworks. Van Gilder it was who stood by Grimm's side when the jagged missile tore through his vitals, and Van Gilder also had led the ex-service men in their demand and purpose that the death of their comrades go not unavenged, by the severest justice obtainable at law. There had been hints and innuendo to the effect that Van Gilder, of all men, knew most of the alleged "plot" to raid the I. W. W. hall, and that he would writhe when defense counsel grilled him. As a grilling the event was over-touted.

O. C. BLAND

I. W. W. Age 40. Married. Brother of Bert Bland. Has been an I. W. W. agitator for some time. Was stationed in the Arnold Hotel with John Lamb. and fired from there. Found guilty of murder in the second degree and given 25 to 40 years in the state penitentiary.

The nonchalant ex-officer gave clear and concise testimony, unshaken by the discomfited efforts of the defense. He described how Grimm met his death, and related the trivial nature of the conversation they were having when the firing opened. The first shots came from the Avalon, testified Van Gilder. He had not even known that there was in all Centralia such an institution as the I. W. W. hall.

The state was nearing the close of its case, though it had yet in reserve, to follow the case for the defense, the introduction of important testimony in rebuttal. Plainly it had demonstrated that the Centralia radicals did conspire to fire upon the Armistice Day paraders, and it had demonstrated that shots were heard before the enraged Legionnaires broke ranks and rushed the deadly portal of the I. W. W. hall.

Where McElfresh Fell

There was one bit of graphic testimony near the termination of the case for the state, relating to the killing of Arthur McElfresh—testimony that came into prominence some days later, when the defense attempted to prove that McElfresh was killed in the very act of attacking the hall. In ghastly fact he was shot through the head with a 22 caliber high-power bullet as he sought cover at the corner of the variety store, a score of paces north of the radical headquarters. One comrade, racing behind him, hurdled the falling body of the young veteran.

Mrs. Helen Schoel, of Chehalis, a trained nurse driving one of the automobiles of the Red Cross division following the troops, saw the stricken body in uniform and hastened to render aid, braving the bullets that even then were thudding in the building fronts along the avenue. She bent above the youthful Legionnaire and saw the red wound in his temple.

"What was the condition of that boy as he lay there?" asked Prosecutor Abel.

"He was dead," came the low-voiced response.

Bear this in mind, and bear in mind as well the spot where Warren Grimm stood as a heavy-caliber bullet shredded his intestines—for the beaten, frustrated, savagely desperate defense was in its own time to advance the claim, supported by weird and shaky testimony, that both Grimm and McElfresh were aggressors when they met death and that they met it at the very door of the hall. And it is the latter contention, false in every syllable, as all Centralia knows—as the defense well knew—that the radical press has set forth as truth in its callous camouflaging of the facts.

Establishing Facts of the State's Case

These facts the state had established when it rested its case on February 18:

That the defendants acted by preconcert in the slaughter of the ex-service men.

That Bert Bland and Loren Roberts fired from the vantage of Seminary Hill, and that a bullet from Roberts' rifle slew McElfresh.

That O. C. (Commodore) Bland and John Lamb were in ambush in the Arnold Hotel, whence came firing, according to several witnesses.

That Elmer Smith, as legal adviser to the radicals, visited their hall immediately before the parade, and asked if all was in readiness, expressing satisfaction when informed that the I. W. W. were prepared.

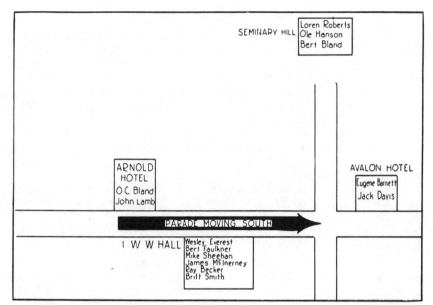

Diagram Showing How Centralia Section of Parade Was Caught in a Pocket.

That there was firing from the Avalon hotel, and that Eugene Barnett, if the identification of the witnesses was correct, was one of the men who fired from that point.

That all of the remaining defendants were in the hall at the time of the attack, and that scores of shots issued from the hall.

That Warren O. Grimm was at the head of his contingent, eyes to the front, laughing light-heartedly, when wounded so terribly that he was to die within an hour.

That the Legionnaires were at ease or marking time when the shots rang out, and that none of them rushed the hall until they realized they were under fire.

That the Legionnaires had no knowledge of any purported raid, and that none of the ex-service men bore arms.

That Grimm, McElfresh and Cassagranda, victims, were all slain at points distant from the I. W. W. hall, and by bullets fired from outside the hall, and that by no possible logic could their killing be ascribed to self-defense.

That the ex-service men were the targets of vengeful visionaries who, however zealous and sincere may have been their fanatical belief in their cause, took four lives without the semblance of provocation—the lives of men who had earned the right to live, through sacrificial devotion to their country's service.

The Spark in the Powder-Train

Why were the marchers fired upon if they did not attack? There are men of unquestioned integrity, men who would permit no allegiance to the American Legion to becloud their testimony, who assert that such was the case. Such is the fact. As well ask why a spark ignites powder, or why oiled waste blazes suddenly into flame when no fire is near. With the I. W. W. waiting in ambush, their nerves tense with a hideous resolve, their targets before them, it may have been that a twitching, spasmodic trigger finger unwittingly loosed the shot that was to be the signal. Or that some radical, more determined upon deadly fruitage, deliberately fired into the marchers. Wesley Everest, by all accounts, was such a zealot. Unfortunately for the state's case his tongue was dumb with death. But his own fellows say that Everest was "a bad bird," who remarked that with all in readiness he meant, somehow, to see that the I. W. W. plans had not been laid for naught.

One of the eleven defendants went free when the state rested, upon motion of the defense for a direct verdict. He was Bert Faulkner, of Centralia, who was in the hall during the attack. No evidence had been brought forward to show that he participated, though there was abundant proof that he knew of the plan. He had gone home before noon on Armistice Day to hide his card of membership in the I. W. W., so that in the event of capture it might not be found on him. But he of all the others was more the typical American youth, erect of stature, fearless of eye, clean in limb and feature—good to look upon. He had served in a home contingent of artillery during the war. But the court listened with leniency to the motion, and Faulkner—whom the jury would as certainly have acquitted—was dismissed and released.

Faulkner was to forfeit this sentiment and solicitude by his testimony for the defense in rebuttal, when he was called to the witness stand as a free man. It was then he defiantly swore that a bullet, fired from outside the hall, had pierced the shoulder of his overcoat—when not a jot of testimony or evidence had been brought forward to show that a single shot was fired by any Legionnaire, and when the defense itself had made no such claim. The bullet-hole in the fabric had been maliciously destroyed, Faulkner intimated, by an agent of the prosecution.

Eugene Barnett, the "Nervy Guy"

By the verdict of the jury Eugene Barnett is guilty of murder. By the evidence and testimony of the prosecution, if guilty at all he was guilty in direct and personal measure of the slaying of Grimm. A word for him, though he be guilty as Cain, before the defense proceeds with its presentation, which takes up as the first thrust an attempted alibi in his behalf.

Of those ten remaining defendants Eugene Barnett was the outstanding figure. His eyes were unabashed and unclouded, friendly eyes with the touch of fierceness in them—far better gauges of a decent human soul than the sullen, shifty and morose brown optics of Elmer Smith, who was to be freed.   One could believe Barnett to be the fighter that report declared him. One could believe that his convictions were deep and desperate and sincere—however greatly one shuddered at the deed he was charged with.   Eugene Barnett, coal miner since his eighth year, moulded and soul-scarred in a trade that undeniably has seen oppression beyond endurance, might ask—as he would not —some word of understanding, if not of extenuation, for the hectic passions that drove him to blinded murder.

Opening With Barnett's Alibi

The alibi for Barnett was the first concern of the defense when it opened its case on February 19.   And the defendant himself was the dominant figure in the testimony which supported it.   He was calmly truculent, given to the logic of the propagandist in reply to question of counsel, and his story of where he was and what he did on the day of tragedy constituted a flat and impressive denial, in orderly sequence of commonplace conduct, to the charge that he passed a portion of the afternoon in Room 10 of the Avalon Hotel, firing a 38-55 caliber rifle and slaying Warren O. Grimm.

Barnett testified that he knew nothing of the plans to fire upon the parade, though he had visited the I. W. W. hall earlier in the day; that he never possessed or had in his possession a 38-55 caliber rifle; that he had no weapon with him on Armistice Day; and that he was in the lobby of the Roderick hotel, adjoining the radical headquarters, during the affray.   He testified that his answer was such, when he saw ex-service men wrecking the front of the hall, that he "pulled" his coat and would have gone out to engage them, had he not realized an instant later that the affair was beyond fistic intervention.

"File Your Bullets Noses Flat"

Grim by-play was in that bit of testimony which concerned a verse from "Christians at War," one of the propagandist songs in the I. W. W. hymnal.   Grimm, so the testimony had developed, was slain by a bullet which had been split at the nose. A number of cartridges, found with the 38-55 caliber rifle, had been similarly treated—the design being to make the missile mushroom and inflict a more terrible wound. Prosecutor Abel had asked Barnett if he was familiar with the song, and had been answered in the affirmative.

"Have you noticed in that song a suggestion about filing your bullets noses flat?" pursued the prosecutor.

"Many times," coolly answered the defendant.

"Ever sing it?"

"No, sir."

"You do not believe in filing your bullets noses flat?"

"No, sir."

Both the defendant and counsel for the defense declared the hymn to be a satire upon modern warfare, intended only as such. But in the minds of those who heard the verse, and who were familiar with the testimony regarding the "mystery rifle" and the death wound of Grimm, arose the hazard that through the song viciousness found its inspiration. These were the words of the verse:

"File your bullets noses flat,
      Poison every well;
God decrees your enemies
      Must all go plumb to hell!"

Barnett asserted that he had ridden his saddle horse into Centralia that day, and had attended to minor business affairs, calling at the Roderick Hotel to see the McAllisters, proprietors of the place, before he returned to his home at Kopiah, ten miles distant. He said that his anger was such, when he saw the hall sacked by the ex-service men in search of radicals, that he rode home at a gallop, intending to procure his rifle and return to the defense of his fellow I. W. W. His wife dissuaded him. His eyes flashed as he told the prosecution that had he returned Wesley Everest would not have died a victim to lynchlaw.

"You were not angered over the shooting of the soldiers, were you?" inquired the state.

"Not at all," was the calm reply. "I approve of anything that's necessary."

That Worthy Couple—the McAllisters

In corroboration of Barnett's attempted alibi came J. C. McAllister, semi-senile boniface of the Roderick, and his wife, Mary, a fleshy termagant who testified far too eagerly and

RODERICK HOTEL

This was rented by the I. W. W. for their hall, and it was here that plans for the ambuscade were laid. Britt Smith, James McInerney, Mike Sheehan, Bert Faulkner, Ray Becker and Wesley Everest were stationed in this hall. After the firing, the enraged Legionnaires rushed the hall and captured all except Wesley Everest, who was caught later. This I. W. W. hall was on the main thoroughfare of Centralia.

glibly for good effect—and who charged that her detention in jail following the Armistice Day tragedy had broken her in health and spirit. Both testified that Barnett was in the Roderick during the shooting, and gave general corroboration to his statement, though in minor details the stories of the three varied somewhat.

"Did you see anyone attack the I. W. W. hall?" the defense asked McAllister, who shook as with palsy.

"No, sir; I never seen anything of the kind," was the tremulous answer.

"What's the matter?" shouted Vanderveer, plainly vexed at the failure of his witness to conform to the testimony of Barnett. "Are you scared to death?"

"I object to counsel bullyragging his own witness," interposed Prosecutor Abel.

The state turned to cross-examination of McAllister, whose nervous tremors had brought him almost to the verge of collapse. Now he was faced with a contradictory statement, made months before, when he had given no thought to his future testimony.

"Did you not tell C. D. Cunningham and J. H. Jahnke, of the prosecution, that there was nobody in the hotel at the time of the shooting?" pressed Abel.

McAllister's voice rose to the occasion with a squeak and a falsetto tremor.

"Yes, but they didn't swear me!" he shrilled triumphantly.

But Mary McAllister was of sterner stuff. Steadfastly, and speaking with such rapidity that the stenographers raced to follow her, she declared that Barnett was in the lobby, and that she saw the paraders rush the hall before the firing began. In passing, it should be remarked that the McAllisters owned the I. W. W. hall and that the radicals were their paying tenants. The witness had every appearance of talented mendacity on the stand, and the defense created a ludicrous situation by referring to the testimony of "this splendid woman, who cannot lie."

If Mary McAllister is a tyro at falsehood she did not betray it by so much as a quiver, when faced with an assertion advanced by Mrs. Ben Cassagranda, widow of one of the four parade victims. Mrs. McAllister had known the dead Legionnaire since his babyhood, and had talked with the widow when all Centralia was rife with gossip of the murders.

"Do you remember that she said Ben was shot, and you said it served him right, that he had no business to be marching with the soldiers?" asked Prosecutor Abel.

"No, sir!" snapped the McAllister woman.

Barnett denied that he had told Preston McDonald, leader of the posse which captured him, that he was seated in the lobby of the Avalon during the firing. He said that he saw the uniformed paraders file past the Roderick, heard an order that he could not distinguish, and saw the men break ranks and charge the I. W. W. hall. Glass crashed and he heard firing from the hall.

Parenthetically, it should be noted that testimony relative to the firing of a volley from the hall, almost simultaneous with the rush of the uniformed men, is without special significance in determining the question of aggression when such statements are contrasted with the testimony of many witnesses that four or five shots were fired first, from outside the hall, and that after a momentary lull a ripping volley, likened to machine-gun fire, broke from the hall and all the points of ambush. It would appear, not questioning the candor of any witnesses who say that

AMERICAN LEGION MESS-HALL
The ground floor of the Montesano City Hall was turned over to the American Legion to be used as headquarters during the trial. Between 80 and 100 Legionnaires from every section of the state were in attendance throughout the trial, and it was necessary to provide a special mess-hall for their use.

the first shots were from the hall, that the initial firing of several shots was unremarked by these witnesses and that it was the volley that riveted their attention.

As for Barnett's statement relative to the firing, it may be passed without comment, other than that voiced by the jury when it declared its disbelief in his alibi and found him guilty— that is, found him to have been where the state declared him to be, in an upper room of the Avalon, its windows snapping with rifle fire.

From February 20th until the 25th there occurred a gap in the continuity of trial, due to the illness of jurors stricken with influenza. Edward Parr, of Hoquiam, eventually was excused from the panel by reason of failure to convalesce speedily and the case was resumed through the substitution of John A. Ball, alternate juror, who thereafter served as a member of the regular panel.

Modern Murderers on Hunger Strike

It was during the pause that the defendants went on "hunger strike" against the prison fare provided by Grays Harbor county. The food was ample, let none be advised to the contrary, but may have been monotonous through lack of variety. It was said that Vanderveer, defense counsel, severely upbraided the recalcitrants for their attitude and the effect it might have on popular opinion. The incident terminated with generous

and wholly voluntary concessions on the part of Sheriff Jeff
Bartell, who ordered that certain additions to the menu be
made.

Enter the American Infantry

And there arose, during the same days of waiting, yet another incident that broke the monotony of court room parley and
testimony and legal sword-play.   It was the summoning of
Federal troops to Montesano to bide throughout the remainder
of the trial. Of the summoning of the troops, and of the suf-
ficiency of cause, the radical press and spokesmen—snarling
as though the sight of uniformed men under the colors were
an affront—made instant material for mis-statement.   It was
Herman Allen, prosecuting attorney for Lewis county, who
called for the troops, it was Governor Louis F. Hart, of Washington, who repeated the request, and it was Lieutenant-General
Hunter Liggett, commanding the western military department,
with headquarters at San Francisco, who ordered the sending
of soldiers to Montesano.

A detachment of 100 men of the 35th United States Infantry,
with full field equipment, arrived in the Grays Harbor capital
on February 25, detrained with the smartness of efficiency,
pitched their camp, and remained until the close of the trial.
Storming into court, the I. W. W. counsel threatened to quit the
trial if the troops were permitted to remain, charging that
their presence was an insult to the civil authorities of Grays
Harbor county, to the court itself, and to the cause of his clients.
Though once he had grown vehement over the "danger" of trial
in that same district—the "peril" to his clients—now he maintained that the entire vicinity was as pacific as a Quaker camp-
meeting.

The glimpse of their country's flag, from the windows of the
jury room, the sound of the bugles lilting at reveille or taps,
would prejudice the jurors against the ten defendants who
had slain certain young men garbed even as these soldiers
were, was the burden of his plaint.   The court ordered an
inquiry into the necessity for military protection.   Governor
Hart sent his secretary to make renewed investigation.   The
adjutant-general's department and the sheriff's office were also
concerned in the inquiry.   Before these representatives of the
state and county, Prosecutor Allen laid his secret information
—and the infantry detachment, with guard mounted about the
jail, was not removed.

"Not Let the Boys Die Like Dogs"

Not the state of Washington alone, but the United States government itself, was deeply and gravely concerned over the likelihood of riot and bloodshed at Montesano. The reports of the secret service agents, of the special investigators of the defense, are not procurable for publication. But there were shrewd and fearless men who donned the rough clothing of the itinerant laborer, procured I. W. W. cards, and moved with vigilant freedom among the radicals of the Pacific northwest —in Montesano, in Centralia, in Seattle, and Tacoma, wherever men congregated to curse their country and its laws.

In a dozen reports this quoted threat was returned to the prosecution:

"We will not let those boys die like dogs!"

What was the portent? Merely this—that the I. W. W. of the Pacific Northwest, ruthless and boastful, were taking the vow that the Centralia murderers should not hang, whatever the verdict. It was well enough that Warren Grimm and his fellow veterans perished ignobly on the streets of Centralia, but for the men who slew these unarmed soldier citizens no propitiatory fate should be invoked.

What actual means of execution armed that threat? Again the records of the investigation—the inquiry that contented all save the self-styled "labor jurors"—are silent. This much is known, that the prosecuting attorney's office of Grays Harbor county had checked the sale of rifles in that county for the period immediately preceding the trial—a matter of several months—and had found the aggregate to be over 600 heavy-caliber sporting rifles, or far in excess of any normal demand. This circumstance may have been coincidence—but public officials, charged with the preservation of law and order, have no right to assume coincidence when the stage is set for revolutionary drama.

There was a marked exodus of strange faces from the court-room following the arrival of the troops. Partisans without occupation or visible means of support, who were accustomed to swagger into the courtroom and sneeze when Vanderveer took snuff, found it convenient to remain absent. For the infantrymen in the courtyard of the little jail were armed with loaded service rifles—quite differently equipped from those defenseless peace paraders who were sniped at from cover in Centralia.

With the resumption of the trial, on February 25, witnesses were called by the defense to support the alibi of Eugene Barnett. Mainly their testimony related to having seen the Kopiah

JEFF BARTELL

Sheriff of Gray's Harbor County for two terms, who was charged with the duty of keeping order in a county where feeling ran high. The situation was so serious that everyone entering the courtroom was searched for weapons. Vanderveer was forced to give up his gun early in the trial.

coal-miner distant from the I. W. W. hall shortly before the shooting, and to having witnessed him ride home, unarmed. One of these witnesses, S. A. Hand, a Centralia dealer in second-hand goods, was forced to admit that he had made no such statements when questioned by C. D. Cunningham, state counsel, immediately after the tragedy.

Lunacy of Loren Roberts

Upon the lunacy of Loren Roberts, youthful lumberjack of the Grand Mound district, the defense had dilated—obviously to discount the worth of the two signed confessions obtained from Roberts, wherein he told of firing from Seminary Hill, with Bert Bland and Ole Hanson as his companions. Now, for the first time, the defendants' counsel turned toward the establishment of proof that Roberts was mentally irresponsible. And in that strangely fortunate attempt—for the jury approved it—was woven such a tissue of obvious improbabilities that all the courtroom was cognizant of the jest.

Loren Roberts, shambling and silent, loose of lip and limb, who heretofore had consulted frequently with Vanderveer in whispered courtroom conferences, and whose face had been keen with thoughtful regard as he listened to the testimony, became a creature who entered the courtroom with a vapid smile wreathed on his features, a madman's titter to greet each witness—an utter alien to both his counsel and his fellow defendants. In all that assembly of persons who daily saw the trial, aside and apart from the scattered partisans of radicalism, was none but believed that "Grand Mound" Roberts was shamming.

Called by the defense to testify regarding the sanity of Loren Roberts was Dr. Arthur P. Calhoun, alienist, of Seattle, a member of the American Legion and a fraternity brother of Warren O. Grimm. The psychiatrist declared under oath that, in his opinion, the defendant suffered from the mental malady of dementia praecox. The delusions which claimed the defendant were genuine and unfeigned, asserted Dr. Calhoun. For example, Roberts believed that the I. W. W. counsel was not Vanderveer, but was none other than Colonel Brice P. Disque, former commander of the spruce division. He fancied, as well, that electric currents were sent through his cot at night to rob him of rest and force him toward damaging admissions. The courtroom, so ran the medley of his clouded mind, was operated entirely by wireless—bench, bailiffs, jurors and attorneys.

But the state, in cross-examination, compelled Dr. Calhoun to admit that the test of Roberts' lunacy was based solely upon the accepted truth of the defendant's own statements regarding his delusions—and that he might be shamming, in certain particulars. The alienist asserted, however, his belief that the malign mental phenomena were not feigned.

But Dr. Calhoun also declared his belief that Loren Roberts was sane and responsible when he uttered the two damning confessions that marked him as the slayer of Arthur McElfresh, and that illuminated the dark folds of the I. W. W. conspiracy to shoot and slay and spare not. In the face of this statement, and in the faces of statements from other alienists, fully as well qualified, that Roberts was and is sane—the discriminating jury found him to be a lunatic, and recommended him for treatment in the state hospital.

"So far as I can see from the statements," said Dr. Calhoun, cross-examined as to the reliability of the confessions, "Roberts was able to give a rational, consecutive account at the time."

"Such as any normal human being would give?" insisted the state.

"Yes."

"And on November 17 he was sane?"

"So far as I can determine from the confessions," was the admission.

"You have to take his delusions for granted in order to form an opinion?" queried Prosecutor Abel, returning to the alleged obsessions of the defendant.

"That is true in any examination for insanity," stiffly replied the alienist.

Fellow defendants were called to give testimony regarding the apparent mental condition of Roberts while in confinement.

Again the state developed the significant fact that the lunacy of Loren Roberts dated singularly from the time the plea of insanity was entered for him. Jackson Hardy, prisoner and cell-mate serving a sentence for "moonshine", testified that the only indication of mental unrest on the part of the defendant was his proneness to sing "Steamboat Bill" all day and well into the night. There was other testimony, notably that of Mrs. Edna B. Roberts, the sad-faced mother of the accused youth, who voiced her belief that her son was of unsound mind, and who testified that two cousins were insane, while a grandfather died in dementia. Cross-examination showed it to be not improbable that the grandfather's ailment was the senility of his advanced years.

Judge Wilson's Inflexible Ruling

Throughout the course of the trial Judge Wilson had shown remarkable forbearance and leniency toward the frequent and studied insolence of the defense—evidently choosing to endure caustic trivialities rather than to afford the vestige of ground for complaint or claims of error. Straight in the judicial face Vanderveer had cast innuendo and almost open insult, only to be met with a calm smile and the request to proceed. Now was approaching, however, the test by which the firmness of Judge Wilson was to be made positively and unmistakably manifest—in his ruling denying the introduction of testimony relative to a purported commercial conspiracy against the Centralia I. W. W., unless it first be shown that Warren O. Grimm, slain Legionnaire, was party to any such plot or was an aggressor against the radicals.

In this position the court was fortified behind the ramparts of the law and exact justice—if there exists any distinction—for manifestly the matter at hand was the justification or non-justification of the killing of Grimm, without any issue of labor and capital unless some proved participation of Grimm drew this element into the vortex of trial.

"The issue in this case is murder, Mr. Vanderveer!" was the court's ruling.

Blackening the Memory of Grimm

Hotly incensed by this failure to introduce testimony relative to a conspiracy against the presence of the Centralia radicals, plans for which were laid at October meetings held in the Elks' club, according to his offer of proof, Vanderveer swiftly reversed his position and made direct assault upon the memory of the murdered Grimm. Such was the strategy demanded of the defense—if it found its scruples easy to swallow, as it did —that the attorney who had absolved the American Legion from all blame now began the bitterest of attacks upon the murdered Centralia leader. He astounded the courtroom with his declaration that the defense would show that Grimm was before the I. W. W. hall, even advancing to the attack, when he received his wound.

"The charge here is murder," said Prosecutor Abel, springing to his feet, his eyes glinting behind their thicklensed glasses. "In order to justify killing in self defense, the person killed must be making an assault. Until today counsel never claimed that Warren O. Grimm was anywhere near the hall or that he knew of the alleged plans.

"We are entirely willing for the defense to prove that there was a raid—reserving for ourselves the right to show that such proof is by perjured testimony!"

Up rose the calm and smiling Cunningham, who marched in the Centralia Armistice Day parade, who knew of his own knowledge that Grimm was stricken at the head of the column, distant from the hall, and who as friend and prosecutor prepared the case against the defendants so that justice might be served and his comrade's death avenged.

"Will you show that Grimm was shot from the hall? he asked, gazing directly at the inflamed I. W. W. counsel.

"Our proof will show that he was shot while attacking the hall!" was the reply.

"You must show an overt act on the part of Grimm, or that he was a party to the alleged conspiracy," ruled the court.

"We will show both," answered the defense.

Let it be said here that neither claim ever was substantiated, that witnesses were faced with perjury charges in the attempt, and arrested as they left the courtroom, and that no righteous-minded man on the jury, or attendant at the sessions, held any other belief than that Grimm met his death precisely where the state declared he did. There were scores of witnesses to prove this—and against them only the lying utterances of a few shady radicals whose lack of character and willingness to falsify was manifest in every facial shift. Yet none of these—procured by promises best known to the defense—quite dared to identify Grimm as having been shot before the hall. The pledge of the defense rested unredeemed, but through no fault of the unscrupulous and dastardly ferocity with which it was pressed. There are creatures more vulpine than the fox, more poisonous than the cobra, and more given to desecration than the hyena—and such are the I. W. W.

BRITT SMITH

I. W. W. Secretary of the Centralia local. Had been an agitator for several years. While in conversation with Elmer Smith, just prior to the shooting, he pointed out the various vantage points from which the I. W. W. later fired. When Elmer Smith asked him if he had men enough, Britt answered that he had. Found guilty of murder in the second degree and sentenced to 25 to 40 years in the state penitentiary.

Britt Smith and His Testimony

It was Britt Smith, secretary of the Centralia I. W. W., towhaired, pale-eyed strategist of the ambuscade, who said when the heat of hatred was past and the bullets sped to their fated targets—said, as he sat in the bull-pen of Centralia's jail:

"God, but I wish that I'd never heard the words, 'Class war!' "

A different, an unrepentant, Smith was the secretary when he took the witness stand in his own behalf. He had been told that he was a martyr, that of such stuff were heroes made— John Browns and other gallant saviours of mankind. Behind him stood the elements of unrest, and before him the manifestation of their might—the high-salaried, clever, fiercely combative lawyer who had been retained to save him from the bitter gallows.

And Britt Smith, quite calmly as though he were discussing economics, made the startling claim that the first shot was fired not from the hall, but from the pistol of an unknown Legionnaire in the street. He had never before uttered such a claim, though statements were made by him following his arrest—statements in which he spun to the uttermost thread the attempted justification of his act. The state passed it by as unworthy of assault.

But Smith did admit that he suggested and approved of the stationing of riflemen outside the hall to fire upon the parade if the hall were attacked, and added that he was aware that several of the I. W. W. had taken such strategic locations. Though in the very center of the reds who fired from the hall, Smith denied that he knew who was armed or who fired the 50-odd shots that swept from the doors of the rookery. He denied the authorship of a roughly penciled map, found on his desk when the hall was searched, showing the exact points at which outside riflemen were stationed.

Corroborative testimony was given by Britt Smith and Mrs. Mary McAllister, owner of the I. W. W. hall, to the effect that they informed Centralia authorities of their belief that a raid was to take place on Armistice Day, and that they asked protection without any definite action being taken to afford it. Circulars were distributed, testified Smith, appealing to the citizens of Centralia. Believing that lawful protection would not be given them, in the event a raid was held, the I. W. W. secretary said that the resolution to arm themselves sprang into being and effect.

"The boys wanted to know what to do," testified Smith. "I believed in the protection of the hall at all times."

Therefore, upon hearsay, and by grace of the lawless doctrines of the I. W. W., on November 11, 1919, certain disciples of desperation constituted themselves the law, violated the principles of manhood and self-defense by assigning marksmen to distant stations, and coolly butchered four followers of the flag. To say that they anticipated a raid is not condonation—as well say that some mad Malay, running amuck with kris and dagger, anticipated personal violence. They had resolved upon slaughter and they achieved it.

From the mouth of one of the defense's own witnesses, plainly on the stand perforce, came denial of the assertion that Warren O. Grimm was before the I. W. W. hall when the split-nosed bullet smashed into his vitals. This witness was Walter Morrill, Legionnaire, who marched in the third platoon of the parade. Under cross-examination he testified that Grimm was at the head of the column, beyond the hall, talking with Lieutenant Van Gilder, when the firing opened and he doubled up at the impact of his wounding.

Two Typical Defense Witnesses

Somewhat of the character of the witness called to support the claim that Grimm was before the hall, and thus by proving him an aggressor open the way to the alleged conspiracy evidence, may be gleaned from the consideration of two typical instances—those of the testimony of Vernon O'Reilly, high school youth of Centralia, and Mrs. May Sherman, cannery worker, of Tacoma. Both sought, in veiled testimony, to redeem the promised proof of the defense.

At this juncture later evidence and testimony should be anticipated by the statement that one Legionnaire was wounded before the I. W. W. hall. He was "Dutch" Pfitzer, of Chehalis, and upon the circumstances of his wounding the defense sought to erect the structure of deceit that was intended to alter the position of Warren O. Grimm. With a bullet through his forearm from wrist to elbow, dazed by the pain of his wound, Pfitzer staggered down the street.

O'Reilly testified that he saw a wounded Legionnaire approach the intersection of Tower Avenue and Second Street, apparently clasping his arms about his middle, and that this man came from the very doors of the I. W. W. hall. He testified that later he saw a wounded man—unquestionably Grimm—being assisted into an automobile on Second Street, and that he noted "a resemblance" to the man he had first seen.

Cross-examination developed that O'Reilly has as his mentor a certain "Pat" Nolan, said to be one of the leading I. W. W. of the district, and that the fluent and brilliant high school youth himself is a convert to modern radicalism.

"Are your father and mother I. W. W.?" queried Prosecutor Cunningham.

"No, sir!" defiantly.

"Arnen't they radically inclined, something like the I. W. W.?" insisted counsel.

"That would depend upon what you call radical inclination," retorted O'Reilly. "My mother goes to Triple Alliance meetings."

"Isn't your mother an agitator in the Triple Alliance?" continued Cunningham.

"My mother is not an agitator in the Triple Alliance at the present time," answered O'Reilly.

Membership in the Triple Alliance, or the Non-Partisan League, was sufficient indication of radical tendencies, in the opinion of the defense, to qualify a venireman for service on the jury when the panel was being selected. Hired investigators of the I. W. W. approached veniremen prior to the case and sounded them upon their attitude toward these two organizations. If it was favorable, the I. W. W. agent reported to his chief that the venireman was desirable for jury service in the trial of the Centralia murderers. If it was unfavorable he was to be challenged and dismissed.

"I'm Liable to Say Anything"

May Sherman, 200 pounds and playful as a kitten, smiled archly at court and spectators, when she testified eagerly that she had seen a wounded man, tall and heavy of stature, gripping his stomach as he left the street before the hall. Inferentially, this man was Grimm—but May made her mistake when she clothed him in an olive-drab overcoat. Grimm wore no overcoat on the day of the parade.

"You knew Wesley Everest well?" inquired Prosecutor Abel referring to the murderer who was lynched.

"Yes," answered the playful May, her composure deserting her.

"Each of you roomed in the same hotel?"

"Yes."

"What name did you go by in the Queen's hotel?"

"Bertha Hope," stammered the woman. Then, swiftly— "My right name is Sherman, but I was going by the name of Hope."

Asked if it were not true that in the courthouse corridor, before she was called to the stand, she had boasted that "we will have evidence to meet anything they (the state) will bring up" the witness said that she did not recall the statement though she had talked with the two women to whom she was alleged to have made it.

ELMER SMITH
Attorney for the Centralia I. W. W. Visited the I. W. W. hall just prior to the shooting. According to the confession of Tom Morgan, "when he turned to go out, he asked Britt Smith if he had plenty of men. Britt said he had. Elmer Smith said he was going up to his own office to protect it. One of the others said it was kind of nice to have your attorney come in and tell you to do your duty." Smith was arrested after the tragedy in his own office, gun in hand. The jury found him not guilty. He is now under indictment for the murder of Arthur McElfresh. Out on bond, he is lecturing about the country, the feted idol of the I. W. W.

"I may have said it," flaunted the witness. "I'm not sure of it. I'm liable to say anything."

She looked toward Vanderveer for smiling approval of this brilliant exit from the difficult lane. But the I. W. W. counsel was frowning his disgust.

Tom Meaden, tailor, and Forrest Campbell, candy-maker, were defense witnesses who swore that they heard cries from the ranks, "Let's go! Come on! Let's get 'em!" and that forthwith the Legionnaires rushed the hall.

Twin Lies and Their Liars

Comment on this testimony may be briefly disposed of. For Meaden, who testified that he heard shots after the rush, admitted under cross-examination that he had specifically stated, following the affair, that he heard no shots at any time. He did not attempt to explain away the discrepancy in his testimony. And Campbell testified that he saw Arthur McElfresh lead the attack on the hall—whereas McElfresh died in his tracks, a bullet through his brain, at the corner of the variety store some distance north of the hall. Despite this proof, plain and unalterable, Campbell asserted that he saw the body of the stricken veteran lying on the sidewalk before the entrance to the I. W. W. headquarters.

At the opening of the sixth week of the trial, on March 1, the defense abruptly gave over its attempt to implicate Warren O. Grimm and in rapid sequence placed the defendants on the stand. By their testimony the defense showed that it had abandoned all subterfuge respecting the location of riflemen outside the hall, and was ready to admit all that had been denied in its opening statement, excepting the question of aggression. As for Bert Bland, companion rifleman of Roberts and Ole Hanson on Seminary Hill, his narration was so candid and incriminating that every listener felt he was being made the sacrificial offering—the scapegoat upon whom the jury might safely fasten the death penalty with the unspoken assent of the defense.

"I Shot Eight Shots"

"At first we decided to go to the Queen rooming house," testified Bland, after he had related the preliminary conference in the hall. "We went up to Wesley Everest's room. He told us we could use it. I did not tell him what we wanted it for, but I guess he knew. We looked out the window and did not like the situation. We came to the conclusion that the soldiers could easily surround the buildings, so we decided we did not want to face that kind of a situation. Then we decided to go to Seminary Hill. We had discussed the hill before.

"I saw a man on horseback at the corner," said Bland, when he had told of their concealment on the hill. "I heard a command. I couldn't tell what it was, but I saw the men break ranks and rush the hall. Then I plainly heard glass fall—then shots sounded. We commenced shooting. I shot between four and eight shots. I shot with one knee on the ground. I was shooting at the people who were raiding the hall."

Bickford the Boomerang

The testimony of Frank J. Bickford, Centralia physician and Legionnaire, who previously had testified at the coroner's inquest that he had suggested a raid on the hall and was in the act of carrying it out when firing opened, proved a boomerang to the defense in that it developed that Bickford was unfamiliar with the occurrences of that tragic day, and that the paraders were under fire before he moved a single step.

"I heard commotion and shouting among the platoons to the rear," testified Bickford, "and turned to look. I saw the platoons

ARNOLD HOTEL

Almost directly across Tower Avenue from the I. W. W. hall. In this building O. C. Bland and John Lamb were stationed, and fired on the passing parade

to the rear breaking up and scattering. Some were going toward the I. W. W. hall, others were going elsewhere, and some were running toward the vacant lot by the variety store."

What Bickford saw was the disruption of the parade after the first rifle fire. Among the men whom he witnessed racing for shelter toward the corner of the variety store must have been Arthur McElfresh, doomed to fall an instant later with a bullet through his head.

Bickford testified that he offered to take the lead in the raid on the hall, making the proffer as he marched with his comrades toward the intersection of Tower Avenue and Second Street.

"Your suggestion about taking the lead was not followed up, was it?" inquired the state.

"No, sir; that was before we halted."

"You say that you heard commotion back of you and saw soldiers scattering in all directions?"

"Yes, sir."

"Is it true that you are somewhat deaf, doctor?"

"Yes, sir."

Perjury Met With Warrants

During the court session of March 2, when the defense again made brazen attempt to place Warren O. Grimm in the attitude of an aggressor, before the I. W. W. hall, the state held to its promise and arrested two defense witnesses on perjury charges. They were Guy Bray and Jay Cook, of Centralia— both of whom had offered testimony tending to indicate that Grimm was shot while in front of the hall. Neither had dared be explicit, but their testimony was so plainly fabricated and its intent so dastardly that warrants for their arrest as perjurers awaited them as they left the courtroom.

Bray dared not testify that Grimm was near the hall, but he attempted to serve the same purpose by openly testifying that Lieutenant Van Gilder, companion of the Centralia leader, when he was stricken, was at the very threshold as the firing began. As the two comrades were known to have been together this fabrication would serve, especially when Bray asserted that Van Gilder's companion was wounded.

"Do you swear that Frank Van Gilder was standing near the door of the hall at the time of the shooting?" asked the prosecutor.

"I do," answered Bray.

"We shall want you a little later," was the dismissal, with an emphasis that stressed the waiting perjury charge.

Cook won his laurels as a perjurer and his subsequent arrest when he testified that the head of the column rested exactly before the I. W. W. hall—a declaration no other defense witness had attempted to utter—and when he capped this triumph of mendacity by declaring the positive identification of Warren O. Grimm as the man he saw running from before the radical headquarters, his hands clasped over an abdominal wound.

Time and again the defense renewed its endeavors to establish falsely the position of the slain Legionnaire, with the jury retiring while Vanderveer made his offers of proof on the conspiracy charge—only to be informed by Judge Wilson that no overt act on the part of Grimm had been proved. In the legal arguments that attended these efforts, the weapons of the prosecution were plied by C. D. Cunningham, whose easy, matter-of-fact and unanswerable exposition of the testimony and the law left to Vanderveer only the portion of the defeated.

The Law of Self-Defense

"Shooting is justified in the defense of your home when you are inside that home," argued Prosecutor Cunningham, during one of these clashes. "I believe the defendants are en-

AMERICAN LEGION BARRACKS

In good old army style, the room over the largest garage in Montesano was fitted up for a barracks for the Legion men in attendance at the trial. These men came from every corner of the state in uniform, to prevent any intimidation of the trial by the I. W. W.—the "silent terrorism" of the I. W. W. which they had used successfully in securing the acquittal of their members in previous murder trials. In addition to these "barracks", the Legionnaires maintained a hospital over one of the offices. The Red Cross were in charge of this feature.

titled to the construction that the hall was their home, but that is as far as this statute can go, and that is as liberal an interpretation as may be placed upon it.

"The law declares that killing in defense of others is justifiable, when the slayer is in the presence of those in whose defense he kills, and not otherwise. Counsel cannot contend, and does not, that the men on Seminary Hill, in the Hotel Arnold and the Hotel Avalon were in the presence of the men in the I. W. W. hall.

"So the men on the hill and in those hotels were not acting lawfully when they shot in defense of the men inside the hall, because they were not in their presence; nor can they claim that they shot out of the building, because they were not inside the building.

"We've proved deliberate murder or killing. They seek to justify it on the ground of self-defense. The burden of proof is upon them. The supreme court has said that you cannot kill a man simply because he has threatened you. What is there in the entire record, giving their proof the most favorable construction, which proves that Grimm committed an overt act or ever made a move against the hall or toward carrying out any purported threats?"

Ruled Judge Wilson: "There is nothing in the testimony which places Grimm in attendance, or convicts him of even attempting to do anyone any harm, and this is giving the defense the benefit of the doubt. The court is of the opinion that the evidence falls far short of being sufficient to show an overt act on the part of Grimm."

"Four or Five—Then a Volley"

Defense witnesses were not lacking to testify that they saw the Legionnaires rush the hall before they heard shots—witnesses of sound repute—but in almost every instance these testified that the first shots they heard came in a rattling volley, whereas it had been demonstrated that four or five scattering shots, with an ensuing lull, preceded the fusillade. It was at these first shots that the uniformed marchers, back from the fields of actual war, realized they were under fire. Some fled, others charged directly towards the bullet-spitting doorway of the hall itself.

Featuring Another Fiasco

The ludicrous nature of much of the testimony advanced by the defense—laughable, indeed, had it not been cited to serve so pernicious a purpose—is again illustrated in the testimony of a dozen witnesses who swore that civilian marchers carried coils of rope, presumably for I. W. W. neckties. How fearsome this testimony sounded, what mystery it engendered—only to be dissipated in laughter when P. H. McCleary, postmaster of Centralia, and Ben H. Rhodes, called by the state in rebuttal, testified that they had carried rope—the frayed fragments of a hempen cord that someone had hitched tin cans to behind an auto, to make a joyous noise on the festal day. The one had picked it up and lashed it at the other, and so the two—both men of advanced years and snowy hair—had played at being boys as they marched down the street. But while that rope endured in the testimony there wasn't an I. W. W. partisan but vowed that it was sinister and ominous.

Timothy the Letter-Writer

But the absolution of Warren O. Grimm was to come from the defense itself, and, most fittingly, from a gentleman of the cloth, the Reverend Thomas T. Edmonds, of Seattle, at present without a parish. Where fly the stormy petrels of the very latest new thought, where is lifted highest the harangue of the revolutionary demagogue, there one should seek the ministerial miscreant who sullied his broadcloth and his calling on the witness stand at the Montesano trial, as that lurid epic of jurisprudence drew to a close.

On the afternoon of March 5, after an interval of humdrum progress, the I. W. W. counsel summoned Dr. Edmonds to the stand. His name had been of frequent mention in previous testimony, as one of the paid investigators of the defense, a witness-seeker, a zealot consumed with impersonal fire for exact justice. Quite frequently state counsel had pricked the defense with caustic reference to Edmonds. There was both malice and purpose in those jabs and gibes—for, of all the motley company of radical adherents, Cunningham and Abel most dearly desired to question the dominie. And there he sat, Vanderveer smiled at him as at a stellar pupil and elected friend, the Reverend Thomas T. Edmonds, to testify for the defendants. The gibes had borne their fruit. The defense had brought forward its trump card, it most excellent witness.

JAMES McINERNEY
Alias James Mack. I. W. W. Had been in America for 12 years but had never become a citizen. Was arrested for murder in the Everett Massacre Trial two years before. He was one of the I. W. W. caught and disarmed in the I. W. W. hall. Was found guilty of murder in the second degree and sentenced to 25 to 40 years in the state penitentiary at Walla Walla.

Absolution of Grimm By the Enemy

Would you know what word it was that Dr. Edmonds wrote for Vanderveer's private reading, after he had made thorough investigation of the Centralia affair—wrote as a guide to the conduct of the case and with particular reference to the policy which must be pursued toward the memory of Warren O. Grimm? Whatever the propagandists may tell you, there on the stand, shifting and twisting under a merciless interrogation, the parishless parson confessed that he had penned this missive to Vanderveer, under date of January 4, 1920:

"And while Warren O. Grimm was not at this time involved in the raiding, the western law of reaching for a gun, (underscored) or motions like that, should apply."

For more than a month this Hessian of the I. W. W. had combed Centralia for evidence to implicate Grimm in aggression, and had not found it. His contribution to this country and to justice, upon that failure to incriminate the dead Legionnaire, was the suggestion to Vanderveer that a deliberate fabric of treacherous falsehood be woven on the witness stand, and that shameless perjury be suborned to fasten upon Grimm the onus of attack—Grimm, but a month or so back from the bitterness and nostalgia of Siberia, with his wife and baby waiting for him when the parade should return, light-heartedly going in soldierly pride to death on the streets of his home city.

Read, if your stomach is immune from nausea, this dialogue of the courtroom, and picture the while that boastful "servant of God" who held the witness chair, dapper and voluble:

Abel: "When were you called as an investigator for the defense?"

Edmonds: "In 1919, November, and I will say I believe it was providential."

Abel: "Do 'the boys' call you 'Timothy?'"

("Timothy" was the signature to the letter in the possession of the state, known to have been written by the chargeless clergyman.)

Edmonds: "They were not the ones who gave me that nickname. It was Dr. Matthews, my friend, who gave me that."

Abel: "Did you write this letter on January 4 to Mr. Vanderveer, about this case?" (The prosecutor thrust forward the penned proof of Edmonds' perfidy.)

Vanderveer: "This is very dramatic, Mr. Abel."

Abel: "Keep your remarks to yourself!"

Edmonds: "Y-e-e-s," stammeringly.

Vanderveer: "Who is opening my mail and reading it?" (His face suffused with anger.)

Abel: "You opened it!"

Edmonds: "I think the last I know of it the letter was in my little grip."

Vanderveer: "Why is it that I didn't get the letter?" (Business of semi-apoplexy.)

Abel: "You got it, and those are your notes on the back!"

Vanderveer: "The next time I will call that statement by its right name!"

Abel: "You may do so now."

Vanderveer's Cue In Timothy's Letter

Glance at this admirable epistle, the cause of such tumult in court, the contretemps of an otherwise dull afternoon—this letter that gave the lie to the I. W. W. counsel and his star witness and impeccable secret agent:

"Dear Mr. Vanderveer: Please forgive the apparent assumption, but I want to relay to you what I felt was an inspiration —in what I believe regarding the Centralia case.

"1.—It would be a line of defense, recognizing seemingly palpable, otherwise unexplainable facts, and so have the strength of truth.

"2.—It would not risk endangering a movement by recoil that might come.

"3.—It would furnish solid ground for an appeal to the latent justice and love for the persecuted in the average man.

"Briefly, to combine the public defense of Lovejoy and the remarkable tactics of John Brown (abolitionist martyrs) who so shrewdly and conciously forced his legal defense to rivet the eyes of the country on the case.

"I have obtained a library copy of 'Decisive Legal Battles of the Country,' by Hill, who described the unimaginable ferocity of public sentiment, local and general, and the way in which John Brown avoided the anti-climax proposed by his friends and attorneys, pleading insanity, and swung sympathy to his cause.

"If interested, will be glad to send it and other J. Brown books to you.

"How the two cases—Lovejoy, who died defending himself, and John Brown, who boldly faced the issue and was convicted—had tremendous historical sequences which no jury would lightly wish to assume.

"It strikes me that there are somewhat interesting legal as well as oratorical possibilities along this line; i. e., could not the outside firing be finally admitted, with Wesley E., Loren Roberts and one or two others involved, as a soldier's attempt to defend their rights—perhaps as legally indefensible as John Brown?

"With Britt Smith defending his home, and all of them actuated by fear for bodily harm, from threats?

"And Elmer Smith and the others not cognizant of any but strictly defensive war measures?

"And while Warren Grimm was not at this time involved in the raiding, the western law of reaching for a gun —(underscored)—or motions like that, should apply.

"And surely there is a case for constructive murder indictments, for the casual connection is positive and logical, reaching to the commercial club.

"In other words, could not Abe Lincoln's absolute honesty be combined with your invincible attack?

RAY BECKER

Alias Rudolph Berkholtz. I. W. W. During the war was convicted of being a draft-evader, and confined to jail in Seattle, Washington. Broke jail and escaped. Was one of the I. W. W. caught and disarmed in the I. W. W. hall following the murder of the parading Legionnaires. Found guilty of second degree murder and sentenced to 25 to 40 years in the state penitentiary.

"Would not this course best suit Britt Smith, et al?

"Would not a photograph of the burned and battered condition of the former raided hall be helpful as an exhibit?

"With hearty congratulations for you victories already,

(Signed) 'TIMOTHY.' "

Supply your own italics. The interrogation of Edmonds was sustained and thorough. In every paragraph of the letter, written with all dissembling dismissed, he declared the hazardous and indefensible plight of the defendants and suggested chicanery and perjury as their bulwark. How that letter came into the hands of the state is, as Kipling says, quite another story and immaterial to the present narration.

Page General Sherman's Nephew!

It is true that Edmonds, lamely struggling, asserted that one ex-service man had told him that he saw Grimm make a motion 'like reaching for a gun." But the smooth defense investigator, queerly enough, had failed to procure the testimony of this super-important witness, and recalled him only as a garrulous individual who said that "he was the nephew of General Sherman."

The epistolary phrase, "not involved in the raid at this time," referring to Grimm, was said by the witness to apply to information he had received that Warren O. Grimm was a participant in a former raid on an I. W. W. hall in Centralia, on April 18, 1918, and that he had been told Grimm led on the rioters, "dancing like a dervish, a flag in each hand, howling at the top of his voice."

It is well that you should know where Grimm was on that 18th day of April, 1918, when the parishless preacher did not scruple to charge, that he raided a radical headquarters. He was in his country's uniform, at Palo Alto, California, taking his marriage vows with the girl who was soon to be widowed —the same who sat through the trial of her husband's murderers, hearing his fond name blackened by most unspeakable calumny.

Rebuttal Testimony of the State

On March 8, at the beginning of the seventh week of the trial, the state opened its case in rebuttal. It had before it the task of refuting the testimony of the defense concerning the alleged attack upon the I. W. W. hall before the firing began, and the "lunacy" of Loren Roberts, as well as the disposal of various minor mis-statements and the plain and fancy fabrications of certain witnesses called by Vanderveer. State counsel turned to rebuttal testimony with confidence born of certainty in the justice of their cause and the truth and candor of their witnesses.

Not until the paraders were under fire, with the whiz of bullets in their ears, and with the windows of the I. W. W. hall bursting to the blast of rifle fire, did Legionnaires break ranks in Centralia's Armistice Day pageant. More than two score of clean-cut youthful veterans, many of them in the uniforms they wore overseas, together with many civilians, testified to that fact in rebuttal for the state. Though defense counsel assailed them with caustic cross-examination in no instance was their testimony shaken.

Three Men Back From Flanders

Then came to the stand three ex-service men who did rush the hall—after the firing began—a trio that gained the deadly portals of the rookery itself in a desperate and foolhardy attempt to carry reprisal to the lurking enemy. And their narratives, as those of their comrades, calmly sustained the thrusts of the I. W. W. attorney and were intact and unrefuted when they left the stand. They were Eugene ("Dutch") Pfitzer, of Chehalis, Loren Stevens, of Centralia, and Elden Roberts, of Portland. These three alone, of all that long parade line, charged directly at the hall when first the ranks were under fire. "Dutch" Pfitzer, for his reckless gallantry, took a bullet through the forearm. His testimony so closely parallels that of his two comrades and fellow witnesses that it suffices for the purpose of setting forth the facts.

Pfitzer testified that he was in the second platoon, and that the parade was in formation when the shooting began. Someone near him cried out that the "wobblies" were firing into the ranks. Pfitzer, with France in his memory, turned and raced for the hall—as thousands of American lads charged, single-handed, the enemy machine-gun nests of Flanders, and Chateau-Thierry and the Argonne forest. He testified that he set his foot to the door and that in the same instant the window-panes crashed to the blast of bullets. At his side were Stevens and Roberts.

With the whine of the missiles in his ears, Pfitzer turned to take cover. It was then that he was shot in the left arm, the bullet traversing it from elbow to wrist. The wound paralyzed the arm, so that he could not hold it out from his body. Gripping it across his stomach he went down the street. It was this gesture which opened the lane of false defense testimony regarding the Legionnaire wounded near the hall, in an attempt to make it appear that Pfitzer was Grimm, hit in the abdomen.

"I did not charge the hall until I found out that the 'wobblies' were shooting at us," testified Pfitzer. "I never heard of any raid."

"Why did you run for the hall?" was the sneering query of Vanderveer, professing doubt that sacrificial bravery is other than a myth.

"I thought the shooting was coming from there," was the somewhat astonished reply of "Dutch," as though the question were superfluous.

As for the score of Legionnaires, members of the parade line, who testified regarding the firing and the attack, this is the comprehensive substance of their testimony: That the ranks were in formation when the firing opened, and that the firing preceded any movement toward the hall or any break in the line, whatsoever. That from two to five shots rang out, with an ensuing lull, and then the air was keen with the flight of a volley. They broke and ran for cover.

Another Lie Pinned and Writhing

Throughout the trial, in his attempt to introduce alleged evidence and testimony that a commercial conspiracy against the I. W. W. burgeoned in slaughter, Vanderveer had charged distinctly that F. B. Hubbard, president of the Eastern Railway & Lumber Company of Centralia, was the leader of this citizens' movement, and that he in person was present in Centralia during the tragedy, enraged to the point of madness by the miscarriage of his plans. Witnesses for the defense had sworn that they saw and conversed with Hubbard in the hours immediately following the ambuscade. Hubbard might well have been enraged, for it was his nephew, Ernest Dale Hubbard, who died at the vicious muzzle of Everest's pistol—but

AVALON HOTEL
Across the street diagonally from the I. W. W. hall. The man in the window is Frank Van Gilder, who was at Warren Grimm's side when he was hit. It was from this window that the fatal shot was claimed to have been fired by Eugene Barnett. With Barnett in the room was another I. W. W. who escaped capture.

Hubbard was not in Centralia on that day. The attempt so to involve him was but part and parcel of the blatantly irresponsible and perjured methods of the defense.

A. L. Weaver, auditor of the Hotel Portland, Portland, Ore., supported by other testimony, proved through the hotel records that F. B. Hubbard was a guest at the Portland on Armistice Day and that he did not return to Centralia until the following morning—broken and swollen-eyed from the sorrow that had come to him in the death of his nephew.

Ghouls Will Be Ghouls

Another prurient, fetid falsehood was bared by state witnesses in the impeachment of the previous testimony of John Patterson, defense witness, who had asserted that he stood at the corner of the variety store, just north of the I. W. W. hall, and saw the body of Arthur McElfresh borne away from the door to be placed almost at his feet. What ghoulish mastermind conceived this perjury, when all Centralia knew that McElfresh, poor lad, dropped in his tracks as he ran for cover, not toward the hall, but away from it? Was the defense even then preparing to forestall, in the Grimm case, the possibility of re-arrest and prosecution for the murder of McElfresh, if the jury freed the defendants? Supply your own answer.

Ruth Godfrey, 15, red-cheeked and dressed in plaid gingham, testified that her home "is just across the road" from the Patterson residence, and that on the morning of November 12 she was in Patterson's home. He had returned but a few moments before from a night in the city jail, where he had been swept when posses raked the city for I. W. W. sympathizers. Ruth testified that this was the conversation between husband and wife.

"John, what did they do to you?" asked Mrs. Patterson.

"They didn't do anything to me, because I didn't see anything," answered Patterson.

J. A. Pollock, another of Patterson's neighbors, testified that shortly after Armistice Day he talked with Patterson and that the substance of the conversation was as follows:

"I'm very sorry to hear that you're mixed up with those I. W. W.," said Pollock.

"I didn't start downtown 'till after two o'clock," had been Patterson's reply. "I got as far as the Randall Hotel. My little girls were with me, and they got scared, so I turned and beat it for home."

The Randall Hotel is far north of the variety store and the I. W. W. hall, where Patterson had testified he stood and watched the removal of the dead Legionnaire. Unshaken by cross-examination was the testimony of both Ruth Godfrey and Pollock.

"Loren Roberts Is Sane"

Remaining for state rebuttal was the plea of lunacy in the instance of Loren Roberts, defendant, slayer of McElfresh. An alienist for the defense had sworn that, in his opinion, Roberts was suffering from dementia praecox and had cited characteristic delusions. Vanderveer had told court, jury and reporters that Loren Roberts was insane, and that he, his counsel, feared attack and bodily harm from the demented defendant. And throughout this farce the prisoner had smiled as imbeciles do. At the conclusion of rebuttal testimony the smile was to fade, succeeded by the thoughtful gravity of one who realizes that his plea is futile and his hope downcast. Of the hundreds who heard the final verdict, when he was held to be insane, none could have been more astonished than "Grand Mound" Roberts.

"Roberts is sane." Five alienists so testified for the state after close observance of the prisoner, and after chats with him in private examinations. They were Dr. William House, of Portland, an internationally noted authority on mental and nervous diseases; Dr. J. F. Calbreath, of Portland, former chief of the Oregon state hospital for insane; Dr. E. R. Ahlman, of Hoquiam, Washington; Dr. L. L. Goodnow, of Aberdeen, Washington; and Dr. Lee A. Scace, of Centralia, Washington. Each of these physicians declared absolute conviction that the delusions of Roberts were palpably feigned.

To Dr. Ahlman the prisoner had said, at a third interview, that he knew that Vanderveer was defending him, that there was no doubt but that the defendants would be acquitted on the ground of self-defense, and that no malign influences were troubling him, and that Vanderveer was the one man he must trust.

MIKE SHEEHAN

I. W. W. Had lived in the United States 25 years, but had never taken out citizenship papers. Was caught in the I. W. W. hall, but claims he was unarmed and took no part in the shooting. Was found not guilty by the jury. Is under indictment for the murder of Arthur McElfresh.

Roy Inmon and J. B. Cooper, jailers of Grays Harbor county prison, testified that Roberts had appeared entirely rational during the many weeks he had been under their charge, and asserted their belief that his mentality was normal and his delusions shammed.

Where Was Eugene Barnett?

In rebuttal attack upon the attempted alibi for Eugene Barnett, the state brought forward witnesses who declared that the defendant had given them varying accounts of his whereabouts during the firing, and that he had not said he was seated in the lobby of the Roderick hotel—the claim upon which his alibi rested. One rebuttal witness testified that Barnett had told him that he stood before the hotel when the firing began.

JOHN LAMB

I. W. W. The village loafer of Centralia. Seemed unable to work more than half a day at any job, and was a charge on the county most of the time. Was arrested on more than one occasion for not permitting his children to attend school. With O. C. Bland, he was stationed in the Arnold Hotel. Found guilty of second degree murder and sentenced to 25 to 40 years in the state penitentiary.

Another testified that he had entered the Roderick, at the time Barnett had sworn he was there, and that the defendant was not present. And one, J. D. Jones, farmer, to whom Barnett talked of the tragedy on his way home to Kopiah, swore that the defendant had given this version of the affray:

"When the soldiers halted, the 'wobblies' thought they were going to raid the hall—and then the shooting started."

Preston McDonald, in the posse which captured Barnett, as he crouched behind a log on a brushy hillock near his home, rifle at ready, testified that the prisoner told him that he sat in the lobby of the Avalon Hotel throughout the firing. It was, indeed a badly scrambled alibi.

Activity of One "Labor Juror"

The status of the pseudo "Labor Jury" stood revealed at the close of the case for the defense, in sur-rebuttal, when Vanderveer called to the stand E. W. Thrall, one of the "labor jurors," to testify in a last attempt to prove that F. B. Hubbard, alleged head of the purported commercial conspiracy against the I. W. W., was in Centralia on Armistice Day. The impartial and disinterested attitude—save the mark—of this "labor juror" was demonstrated when the state forced him to admit that he had, while ostensibly relaying to organized labor an unprejudiced opinion of the facts, busied his spare hours in recruiting witnesses for the defense.

With this last exposure of the unprincipled character of the defense, the taking of evidence and testimony came to a close, on March 11—just four months from the day on which Centralia witnessed the savage butchery of her sons. Seven long weeks of trial, fraught with constant contest and struggle, had been consumed in disentangling the weave of treacherous intrigue that had culminated in scarcely more than seven seconds of deadly rifle-fire.

Judge Wilson to the Jury

On March 12 Judge John M. Wilson delivered his instructions to the jury. They were ably and thoroughly couched in language so clearly expounding the facts and the law that none could misread them, unless willfully. And through the court's charge, as though a giant lens were held above the shifting colors of testimony and the mass of evidence, one saw that the case of the defendants was without comfort—that ranged in the prisoners' dock sat ten men in the very shadow of that bitter tree which bears dead murderers for fruitage.

"You are instructed," said Judge Wilson, "that any person, or persons, has or have the right to defend himself, or themselves, or their property, from actual or threatened violence, and to that end to arm themselves; but this right does not go to the extent of stationing armed men in outside places for the purpose of shooting the persons from whom violence, real or apparent, is expected.

"If you find that any two or more of the defendants, in the manner and form and at the time charged in the information, planned to defend the I. W. W. hall or the property therein, by the stationing of armed men in the Avalon Hotel, the Arnold Hotel, and on Seminary Hill, for the purpose of shooting from those points, the placing of such men and the shooting from outside points would not be lawful acts.

"And if you find that any two or more of the defendants so planned, and any two or more of the defendants carried out such plan, and as a natural, necessary or probable result thereof Warren O. Grimm was shot and killed, then such killing would be unlawful and would be murder.

Further interpreting this instruction, Judge Wilson advised the jury that a conspiracy may be established by circumstantial evidence as well as by fact, whether the identity of the individual who committed the act be established or not.

"If the jury believes in this case," said Judge Wilson, "beyond reasonable doubt that the defendants, or any of them, conspired and agreed together, or with others, to do an unlawful act, or a lawful act by unlawful means, and that in furtherance of the common design, and by a member of such conspiracy, Warren O. Grimm was killed, then these defendants, whom

JUDGE WILSON
Who presided at the trial in Montesano. Judge Wilson was appointed by Gov. Hart to preside at the trial in the place of Judge Abel on account of the fact that Judge Abel's brother was acting as special prosecutor in the case. Judge Wilson refused to become excited at Vanderveer's repeated and deliberate insults. And when Vanderveer attempted to force the issue of labor and capital into the trial, Judge Wilson brought him up short with: "The issue in this case is murder, Mr. Vanderveer."

the jury believes were parties to such conspiracy, are guilty of the murder of Warren O. Grimm, whether the identity of the individual doing the killing be established or not, and whether such defendants were present at the time of the killing or not.

"You are instructed," said Judge Wilson, "that while the law requires, in order to find all the defendants guilty, that the evidence should prove beyond a reasonable doubt that they all acted in concert in the commission of the crime charged, still it is not necessary that it should be positively proved that all met together and agreed to commit the crime; such concert may be proved by circumstances, and if from the evidence the jury is satisfied beyond a reasonable doubt that the defendants are guilty, they should find them guilty."

Had the court in mind the memory of certain shady testimony for the defense, divers witnesses whose faces were the transparencies of untruth, when he issued an instruction covering the credibility of witnesses? For the court charged the jurors to take into consideration, in weighing testimony, the manner of witnesses on the stand, their candor and their intelligence, and to give credit accordingly.

At 10:15 o'clock on the night of March 12 the case went to the jury. Arguments of state and defense had thrown but little additional light upon the circumstances of the crime and its trial—for the trend of evidence and testimony had focused so closely upon the certainty of guilt that all who had followed the case were agreed that the deliberations of the jurors would be comparatively brief. It had become of general knowledge that at least two of the jurors were of radical adherence, and possibly another shared kindred views. But confidence in the staunch Americanism of the remainder led to the prediction that verdicts of first degree murder for all, with the possible exception of Mike Sheehan, would speedily be returned. And the instructions of the court left no other course open save that of conviction in the first degree or of acquittal, for proof of conspiracy and concert, essential to conviction, had been offered in conclusive abundance, and remained uncontroverted. And if a murderer conspires it follows, logically and as a matter-of-course, that he premeditates—and premeditated murder is none other than murder in the first degree.

"Before Your Country and Your God"

"For five long days," said Prosecutor Abel, in his closing address to the jury, "we dared the defense to prove that Warren O. Grimm was anywhere near the I. W. W. hall. Finally counsel was absolutely driven to the wall—and then came the perjured testimony, the testimony that was untrue!

"The I. W. W. organization is not a shield for murderers. Behind the shield of that organization no man may say that he can shoot down at will peaceful men in the street.

"You understand, gentlemen, that what was done that day was intended. The killing of Grimm was willful murder. There can under no circumstances in this case be a verdict of murder in the second degree.

"Counsel for the defense tells you that he has for years fought the battles of the underdog. I'm not so sure about that. I'm not so sure that he hasn't been fighting the battles of the vicious, of the disloyal, the criminal. I'm not sure but that his voice has been raised more often in defense of treason than of right!

"I want you to remember, you jurors, that there are other people besides these defendants who are interested in this case. Shall we say that the widow of Warren O. Grimm and her little daughter are not interested? Shall we say that Grimm could be slaughtered in his uniform, in the broad light of day, and that a thing so cruel as that could go unpunished?

"All that we ask is justice, and we do say, in dealing justice, these men will every one be convicted of murder in the first degree. Before your country and before your God you can find no other verdict!"

"I Find No Fault In This Man"

And Cunningham, easy, persuasive, eloquent, forceful, held forth to the jury the participation of each defendant in the lurid events of Armistice Day, analyzing the share each bore, as shown by the testimony and evidence. Concerning the lunacy plea of Loren Roberts the prosecutor told the jurors that it was too trivial to argue—constituting a matter upon which their minds already must have attained fixed conclusions.

"So interested was the Reverend Timothy Edmonds in truth and justice," said Prosecutor Cunningham, "that he devised a plan whereby these men would be acquitted. One of the most humorous features of this case is that the very plan, proposed by the frock-coated preacher, has been followed by the defense. I do not charge that counsel accepted it—it was merely the queer meeting of two great minds.

"What did Edmonds find, with respect to Grimm, after 35 days' investigation? That, "Grimm was not at this time involved in raiding."

"If these defendants are freed as guiltless, such action will mean that good government in the United States is at an end. It will mean anarchy and red murder, such as I saw on the streets of Centralia, on the 11th day of November, 1919."

Vanderveer to the Red Juror

Vanderveer had the appearance of weariness, body and soul —the listless apathy of a lost cause—when he spoke to the jury. The passionate plea and exhortation for which the auditors waited was not lifted. The fires of his enthusiasm had deadened to ash. He told the jurors that evidence and testimony had been introduced to show that the rush preceded the attack, he declared that the I. W. W. acted solely in self-defense, he quoted a homely adage to the effect that a kicked dog will turn and bite—but the zest of battle was gone from his tone. And at the end of his address he launched one meaningful warning to jurors whose identity was best known to himself. For he spoke as one radical speaks to another, bidding them stand fast, whatever transpired in the jury room.

"Do not be influenced by your cowardice," urged Vanderveer. "If you haven't the courage to do what I am doing, then never again pretend to believe in this cause."

From the mouth of defense counsel came this testimony, that, known to him, there sat as jurors certain men who were allied with the cause of radicalism and who had falsified under oath when they took their places in the panel.

The Abortive First Verdict

The jury slept upon it. They rose and breakfasted. The interest of a nation—and the peculiar interest of those who seek its downfall—centered in that isolated, lonely jury room on the upper floor of Grays Harbor courthouse. The air was

THE JURY, ALTERNATES AND BAILIFFS
From reader's left to right: Bottom Row—Bailiff; A. T. Fisher, relator; Edward Parr, logging engineer; John A. Ball, blacksmith, the alternate who succeeded Edward Parr on the jury; Harry Sellers, laborer; W. E. Inman, rancher. Upper Row—Frank Glenn, farmer; Carl O. Hulten, farmer; E. G. Robinson, carpenter; E. E. Sweitzer, farmer; E. E. Torpen, farmer; F. H. McMurray, teamster; A. W. Johnson, storekeeper, alternate juror; P. V. Johnson, paver; Bailiff. Top Row—Bailiff Samuel Johnson, fisherman.

pregnant with eventful promise. And then, almost in time for dinner, the jurors reached their first conclusion, notified the court that they were agreed, and filed solemnly into the judicial presence. They bore with them an abortive document that found Eugene Barnett and John Lamb guilty of murder in the third degree, or manslaughter, a verdict incompatible with the laws of Washington and unacceptable by the court. Plainly the jurors had disregarded the specific instructions of the court, had sought to evade responsibility and rancor, and had cowered under dread of the I. W. W.—vengeful and terrible. In this first verdict, as in the final, the jury found Loren Roberts to be insane, and the other defendants to be guilty of murder in the second degree. Judge Wilson ordered the jury to return and resume its deliberations.

A Verdict That Suited None

Two hours later the final verdict was returned, as follows:

Guilty of murder in the second degree—Britt Smith, O. C. Bland, Ray Becker, James McInerney, John Lamb, Eugene Barnett and Bert Bland.

Acquitted—Mike Sheehan and Elmer Smith.

Insane and irresponsible—Loren Roberts.

"A hell of a verdict and a hell of a jury!" is said to have been the comment of one of the convicted men.

It was. Grays Harbor county and the entire Pacific Northwest declared it an impossible, monstrous miscarriage of justice. Both state and defense were agreed, for the once, that but one of two verdicts could logically have been returned—guilt in the first degree, or acquittal. And local belief declared that unworthy fear of I. W. W. reprisals, together with a desire also to placate public sentiment, led that incomprehensible jury toward a verdict which its members considered a compromise.

Later it was to be known that two jurors were violently radical, and that a third favored their attitude—these three holding out for acquittal. Nine Americans, therefore, against their own belief in the extreme guilt of the accused, permitted the prejudiced opinion of openly avowed radicals to force them into a shameful and illogical decision. Let their own consciences walk with them to keep this fact forever in mind. For they, as jurors, in the most important case with which Americanism has been concerned since the bomb outrage in San Francisco, deliberated for a lesser number of hours than is customary in the settlement of hog stealing litigation and farm boundary disputes.

"For the Murder of McElfresh"

On information charging them with the murder of Arthur McElfresh, even as they walked out to freedom, Mike Sheehan and Elmer Smith were re-arrested as they left the courtroom. They are now at liberty under bail, and the time of their trial is unfixed and nebulous—at liberty as the Homeric heroes of the reds. Prosecutor Allen, of Lewis county, has vowed that the charge will be pressed.

Sentence Upon the Seven

On April 5, at Montesano, Judge Wilson passed sentence upon the seven convicted men, decreeing that each shall serve from 25 to 40 years in the Washington state penitentiary at Walla Walla—a firm and righteous sentence under the lenient verdict of the jury. Vanderveer has served notice that he will appeal the case. Perhaps. But there is a likelihood that the I. W. W. defender is secretly content, and roundly amazed at the escape of his clients from the noose itself. He has filed affidavits of prejudice against one of the jurors, alleging that this man declared, upon learning of the Centralia murders, that the slayers should be hanged. Unhappy and unworthy fellow —if so he spoke—to have ventured an assertion with which all America was ringing. To have dared to utter a patriot's opinion.

The Truth About Montesano

Radicalism once issued a brochure entitled, "The Truth About Centralia." It issued from a printery that later was raided by Federal officers seeking alien revolutionists—whom they found there. And from the pedestal of the shining goddess, in whose light all men must walk if the world go forward, it was more remote than pole from pole. But these facts which have been set forth in the foregoing pages are literally the truth about Centralia and Montesano, the cause and the effect; the sanguinary crime and its punishment.

There are those who will say it is propaganda. So it is—but it is the propaganda of truth and the records will bear it out. Upton Sinclair, brilliant and embittered intellectualist, defender of the I. W. W. faith, has said, in "The Brass Check," that American journalism is putrid to the heart, that it is in the chains of capital, a willing and mendacious helot. He has charged that the "capitalistic press" lied when it told the story of Centralia. The Sinclair attack is as zealously misdirected and futile as are the vocal aspirations of the terrier that bays at the moon. The fact is that it was the radical press that lied—both of Centralia and Montesano.

One test—though there are hundreds—of the misrepresentation and suppression of truth in the Montesano trial, on the part of the radical newspapers, is that of the narration of the testimony of the Reverend Timothy Edmonds. In the staff correspondence of the Seattle Union Record, paladin of the defense, appeared no mention of the incriminating letter written by Edmonds and admitted by him on the witness stand—the letter that absolved Warren Grimm from blame. The account of the staff correspondent, on the contrary, cleverly sought to portray portions of the courtroom dialogue as showing that Edmonds defeated and discomfited the prosecution. Let this charge stand—by the files of the various radical publications printing accounts of the trial, in comparison to the court records, it may be proved that deliberate distortion was the fixed policy of the red publicist, when he did not entirely omit the testimony and evidence prejudicial to the men on trial. Proof to the contrary is challenged, but the challenge never will be caught up.

The staff correspondents of metropolitan dailies, and the representatives of news service associations, on the other hand, were almost meticulous in their endeavor to portray the exact facts of the trial, crediting defense as well as prosecution with the points in testimony or argument. The sympathies or prejudices of the individual reporters were restrained in the presentation of the news. These men knew the charges that would be laid against them if they deviated. Their respective newspapers were responsible to the public for the truth. That trust was kept.

Have You a "Wobblie" In Your Town?

A word about Centralia. The defense declared that there existed a commercial conspiracy to rout the I. W. W. from the city. Of such there was no proof in the trial, nor does this review concern itself with the accuracy or falsity of the statement. The defendants were on trial for the murder of Warren O. Grimm, and even perjury did not serve to link him with alleged hostility and intrigue against the radicals. But if there did exist a purpose to evict the I. W. W., whose voice will be raised to say that these unwelcome civic tenants should remain? Remember well that Centralia, as all the Pacific Northwest, had seen her sons march off to war and death, while at home this very organization obstructed the draft, practised sabotage in the delay of production, committed a myriad cloaked and treasonable acts, and sought to delay and impede righteous progress of our war with Germany.

These are the same men who seek the shield and shelter of American institutions when justice cries a halt. And such as these were the men, misguided and blinded, spurred on by lurid press and flaming oratory, who fired into the Centralia Armistice Day parade. The facts convict them of wilful murder, and the jury so held. Established indisputably, whatever rumors may have spurred the I. W. W. fear, is the truth that the marching Legionnaires did not attack until fired upon, and that four lives were sacrificed because radicalism had taught the creed of bloody violence.

Orators and Dragon's Teeth

Hatred against these men as individuals should be reproved and restrained. As individuals there were those among them, had destiny shaped another course, who might well have been honored as citizens and friends. And punishment for their crime rises above mere personality—it should strike, through the individual, at the slavering beast which incited and encouraged them to crime, the organization known as the Industrial Workers of the World. Not blood-thirst dictated that these men should suffer condign punishment. It was the safety of the commonwealth itself which cried out for such a sentence as would serve notice that America is done with treason at home.

When Americans hear the plaza orator pour out his vitriol, as he does, the smile of tolerance should fade and never re-appear. For the scored and ensanguined seeds he sows are the same dragon's teeth from which Centralia reaped her harvest of most lamentable death.

Address of
National Commander Franklin D'Olier at the
Grave of Warren O. Grimm
Centralia, Washington, August 10, 1920

"I come to Centralia today in a double role, as national commander of the American Legion, and also as a plain American citizen, but with the single purpose of paying homage to the memory of four men who died as truly in the service of their country as though they had actually fallen on the battlefields of France. Officially, I come here as to the shrine of the American Legion hallowed by our first martyrs, because Centralia will mean to the Legion what Bunker Hill, Gettysburg and Chateau Thierry mean to our nation. At these places the spirit of America met the enemy and triumphed. Here in Centralia the spirit of the American Legion likewise met the enemy of our nation and triumphed.

"Nine months ago, the first anniversary of the signing of the armistice here in this town, a murderous blast was fired into the ranks of parading Legionnaires. The event is too close for us to appraise it, but we are beginning to appreciate the significance of Centralia. We, who were delegates to the first convention of the American Legion at Minneapolis, recall the dramatic tenseness when the news was received. The ink was scarcely dry on the words of the preamble of the constitution of the American Legion, pledging ourselves to uphold and defend the Constitution of our country, to make right the master of might, to maintain law and order and to transmit to posterity the principles of justice, freedom and democracy when the Legion men of Centralia proved how sincere was their stand for law and order. It was Centralia's sorrow to bear the tragedy, but it was Centralia's honor to show how lofty were the ideals of the ex-service men and how sacred their pledges.

"These four men, Warren O. Grimm, Dale Hubbard, Arthur McElfresh and Ben Cassagranda, died as heroically as though they had made the supreme sacrifice over there. They will be the beloved martyrs of the American Legion, and it is not what we say today, but rather what we do tomorrow, that will show how truly we appreciate the great sacrifice made by our fallen brothers in arms.

"And so it is fitting that here today we should renew our pledge of patriotism and law and order and thus serve notice upon the forces of anarchy that over 4,000,000 ex-service men who fought and defeated the foe without our borders are now sworn together to fight to the death the foe within, who would do injury to our sacred institutions. Our inspiration shall be our beloved martyrs and the restraint shown by our outraged comrades, and by dedicating ourselves anew to the defense of our flag and all that it means, a defense in fair play and justice, we shall thus prove that our comrades shall not have died in vain."

The Americanism Program of the American Legion.

By NATIONAL COMMANDER F. W. GALBRAITH, JR.

The resolution adopted at Minneapolis by the first national convention of the American Legion authorizing the creation of the National Americanism Commission of the American Legion sets forth the aims of that body in these words:

"The establishment and conduct of a continuous, constructive, educational system designed to:

"1. Combat all anti-American tendencies, activities and propaganda;

"2. Work for the education of immigrants, prospective American citizens and alien residents in the principles of Americanism;

"3. Inculcate the ideals of Americanism in the citizen population, particularly the basic American principle that the interests of all the people are above those of any so-called class or section;

"4. Spread throughout the nation information as to the real nature and principles of American government;

"5. Foster the teaching of Americanism in all schools."

The program there set forth may be compressed into two phases:

First—The problem surrounding immigration—the making of Americans of the arriving and newly arrived residents of America from other shores.

Second—The "domestic" problem—the making of Americans of unassimilated aliens who are in America but not of it, and all other individuals and groups who for one reason or another seem to have failed to appreciate the fact that the form of government under which this nation has grown great is the form under which it must grow greater.

The Legion's Americanism Commission was organized by and until the recent convention at Cleveland functioned under the guidance of Arthur Woods, of New York. With virtually no resources it has made a splendid beginning at its vital and stupendous task. The Commission is now in the process of reorganization and shortly will enlarge greatly the scope of its activity. It is my hope and belief that means will be found to enlist the co-operation of various other organizations whose aim is common with ours. There must be co-ordination. There must be a distribution of work that will eliminate duplication of effort. Specific tasks must be assigned to specific bodies who are best constituted to deal with the situations in question. These are basic considerations which must guide us or we will not scratch the surface.

The fundamentals to which shall adhere in the matter of immigration are selection, assimilation, rejection.

By selection the Legion proposes that the United States, being a sovereign nation, shall exercise more stringently its right to say who shall and who shall not take up residence and citizenship within our gates. There is need for more rigorous standards governing the admission of aliens. Too many that come are simply good riddance for the country from whence they came. We should inquire more painstakingly into the history and antecedents of those who come to live among us. If they are desirable let them come and be Americans. If not, shut the door.

By assimilation the Legion proposes a method by which the newly arrived may become an integral part of America. The Legion proposes to station its agents at the ports of debarkation. These Legion bureaus will receive rosters of incoming immigrants which shall give the destination of each. A Legion committee in the local post where these aliens settle will extend the hand of welcome to these selected newcomers; the committee will, according to forms laid down, help the newcomers to appreciate the advantages of life in America and start them on the highroad which leads to American citizenship in fact as well as name.

American Legion members will be the alien's friend, confidant, defender and critic. They will help him get a job, help him learn English, settle his grievances, explain his difficulties, show him how to make use of libraries, playgrounds, schools and other community benefits. They will not tell him how to vote, how to worship or how to think. They will respect his opinions as a man, providing he respects America's opinions as expressed in our form of government.

By ejection the Legion proposes that we shall reserve to ourselves the right to send back to the land from whence he came, any alien who fails to respond to the assimilation process. *It must be understood that an alien comes here on probation.* If he does not measure up, if it is apparent that after sufficient time he is not on the way to real Americanism, out he should go.

Then there are the millions already admitted to residence and some to citizenship who need Americanizing. Some, indeed, were born here. What shall Americanization mean to them?

The answer varies. With some it will be purely a problem of assimilation to be gone about by the same way we propose to go about assimilating the newly arrived. With others the destruction of preconceived and false ideas must precede the constructive work. This means education. It means also the elimination of the cause; the deportation of these radical firebrands who prey on the ignorance of the aliens and implant in their minds false conceptions of American institutions before the alien has had the opportunity to learn the truth.

THE I. W. W. AND IT'S TEACHINGS.

Nothing So Damns the I. W. W. Organization as It's Own Literature. No Comment is Necessary; the Following Speaks for Itself.

Preamble to the Constitution of the Industrial Workers of the World

"The working class and the employing class have nothing in common. Between these two classes a struggle must go on until the workers of the world organize as a class, take possession of the earth and the machinery of production, and abolish the wage system.

"Instead of the conservative motto, 'A fair day's wage for a fair day's work,' we must inscribe on our banner the revolutionary watchword, 'Abolition of the wage system.'

"By organizing industrially we are forming the structure of the new society within the shell of the old."

Quotations from I. W. W. Publications

"If the I. W. W. had the power to make good we might depend entirely on direct action. All we need is the power to make good."
—*One Big Union Monthly.* (I. W. W.). Sept., 1919.

"We are building the new society within the shell of the old. Where the General Executive Board of the I. W. W. shall sit, there shall be the nation's capitol."—*Why Join 300.* I. W. W. publication, Seattle, Wash.

"Unlike the trade unions, the I. W. W. organizes always with a view to the ultimate revolution. The existing parliamentary government will crumble into uselessness. The existing industrial unions will become the supreme national power."—*The Industrial Commission* of the I. W. W.—By H. L. Varney.

"As a revolutionary organization the Industrial Workers of the World aims to use any and all tactics that will get the results sought with the least expenditure of time and energy. The tactics used are determined solely by the power of the organization to make good in their use. The question of 'right' and 'wrong' does not concern us."—*The I. W. W.*—By Vincent St. John, I. W. W. writer.

"The I. W. W. opposes the institutions of the state." "Toward the existence of the government, the I. W. W. is openly hostile."
—*The Industrial Worker*, Spokane publication.

The Centralia Case

A Joint Report

THE
CENTRALIA CASE

A Joint Report on the
Armistice Day Tragedy at Centralia,
Washington, November 11, 1919

Issued by
The Department of Research and Education
of the
Federal Council of the Churches of Christ in America
The Social Action Department
of the
National Catholic Welfare Conference
and
The Social Justice Commission
of the
Central Conference of American Rabbis

October, 1930

CONTENTS

FOREWORD

THE study on which this report is based was made jointly by our three church organizations in response to urgent requests received from the Washington Conference of Congregational Churches and the Pacific Northwest Conference of the Methodist Episcopal Church. There are those who feel that the members of the Industrial Workers of the World involved were treated unfairly and with unwarranted harshness, that they were denied the full safeguarding of their right to a fair trial and a sentence consistent with the offense of which they were convicted. On the other hand, there are those who take the position that the situation was largely of the I.W.W.s' own making, that they committed a crime more serious than that of which they were found guilty and that the verdict reflected a conflict in the minds of the jurors between patriotism and a desire to placate public sentiment on the one hand, and fear of the I.W.W. on the other. The desire for a reexamination of the events was brought to a head when an officer of the American Legion stated that in studying the history of the conflict in order to exonerate his organization from criticism for its part in the affair, he became convinced instead that there was ground for this criticism, reversed his position, and began to work for the liberation of the prisoners.

For the purpose of this investigation a cooperating committee was appointed by interested church groups in the State of Washington. This committee has been earnest, active and efficient in its cooperation. Certain of its members participated in conducting interviews. An extensive study has been made, with the aid of legal counsel, covering the entire court record, newspaper files, and much other documentary material. Many personal interviews were had, with the Governor, the trial judge, the present chief justice of the State Supreme

Court, who wrote the opinion of that Court in the case, members of the staff of the prosecution, ministers, American Legion members, members of the Industrial Workers of the World and their sympathizers, nine of the jurors, and all the prisoners. The evidence has been thoroughly examined and weighed with care.

In reviewing the circumstances surrounding the fatal shooting in Centralia it is not our purpose to pass final judgment on the guilt or innocence of the prisoners. We have endeavored, however, to throw new light on the question, Was justice done? To this end, we begin our study with a review of the factors, physical and psychological, which produced the situation that resulted in the tragic events of Armistice Day, 1919.*

In the interest of conciseness and brevity we have omitted detailed documentation in summarizing evidence. Reference to sources on which statements of fact are based can be supplied on request.

THE DEPARTMENT OF RESEARCH AND EDUCATION,
The Federal Council of the Churches of Christ in America.

THE SOCIAL ACTION DEPARTMENT,
The National Catholic Welfare Conference.

THE SOCIAL JUSTICE COMMISSION,
The Central Conference of American Rabbis.

---

* Since this report was prepared, James McInerney, one of the men under sentence as a result of the Centralia tragedy, died in prison, in August of this year. He had served ten years and four months of his sentence of from twenty-five to forty years.

I

THE FACTS OF THE CASE

1. THE BACKGROUND OF THE TRAGEDY

THE event known as the Armistice Day Tragedy at Centralia, Washington, occurred in the early afternoon of Tuesday, November 11, 1919, when a violent clash took place between parading ex-soldiers and members of the Industrial Workers of the World before whose hall the parade had halted. Under circumstances that will be examined in this report, four of the paraders—Warren O. Grimm (local Legion commander), Ben Casagranda, Dale Hubbard, and Arthur McElfresh—were shot to death; the I.W.W. hall was wrecked; and one member of the I.W.W.—Wesley Everest—was lynched. Eleven members of the I.W.W. were tried for the murder of Grimm on the basis of an alleged conspiracy to kill. Their defense was that they had not conspired to kill but had undertaken lawfully to defend their hall from an expected raid. The trial resulted in the conviction of seven of the defendants for murder in the second degree and a sentence of from twenty-five to forty years.

The tragedy thus briefly described stands against a background that must be clearly seen before the events of that day can be understood.

For many years conditions in the logging camps in the State of Washington had been intolerable. Hours were long and wages low. Provision for sanitation was negligible. The logger, usually a casual laborer without home or family, was deprived of normal social contacts. He felt that the labor leaders were failing him. Then came the Industrial Workers of the World, a radical fighting organization, and the loggers rallied to it as an instrument of economic and social emancipation.

In 1917 a widespread strike led by the I.W.W. resulted in marked gains for the loggers in the Pacific Northwest, including the eight-hour day. This stimulated resentment against the organization among the lumber interests, which was enhanced by the syndicalist philosophy of the I.W.W., whose avowed purpose was the establishment of a new economic order by revolutionary methods.

7

It was commonly believed in Washington and elsewhere throughout the United States that the I.W.W. was in effect a criminal organization; that its members freely practised sabotage, destroyed farm crops and burned buildings. They have been charged in countless instances with acts of violence against property, involving hazard to life. It is true that extensive investigations failed to elicit proof of such charges, but the significant fact is that they were generally believed. The I.W.W.s have been regarded as trouble makers and outlaws, the Ishmaelites of the industrial world, and they have been treated accordingly.

The widely felt antagonism against the organization was immeasurably sharpened when the United States entered the war. The I.W.W.s opposed the war, contending that it held nothing of value for labor, that it was a war of capitalists. They believed that there was only one legitimate war—the struggle to liberate the working class. Their organization was utterly uninterested in national aims and purposes and felt no loyalty to the government.

Thus, in the hostile attitude of the community toward the I.W.W. there were two distinct elements, the one economic and industrial and the other pertaining to patriotism, national loyalty, and the effective prosecution of the war. These two factors reinforced each other and frequently became inextricably blended.

Attempts at suppression of the I.W.W. became violent and the organization and its members were ostracised to such a degree that they found difficulty in obtaining legal redress of grievances. They were practically at the mercy of their enemies, including both employers and those who opposed them on patriotic grounds.

It should be said that neither national nor race prejudice enters into the picture. Most of the loggers were American born, as were all those involved in the Centralia affair, except two who were born in Ireland.

Earlier Clashes with the I. W. W.

Numerous clashes with the I.W.W. had occurred in the Northwest, of which the shooting at Everett, Washington, in 1916 was the most serious. Two hundred and fifty I.W.W.s had chartered a steamboat in Seattle on November 5, 1916, and proceeded to Everett with the avowed intention of forcing the issue of free speech, which had been interfered with by the activities of the vigilantes. They were met on the pier by armed deputies and in the clash which ensued at least five I.W.W.s were killed and two of the deputies. One of the I.W.W.s was tried for murder, but was acquitted.

Centralia, a town of some 11,500 inhabitants, in Lewis County, located at the center of a lumber industry, has a history in connection with the outlawry of the I.W.W. Several violent outbursts against them had occurred in the vicinity before the Armistice Day tragedy. In the spring of 1918 the hall then in use by the I.W.W. was raided by a group of business men who broke away from a Red Cross parade and destroyed the contents of the building. The men found in the hall were manhandled and expelled from the town. In June, 1919, Tom Lassiter, a blind newsdealer who sold I.W.W. and other radical literature, was kidnapped. On two occasions his stock was destroyed. In broad daylight he was forced into an automobile, carried out of town and given warning not to return. Although the matter was brought to the attention of the Lewis County prosecuting attorney and, on his failure to act, to the attention of the Governor, no one was prosecuted for the offense.

Citizens' Protective League and Meeting of Employers

A Citizens' Protective League was formed in Centralia in June, 1919. The opening of a new I.W.W. hall in September was followed by a meeting of employers on October 20. Community sentiment regarding this meeting is indicated in the following "want ad" which appeared in the *Centralia Daily Hub:* " 'Wobblies'—How to get rid of them and stay rid is the question before the meeting of all employers of Centralia and vicinity at the Elks Club, 8 o'clock Monday evening. Be there. Signed, 'Committee of Citizens' Protective League.' " On the 21st the *Hub* carried a statement under the caption: "Discuss Plans for Combating I.W.W. Menace" in which the following appeared: "The Citizens' Protective League recently organized in this city to combat the I.W.W. problem, held an interesting session at the Elks Club last night at which plans for handling the matter were discussed at length. . . . About 100 business men were present. . . .

"While the meeting brought forth many suggestions as to how the problem of ridding the city of undesirables might be handled,

9

none of these was finally adopted, and it was decided that the 'inner workings' of the organization should be conducted with as little publicity as possible, because that was the best way, it was thought, to meet an organization which used similar tactics."

The Centralia *Daily Hub* on October 19 stated, "Members of the committee state that they have a definite plan to advance at the meeting Monday night which plan will not be made public until that time."

An account of the meeting which is apparently correct relates that the president of the Eastern Railway and Lumber Company became highly incensed when the Centralia Chief of Police informed the gathering that the I.W.W. had a legal right to remain in Centralia. The local Legion commander, predecessor in that office to Warren O. Grimm, acting as chairman, said that while he was personally not in favor of raiding the hall, in his opinion no jury would convict men who might conduct such a raid. (He later acted as color bearer for the Centralia contingent in the Armistice Day parade.) When a trade union representative objected to serving on a committee to oust the I.W.W. and the effort to appoint a committee in open session failed, it was agreed to appoint a secret committee. However, it has not been established conclusively that such a committee was actually appointed.

Efforts to Obtain Protection

Mrs. J. G. McAllister, who, with her husband, owned the Roderick Hotel, part of which had been rented as an I.W.W. hall, testified at the trial that she had appealed to the chief of police for protection but had received no satisfactory assurance. She had reported this to Britt Smith, the secretary of the local I.W.W., who testified at the trial that he had tried unsuccessfully to see the mayor. Elmer Smith, the attorney for the I.W.W., testified that he had appealed to the Governor for protection against raids. The above testimony was not contradicted.

About a week after the meeting at the Elks Club the I.W.W. distributed from house to house a thousand leaflets which read in part:

"TO THE CITIZENS OF CENTRALIA WE MUST APPEAL.

"*To the law-abiding citizens of Centralia and to the working class in general:*

10

"We beg of you to read and carefully consider the following:

"The profiteering class of Centralia have of late been waving the flag of our country in an endeavor to incite the lawless element of our city to raid our hall and club us out of town. For this purpose they have inspired editorials in the *Hub*, falsely and viciously attacking the I.W.W., hoping to gain public approval for such revolting criminality. These profiteers are holding numerous secret meetings to that end, and covertly inviting returned service men to do their bidding."

The leaflet also sought to exonerate the I.W.W. from charges of crime and made counter charges.

2. EVENTS OF ARMISTICE DAY

On November 11, 1919, an Armistice Day parade was held under the auspices of the American Legion, in which the Centralia Post was joined by others from the vicinity. Several days before the parade the line of march was announced. A simple diagram showing the location of the I.W.W. hall is given on page 12. The parade was to march northward on Tower Avenue to Third Street, turn there, and march southward on Tower Avenue. This would take it twice past the I.W.W. hall, which was on the west side of Tower Avenue north of Second Street.

Members of the I.W.W. were gathered in their hall, having armed themselves. They had been advised by their attorney that they had a right to defend their hall from attack. They had also stationed armed men on Seminary Hill, about one-quarter mile east of the hall, in the Avalon Hotel, south of Second Street on the east side of Tower Avenue, and in the Arnold Hotel, which also is on the east side of the Avenue but a little north of the hall.

The parade, which began at about 2:00 o'clock, consisted of several divisions. Boy Scouts led the march, followed by Canadian veterans, ex-navy men, the Chehalis Lodge of Elks, and the Centralia Lodge of Elks. A Centralia contingent, consisting of Centralia and other World War veterans, was in the rear, save for a few automobiles which followed carrying persons in Red Cross uniforms. Ahead of the Centralia contingent was the Chehalis section, composed also of veterans. (Chehalis is a nearby town.) On the return march the Centralia veterans stopped in front of the hall. Following closely upon the

11

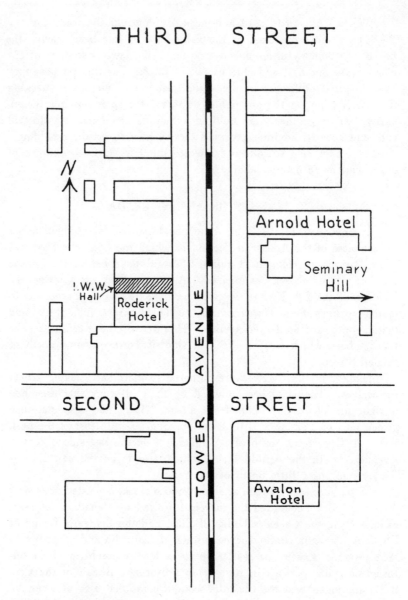

DIAGRAM SHOWING THE LOCATION OF THE I. W. W. HALL

halt of the Centralia veterans shooting began, under circumstances which are much in dispute and which will be considered later. Three Centralia Legionnaires were mortally wounded, Warren O. Grimm, newly elected commander of the Centralia Post of the American Legion, Arthur McElfresh, and Ben Casagranda. Several others suffered less serious wounds. Great excitement followed. The hall was entered by paraders and its contents destroyed; the porch was torn from the building and, together with the furniture, burned in the street.

Wesley Everest, who had done much of the shooting from the hall, escaped from the building but was pursued by armed men. He shot and mortally wounded Dale Hubbard, one of his pursuers. Everest was immediately overpowered and knocked insensible. A little later he was led down the street with a rope or strap around his neck, then barely escaping lynching.

The story of the clash spread rapidly and before nightfall many Legionnaires and others came pouring into Centralia. About seven o'clock the lights of the city went out for about fifteen minutes. Under cover of the darkness a party of men took Everest from the jail, apparently without opposition. They proceeded in automobiles, which were at hand, to a bridge, and there hanged and shot him. It was not until several hours after the lynching that Dale Hubbard died.

Further lynching was threatened that evening but some of the cooler-headed citizens summoned federal troops from Tacoma and, in the interim, used their influence to prevent further loss of life.

The American Legion took over the policing of the community and pursued the round-up of I.W.W.s with vigor. On November 15, John Haney, participating in a man hunt, was shot and killed by a member of another posse who mistook him for an I.W.W. The reason given by the Legion for its action in taking charge was that ordinary processes of administration had broken down and there was no other body which could or would exercise control.

Because no undertaker would handle it, Everest's body was taken to the jail and placed in a cell near those occupied by the prisoners. Later, according to the Seattle *Post-Intelligencer*, four I.W.W.s from the jail, "accompanied by a squad of 17 armed national guardsmen were sent to the pauper section of the local cemetery with the body, dug a grave, dropped in the box and covered it up. There were no prayers and no services of any nature when the body was lowered into the grave." No members of the family were there; nothing was left to mark the spot. It was said that Centralia people "would not let such a mark stand."

Public funeral services were held for the four Legionnaires. Thousands were present. Prayer was offered by the Washington State Legion chaplain. "Oh, thou who didst put the mark upon Cain," he prayed, "put the brand upon those who have brought us together this dark afternoon." (*Morning Oregonian*, Portland, Nov. 15, 1919.)

3. PRINCIPAL QUESTIONS OF FACT INVOLVED

A. FACTS ESTABLISHED

The I.W.W.s' Belief That a Raid Was Planned

It is admitted even by the American Legion that the I.W.W. believed that a raid was to be made on their hall during the parade. The line of march, which brought the paraders twice opposite the hall, had been publicly announced. In their various stations the I.W.W. men were watching for signs of aggression. The defense admitted an agreement among the I.W.W.s to defend their hall against attack.

Stations Occupied by the I.W.W.s

O. C. Bland and John Lamb, members of the I.W.W., were in the Arnold Hotel; the former testified that he intended to shoot at any persons seen attacking the hall. "John Doe" Davis was in the Avalon Hotel. On Seminary Hill were Loren Roberts, Bert Bland, and Ole Hanson, who were to fire when they heard shots or saw an attack. Wesley Everest, Britt Smith, secretary of the local I.W.W., Ray Becker and James McInerney, with others not convicted, remained in the hall.

It is admitted that the three on Seminary Hill took part in the shooting. Several shots were fired from the hall. Everest was responsible for most, if not all, of these. He used a .45 caliber Colt automatic pistol.

B. POINTS OF FACT AT ISSUE

The Question of Aggression

The most important question in dispute is: Which side was the aggressor? Many accounts are given of what happened after the

14

halting of the Centralia contingent. Some testified that the paraders marked time, some that they stood still, and others that there was a "bunching together" in front of the hall.

The testimony at the coroner's inquest is especially valuable because it was given only two days after the event and before battle lines were drawn in preparation for the trial. According to the official digest of the statement of Dr. Frank J. Bickford, a Legionnaire, at the inquest, "he heard some one say something about raiding the I.W.W. hall and he offered to take the lead if enough would follow. There were six or eight men in the lead. McElfresh was at the right of Dr. Bickford. Some one larger than McElfresh put his foot against the door of the hall and shoved. Immediately a shower of bullets came through the door. The first volley consisted of from 15 to 20 shots, after which everybody scattered." An attempt was made to discredit Dr. Bickford's testimony on the ground that he was somewhat deaf, that earlier shots might have been fired which he did not hear. No marked degree of deafness was established at the trial. In any event, his statement makes it clear that one Legionnaire, at least, on his own admission, started for the hall while still unaware of any gun fire.

Dr. Herbert Y. Bell is quoted in the inquest record as saying that he "wondered why the halt when he heard a yell and shots simultaneously," and that the shots were heard at the same time that "the boys" started toward the building.

In the record of the inquest there is no suggestion that an appreciable time elapsed between the first shot and the "volley." Evidence on this point at the trial, however, was conflicting. Also, in its published account of the affair, the Legion maintained that "four or five scattering shots, with an ensuing lull, preceded the fusillade."*

Their own rush on the hall was admitted by "Dutch" Pfitzer, Eldon Roberts and Loren Stephens. They testified, however, that they were in regular formation in the parade at the time of the first scattering shots and that, independently of each other (they were in separate platoons), they left the ranks unarmed and went toward the hall in order to prevent further shooting. This testimony was not mentioned in the opening statement by the prosecution to the jury nor in the direct case for the prosecution but in the State's rebuttal, after the

---

* *Centralia Tragedy and Trial*, the *American Legion's Account of the Armistice Day Massacre*, by Ben Hur Lampman, special correspondent for the *Portland Oregonian*, covering the trial.

15

defense had introduced evidence that Pfitzer had been shot in front of the hall and had gone down the street leaving a trail of blood.

The testimony on this question of aggression is so confused by conflicting statements regarding details that the relative reliability of witnesses becomes an important consideration. On this point direct evidence is lacking, but, manifestly, evidence supporting the defense by members of the Centralia contingent should be given especial weight. While a prior rush toward the hall is not conclusively shown, it appears more probable that this occurred than that the shooting took place first.

The pursuers of Wesley Everest had guns but there is evidence to show that these were obtained after the first shooting. The testimony makes it fairly clear that the marchers were not armed. It is true that one of them carried a rope, but that any violent use of it was intended could not be established.

Agreement to Defend the Hall

Both sides agree that the I.W.W. had advice from Elmer Smith, a young Centralia lawyer who acted as legal adviser to the local I.W.W.; this advice they apparently interpreted to mean that they had a legal right to defend their property even to the extent of using firearms both inside and outside the hall. At the trial Smith admitted having advised that defense by physical force was lawful but denied having mentioned the use of guns or having entertained any such thought. It seems reasonably certain that the collection of arms and the placing of men in outside stations were part of a general plan of defense.

Implication of Barnett

The prosecution contended that Eugene Barnett fired the shot that killed Grimm, from the Avalon Hotel. On appeal, the prosecution offered the alternative possibility that Barnett was present with "John Doe" Davis when the latter fired the fatal shot. The testimony for the prosecution, however, was unsatisfactory; some statements by witnesses were inaccurate; one witness failed to identify Barnett after his position among the defendants in the courtroom had been changed during a short recess.

A rifle of the same caliber as that with which Grimm was shot— 38.55—was found about two weeks after Armistice Day under a billboard near the route from the hall to Barnett's home. The prosecution was not able to prove, however, that Barnett had concealed it there, and it is contended on his behalf that it was "planted."

Barnett testified that he was not at the Avalon but in the lobby of the Roderick Hotel (adjacent to the I.W.W. hall) with the proprietors, old friends of his. The testimony of these people, Mr. and Mrs. McAllister, is substantially similar to his. Many witnesses testified in Barnett's behalf, some to seeing him after the shooting under circumstances which would preclude his hiding the gun under the billboard and which would indicate that he was in the Roderick and not the Avalon Hotel.

The mass of evidence cannot be digested here but it casts serious doubt on the charge that Barnett was present in the Avalon and participated in the defense of the hall. The State contended that he fired the fatal shot and therefore he, if any of the defendants, stood in danger of a first degree verdict. However, the jury (in its first verdict) found him guilty of "third degree murder" which indicates that the jury did not believe the prosecution's contention that he was in the Avalon. This first verdict weighs heavily in Barnett's favor. Moreover, one of the State's attorneys has written to the Governor expressing his opinion that the evidence was inconclusive as to his guilt.

Circumstances of Grimm's Death

The prosecution claimed that Grimm, for whose murder the I.W.W.s were tried, was in the street at the head of the Centralia contingent near the intersection of Second Street and Tower Avenue when he was shot; the defense insisted that he was, or had been, breaking in the door of the hall. Those who testified for the State on this point were far more numerous and much more definite than those for the defense. The weight of the testimony at the trial indicates that Grimm did not participate in an attack. Dr. Guy Scace testified that part of the jacket of a 38.55 bullet was lodged in the wound. The only 38.55 rifle that figures in the case had been taken from the I.W.W. hall to the Avalon Hotel by "John Doe" Davis. The coroner's jury found that the bullet that killed Grimm came from that point. George F. Vanderveer, the defense attorney, who fought the case with every resource at his command, admitted, after the prosecution's evidence was presented, that the fatal shot came from the Avalon, although he had contended at the outset that no shots were fired from that point.

Grimm was shot in the abdomen, the bullet entering at the front. If, as was admitted at the trial, the shot came from the Avalon, Grimm was facing the Avalon at that moment. While this suggests that he was not participating in the raid it is, of course, not conclusive evidence to that effect, since, conceivably, he may have joined in the rush, have turned away from the hall when the firing from within began, and received his death wound immediately afterward. It is positively asserted by those working for the release of the prisoners that Grimm took part in the attack and was shot from the hall. This assertion is based on affidavits and statements by eye-witnesses which stand in contrast to the main body of evidence presented at the trial. Such extra-judicial statements are generally considered much less reliable than testimony given in court, primarily because they are not subjected to cross-examination. This is a powerful weapon in the hands of a skillful attorney, bringing to light bias and prejudice, completing partial statements and exposing falsehood. Such cross-examination is especially important when the question is one of the identification of a man who is a member of a uniformed company of men moving about in a state of confusion.

Treatment of the Prisoners

The story, widely circulated, that on the way to the bridge where he was hanged Everest was atrociously mutilated, while it had a tremendous emotional effect, has not been clearly established and is not of primary importance in this study. While some of the prisoners state that they personally were not subjected to the "third degree," others assert that they were. It is alleged that references were made in their hearing to the killing of Everest, questions were asked as to whom "they will get" next, and such terror created that for nights sleep was practically impossible.

4. THE TEMPER OF THE COMMUNITY

Prevailing Excitement

The Centralia *Daily Chronicle* for some time following November 11 carried numerous significant statements indicating the general temper of the community and showing that the American Legion was still in charge of the situation almost two weeks after the event.

The following are examples:

November 12. "Keep Off Streets—Chief of Police Hughes asks all law-abiding citizens to keep off streets tonight as the best means of preserving order."

November 21. "Centralia police affairs are still under complete control of the American Legion, a special committee of the local post, headed by Lieutenant Frank Van Gilder, directing all investigations of Wobblies arrested and organizing the man hunts."

November 24. "American Legion headquarters in the city hall were mopped and all cleaned out this morning. There were two alleged I.W.W. in the city jail who said they would much rather do that work than stay in jail, so they were given the opportunity."

A Centralia despatch in the Aberdeen *World* for November 14, stated: "While Sheriff Berry announced today that he considered the emergency had passed and that no more arrests of alleged I.W.W. would be made except upon warrants, American Legion men, who had been engaged in a round-up of reds since the Armistice Day massacre here Tuesday, kept steadily at work this morning."

A newspaper account of the death of Haney states: "One man shot him, and he rolled over against a tree, and when he attempted to rise, one of the men shot him twice more. The man who did the shooting—all in good faith since he thought Haney was an I.W.W.—is prostrated with grief. Everyone states that it was entirely an accident."

The fact that Haney had been killed by a member of a posse was concealed when it was first discovered, and news of a battle was allowed to circulate. His 20-year-old son absolved the posse of blame. A state official who described the killing as "accidental" told an investigator that no jury would convict.

The Lewis County Bar Association resolved that no member would defend or aid in the defense of those who took part in the Armistice Day shooting.

The Legion Fund

The Legion Post at Centralia raised a fund which in the middle of January, 1920, amounted to $11,751.57 and which, it claims, was used "for the prosecution of those responsible for the Armistice Day Mas-

sacre" and "to defray their [the Legion's] many expenses during the
. . . week" following Armistice Day.

The I.W.W. organization has charged that the fund was raised "to
pay certain of the expenses that the prosecution did not dare to make
a matter of public record." It is admitted that from it Legionnaires
in uniform at the trial were paid $4.00 a day.

Funds of the Citizens' Protective League were turned into the
Legion fund. Among the contributors were the H. H. Martin Lumber
Co., $50; Lincoln Creek Lumber Co., $100, and 118 of its employes,
$277.50; the Eastern Railway and Lumber Co., $100; J. P. Guerries
Lumber Co., $100; the Lumber Manufacturers Agency, 100; the West
Coast Lumbermen's Association, $1,000; First Christian Church, $8.36;
the minister of the Christian Church, $3; the Presbyterian Ladies
Aid, $5.

When Vanderveer offered to prove at the trial that "funds for
prosecution" were being "raised by the [lumber] mill owners and
their employes" this was denied by Prosecutor Allen.

5. SET UP OF THE TRIAL

The Charge Against the Defendants

The charge on which the defendants were tried was the murder of
Warren O. Grimm, those not accused of shooting Grimm being implicated on the basis of conspiracy to kill. Every participant in a
conspiracy is held guilty of any crime committed within the scope of
the conspiracy. The defense maintained that the accused had not conspired to kill, but had lawfully agreed to defend their hall and themselves.

Change of Venue

The prosecution resisted the efforts of the defense to have the trial
removed from Lewis County. It got some 300 persons to swear to a
printed affidavit which stated, "there is no prejudice, so far as your
affiant knows, against said defendants charged with said crime, in
Lewis County, Washington, and in any event, there is no more prejudice
against said defendants in Lewis County, than there is in any other
county in the State of Washington, if any prejudice exists at all."
Prosecutor Allen and Special Prosecutor Cunningham argued for the
retention of the trial in Lewis County.

An editorial in the Centralia *Daily Chronicle* contained the following: "The people should be unified in the one proposition of insisting that a Lewis County jury shall try these criminals so that no miscarriage of justice may follow."

Upon the filing of an affidavit of prejudice against Judge Reynolds of the Superior Court of Lewis County the case was assigned to Judge George D. Abel of Grays Harbor County. He decided that public sentiment was such that the trial should be transferred to Grays Harbor County, the county seat of which is Montesano.

Selection of the Trial Judge

The prosecution retained as special counsel William H. Abel, a brother of the judge. This relationship led to Judge Abel's retirement from the case at the instance of the prosecution. In the normal course of events Judge Ben Sheeks, the other Superior Court Judge of Grays Harbor County, would then have taken the case. The Governor, however, appointed Judge John M. Wilson of Olympia. Judge Sheeks is reported to have been popular with the laboring class and was supported by labor in his campaigns for office.

A charge of bias has been made against Judge Wilson, based in large part on his address at an annual memorial service of the Centralia Elks Lodge for its members who had died during the preceding year, including Grimm, Hubbard and McElfresh. According to a newspaper report he also addressed a meeting in Bucoda assembled to form a citizens' club, the purpose of which was to be "to use all necessary measures in the expulsion of I.W.W. propaganda in the vicinity of Bucoda." A later newspaper report stated, however, under the heading "Bucoda Residents Renew Loyalty Oath," that "the present unrest in the industrial world Judge Wilson laid to the conditions under which laboring men have worked and to the fact that so little attention has been paid to the Americanization of the foreigner. He assailed the employer who in his eagerness to make money left unheeded the conditions under which his men worked."

The attorney for the defense stated that "the defendants were powerless to disqualify Judge Wilson except for actual bias. Being assured by him that he could try the case impartially, they elected not to attempt this."

Second Change of Venue Denied

The I.W.W. organization, some little time after Armistice Day, sent out an appeal for funds which was accompanied by an attempted justification of the shooting. It was circulated not only in Grays Harbor County but throughout the whole State of Washington as well as other states. This was followed by the anonymous distribution, in the county only, of leaflets bitterly hostile to the I.W.W. and the defendants. One of these was headed, "Will I.W.W. Threats Affect the Jury's Verdict?" and appealed directly to the prospective jurors, saying: "If, at their trial, their guilt is proven beyond a doubt, and this guilt is practically admitted by the I.W.W. themselves, it is the duty of every juror, as an American citizen, to cast his ballot for conviction and maximum punishment and thus sever a few heads of a many-headed monster that is eating at the heart and vitals of the nation Centralia's Armistice Day victims sought to save." Much more in similar strain was included. Several persons swore that the publications of the opposing groups "neutralized" each other.

A second change of venue was applied for on the ground of existing prejudice. On January 3, the court approved the application in the following language: " . . . Now while the question of accommodations [for witnesses, officers of the court, etc.] cannot be taken into consideration to any extent yet the effect and result of those accommodations . . . must be taken into consideration." Opposing factions would be housed in this community, the court said, "where there is absolutely no police protection and no assurance of any adequate means" of preserving the peace of the community. "These eleven defendants are entitled to a fair trial and the state is entitled to a fair trial in a community of fair-minded citizens and I have come to the conclusion after very careful and serious thought upon this question that this case . . . must not and cannot be tried in this county."

On January 7, however, the court reversed itself, deciding that the trial should be held in Grays Harbor County and stating that the former ruling was based on the statute relating to civil cases rather than that relating to criminal cases, which limits the grounds for change to prejudice of the judge "or to excitement or prejudice against the defendant in the county, or some part thereof." The matter of police protection was held to be irrelevant and the showing of prejudice was deemed insufficient.

The motion was renewed and finally denied on January 26, 1920, and the additional reason was given that "the court is of the opinion that the law does not permit a second change of venue in cases of this kind."

Evidence of the attitude of Grays Harbor County toward the I.W.W. is found in the severe denunciation of them by the press of that county. The Aberdeen *World* on November 17, 1919, printed the following from a letter to the editor, referring to the I.W.W.: "Boycotting and sabotage are their favorite methods. All right try that on them also. Let our physicians and surgeons ignore them in their hours of sickness and death. Bar them from all kinds of labor and let them feed upon each other; refuse them admittance to our schools and churches. They have no respect for them. Let the merchants refuse to sell them merchandise." The boycotting was to extend to "branding as a shyster any lawyer who defends them and barring him from any further practice before the bar of justice."

The Elma *Chronicle*, November 20, said: "Hanging is too good for them." Articles and editorials in the weekly Montesano *Vidette* were of the same general tenor. On November 14, an editorial referred to the I.W.W. as "copperheads" and "human reptiles," and a news item states that the commercial club sent a petition to the Governor for a special session of the legislature in order to make membership in the I.W.W. a crime. "Many of the members were in favor of making the penalty" for membership in the I.W.W. "a life sentence or capital punishment." The issue of November 21 notes that "the American Legion of Montesano is making the prosecution of Wobblies their chief concern. Nearly every other organization and lodge in the city has taken some action either by resolution or otherwise pledging themselves also to the task." And so on.

The editor of the Montesano *Vidette*, quoted above, was asked as a witness on the motion for a change of venue: "Are you prejudiced against the defendants in this case?" "I am not," was the reply. Many other sworn statements, mostly in the form of affidavits, denied public excitement, hysteria, hostility and hatred. At least one affiant denied that he had heard any expression of hostility. Other affidavits, on the contrary, asserted that there were hysteria and hostility. One sworn statement is discriminating: "The laboring class in this community are inclined to be in sympathy with the accused and the others are very much against them."

23

On appeal to the Supreme Court, Vanderveer quoted from the affidavit of Judge Abel, taken for the prosecution, to the effect that the reason for the lack of accommodation for the defendants' friends and witnesses was "that the people might hesitate to subject themselves to criticism by renting rooms to such persons." The attorney asked: "What more eloquent evidence could one ask of the hysterical condition existing in that county? Again why should the court comment on the absence of police protection?" The appellants also stated: "Let us again call the court's attention to the fact that at all times the defendants expressed themselves as perfectly willing to be tried in Pierce County," of which Tacoma is the county seat. "There was probably no place in the whole State of Washington," they said, "nor perhaps in the whole United States, where the defendants and their case would have been entirely free from prejudice; and in these circumstances we believe it was the court's plain duty, having conveniently at hand a county which was wholly unobjectionable to both parties, to transfer the case to that county for trial."

Although the reason assigned by the prosecution for objecting to Tacoma was that the jail and transportation facilities were inadequate, it is asserted, but cannot of course be proved, that the court and counsel for both sides believed that a trial in Tacoma would result in acquittal. The trial for the Everett I.W.W. shooting, held in Seattle, another fair-sized city, had resulted in acquittal.

The Supreme Court affirmed the ruling of the lower court on the ground that there had been no arbitrary action and no gross abuse of discretion. It did not pass upon the question whether the motion should or should not have been granted.

A field investigator found, even after the lapse of ten years, excitement and tenseness in Montesano over the Centralia affair. The prevailing opinion there at the present time is that considerable hysteria existed in Grays Harbor County at the time of the trial.

Preparation for the Trial

The prosecution had a staff of six attorneys, two of whom were outstanding members of the bar, and also numerous investigators. The facilities of the State Attorney-General's office were at its disposal. Vigorous preparation was begun immediately after the tragedy. Efforts were made to obtain statements from all who had any relevant knowledge.

The jailed I.W.W. did not consult counsel until November 18, a week after the shooting. They secured an attorney, Ralph Pierce, who was shortly succeeded by George F. Vanderveer of Seattle. The latter had defended the I.W.W. in the famous Chicago trial before Judge Landis and also in the Everett case. He was unable, however, to be personally present until a few days before the trial began. The defendants had the aid of certain investigators in preparing their case, but these worked at a great disadvantage as compared with those of the prosecution. It is conceded on all sides that Vanderveer safeguarded the interests of the defendants with all the skill and ingenuity that could be expected from any attorney.

Eleven days were spent in the selection of the jury. It consisted of four farmers, two stationary engineers, a teamster, a real estate agent, a telephone employe, a fisherman, a carpenter and a construction laborer. Two alternates were chosen. The illness of one of the engineers during the trial resulted in the substitution of a blacksmith. Except in the case of Juror Sellers, further consideration of the jury may await the discussion of the verdict.

Juror Sellers' Statement

Sellers, a laborer employed by a telephone company, when examined by Vanderveer gave no evidence of prejudice or of having made any statements hostile to the defense. After the trial, on the motion for a new trial, affidavits were produced, sworn to by four persons, alleging that before his selection as a juror Sellers had made the following or a similar statement: "I am going to be one of the jurors and I will hang every G—— d—— one of them," referring to the defendants. Vanderveer has made an affidavit to the effect that during the trial he received information concerning such statements and requested the court to interrogate Sellers so that, if the report were verified, an alternate juror might be substituted without interruption of the trial, but that the court denied having the power to take such action.

Sellers swore that the charge was made by I.W.W. sympathizers. This was corroborated by affidavits. One affidavit stated that one of Sellers' accusers was reported to have been a paid investigator for the defense. The defendants' brief on appeal to the Supreme Court takes the position that the four who swore that they heard the remarks could not all have been "honestly mistaken." The State replied: "If the Juror Sellers made the threat, if he was prejudiced, the verdict failed to disclose it. The evidence was amply sufficient for the jury to have done exactly what it is claimed the Juror Sellers said he would do. . . . It possibly may be outside of the record, but it is known to everyone in the State of Washington and elsewhere, if not to this court, that the I.W.W. as an organization has heretofore advocated crime, violence and intimidation and the overthrow of orderly government by force as a means to accomplish its end. It is too plain for argument that anyone believing in and advocating crime and violence and sympathize [sic] with those who do, would perjure themselves [sic] whenever it was to their advantage or to the advantage of their fellows, to do so. If the lower court rightfully believed that Mr. Vaughn and Mr. Tompkins and the others who swore to supporting affidavits on behalf of the defendants were sympathizers with the Industrial Workers of the World, it in itself, we say, was sufficient reason to reject their affidavits altogether. So we do not care whether the affidavits filed by appellants are wilfully false or not, nor is it necessary for this court or the lower court to so find, but from the record before us, there is ample ground upon which to base a finding of falsity. The Juror Sellers was not prejudiced."

On his examination prior to being sworn in, Sellers had been asked, "Can you weigh the testimony of" an I.W.W. "and give it that credit which you could give to the testimony of any other witness?" "Yes, Sir," was his answer.

The trial court refused to order a new trial on the ground of Sellers' alleged statement. The Supreme Court did not decide this question "upon the merits." It refused to overrule the trial court's exercise of its discretion.

Loren Roberts' Statements

Loren Roberts, who pleaded insanity, was denied a separate trial. The result was that statements by him, commonly referred to as his "confessions," obtained at the instance of the prosecution and implicating the other defendants, were admitted in their joint trial. The court instructed the jury that these "confessions" should not be considered as evidence against any but Roberts.

26

6. CONDUCT OF THE TRIAL

Exclusion of Evidence

The court has been severely criticized for its exclusion of evidence. The evidence rejected is too extensive to be treated in detail; that here considered is representative.

The defense wished to prove the details of the history preceding the tragedy, including among other things the details of the raid on the former I.W.W. hall, the kidnapping of Lassiter, the organization of the Citizens' Protective League and the meeting of employers at the Elks Club on October 20, 1919. The newspaper accounts of the meeting on October 20 were excluded. Elmer Smith's testimony that "some time previous" to Armistice Day he made an "appeal to the Governor of the State of Washington for protection against raids and violent acts of this kind threatened against the I.W.W." was stricken out.

The defendants were not permitted to state why they anticipated the wrecking of the hall and personal violence and what specific events they had in mind in arming themselves. Although defendants were permitted to testify that they understood the hall was to be raided and extended testimony was given by defendants on this point neither the defendants nor their witnesses were permitted to testify to the fact of a previous raid or to other relevant facts upon which their expectation of a raid was based. The court excluded answers to the question "whether it was a matter of common knowledge known about Centralia that there was going to be a raid on the I.W.W. hall on the 11th of November" and whether the witness "had heard talk of a threatened raid on the I.W.W. hall that afternoon."

The ground for exclusion of evidence of a conspiracy to attack the hall was that "there had been no proof of an overt act on the part of Warren O. Grimm.". Vanderveer argued that such evidence was admissible: (1) to prove apprehension, in order "to explain why they armed themselves, to explain the presence of some of the defendants in sheltered spots remote from the hall, to rebut the suggestion made in Mr. Allen's opening statement that their discussion . . . of the threatened assault was pure bunkum and a ruse to conceal their true purposes, to prove which party was the aggressor on November 11, and to prove that the defendants acted as reasonably prudent men in their attempts to avert the threatened difficulty"; (2) to rebut the

27

State's contention that a conspiracy existed to shoot down marchers in the Armistice Day parade. "Only by proving what they actually did, and why they did it, could the defendants hope to negative the charge of a criminal conspiracy," he said. The contention was made also that there was ample evidence "of either actual or apparent aggression on the part of Mr. Grimm."

The State in its brief on appeal took the position that Grimm was neither an actual nor an apparent aggressor; that consequently the rejection of the offered testimony "of the purported threats of Warren O. Grimm, the purported conspiracy to which he was not a party, the purported raid on the hall in which he was not involved, the purported statements of others, became immaterial, and the ruling of the lower court was manifestly correct."

Jurors Inmon, Sweitzer and P. V. Johnson have made affidavits to the effect that if they had known what they now know they would never have returned a verdict of "guilty." Juror Hulten has sworn that those affidavits coincide with his views. One juror, however, has stated that he understood from the record that a conspiracy existed among the business men.

Details regarding the lynching were excluded, although testimony that lynching occurred was admitted without objection. Objection to evidence of non-prosecution of the lynchers was, however, sustained. Notwithstanding this exclusion of evidence, Vanderveer, by tactics known to a skillful trial lawyer, succeeded in suggesting much that was technically ruled out. In many cases the jury actually heard the answer which was stricken out.

Where the admission of evidence depends upon proof of a prior fact, the question whether the evidence offered to prove such fact is sufficient is, in general, for the jury to decide rather than for the court. The regular procedure is to admit the evidence where there is sufficient proof for the consideration of the jury with instructions to the jury to disregard it if they do not deem the prior fact proved. In this case, the court excluded evidence of the sort referred to above in spite of testimony to the effect that Grimm was implicated in the raid. As a matter of fact, the position taken in this report is that Grimm was probably not a participant in the raid, but no grounds appear, either technical or otherwise, for the exclusion by the court of so much relevant and important testimony concerning previous use of violence against the I.W.W.

Arrest of Witnesses

Guy Bray and Jay Cook, witnesses for the defense, whose testimony placed Grimm near the I.W.W. hall, were arrested for perjury after they left the court room. This fact was revealed when Vanderveer recalled the two as witnesses. The cases were never brought to trial. Whether the arrests were made in order to intimidate other witnesses is a matter of conjecture. None of the State's witnesses were so treated, although the testimony of some of them was badly discredited. Furthermore, no attempt was made to punish a witness for the State who admitted having attempted to influence a defense witness.

Charge Against Bailiff Jackson

Vanderveer sought during the trial to have Bailiff Jackson removed on the ground that he had been illegally imparting information to the jury. Vanderveer would not state the source of his information, saying that it was given in confidence and that disclosure would close a channel of information. Lacking this knowledge, the court refused to remove the bailiff.

Military Aspect Given to the Trial

On February 25, federal troops arrived in Montesano and remained until after the close of the trial on March 13. Prosecutor Allen, without consulting either the court or the sheriff, had asked the Governor to intercede with the federal authorities to have soldiers sent. They were stationed near the court house and the jurors saw them. Vanderveer objected vehemently and asked that Allen be punished for contempt, on the ground that the troops created the impression of an I.W.W. menace and gave the trial a military aspect. The prosecution gave the court information bearing on its action. Vanderveer's request for such information was denied. The court took the position that since it had nothing to do with the calling of the troops it would not take responsibility for requesting their removal.

An added military aspect was given to the trial by the presence of ex-soldiers in uniform. These were paid $4 a day from the American Legion fund. It was asserted that their presence was intended to prevent the practice, resorted to on some occasions by the I.W.W., of packing court rooms with their sympathizers to create a favorable atmosphere. The possibility of their doing so in this case, when every I.W.W. who showed himself was in danger of attack or arrest, was, of course, out of the question.

The Verdict

The jury was given the case for formal deliberation on the morning of Saturday, March 13, 1920. About 5 o'clock in the afternoon they had agreed on a verdict. At 6:30 it was delivered to the court. This first verdict, in part, found Eugene Barnett and John Lamb guilty of third degree murder.* The court refused to accept this verdict and sent the jury back. The final verdict was rendered at 8:40.

By the final verdict Eugene Barnett, John Lamb, O. C. Bland, Bert Bland, Britt Smith, Ray Becker, and James McInerney were convicted of second degree murder. To this verdict was attached the following plea, signed unanimously by the jurors: "We the undersigned jurors respectfully petition the court to extend the [sic] leniency to the defendants whose names appear on the attached verdict." This referred to all those convicted.

Elmer Smith and Mike Sheehan were found "not guilty." The court had definitely instructed the jury that the verdict against Elmer Smith, the attorney who was charged with being a party to the planning but who was not present at the shooting, must be "guilty of first degree murder," or acquittal. It was proved that Mike Sheehan was not used to the handling of arms and took no part whatever in the shooting. Bert Faulkner had been dismissed by the court at the close of the State's case on the ground of insufficient evidence. Loren Roberts was found guilty but insane.†

Juror Torpen has made affidavit that when the jury retired to deliberate, before any discussion took place, a trial ballot was taken and "it was unanimous in favor of acquitting the defendants in the case." Jurors Hulten and P. V. Johnson swore that they agreed with these statements. Other jurors, when interviewed, stated that the first ballot

---

* First degree murder, as applied to the facts here, is defined by the Washington statute as premeditated murder. The statutory definition of second degree murder, so far as applicable, is intentional but unpremeditated murder. The statute does not recognize any such technical offense as third degree murder. Homicide other than first and second degree murder is manslaughter.

† Loren Roberts was confined for a brief time in an asylum for the insane and then was transferred to Walla Walla where he was confined with the other prisoners, although he had been adjudged legally irresponsible. His imprisonment continued until August 20, 1930, when he was released by virtue of a judgment based upon the verdict of a jury that he was now sane.

was unanimous for conviction. Jurors Inmon and Sweitzer made affidavit that Sellers "at all times voted for and insisted upon a conviction."

Interviews with the jurors, held during this investigation, gave the definite impression that the verdict was a compromise between those who desired a first degree conviction and those who wanted acquittal, but that practically all the jurors were fairly well satisfied with the second degree verdict as representing rough justice, on the ground that a rush was made upon the hall before the shooting but that the I.W.W.s fired from outside stations. It also appeared that the petition for leniency was a part of the compromise, those who desired acquittal forcing some of the others to sign it on the threat that otherwise the jury would be "hung."

Neither prosecution nor defense was satisfied with the verdict, and the defense appealed. That "the court erred in receiving a verdict of murder in the second degree" was a major contention of the prosecution before the Supreme Court. This was on the theory that the basis of prosecution was conspiracy. Conspiracy involves premeditation, but second degree murder means unpremeditated killing. Vanderveer's argument before the Supreme Court contained the statement that "the function of a verdict is to decide the issue. This verdict decides nothing. Did the defendants conspire or did they not? Yes, for otherwise they should have been acquitted. No, for otherwise they should have been convicted of murder in the first degree."

If a prior opinion of the Supreme Court of the State of Washington be applied to this case the fact that the defendants were not "present" at the firing of the shot that killed Grimm (i.e., in the Avalon Hotel from which it was admitted the shot was fired) would, except upon a tenuous line of reasoning, preclude any verdict other than "first degree" or "not guilty." (State v. Robinson, 12 Wash. 349, 41 Pac. 51.)

A contention of the State which would sustain a second degree conviction was stated in the Supreme Court opinion as follows: "If a homicide is proven beyond a reasonable doubt, the presumption of law is that it is murder in the second degree, and if defendant would reduce it to manslaughter or justify it the burden is upon him to do so. . . . In this case the crime of manslaughter is not involved and it cannot be held as a matter of law that the appellants' proof justified the homicide."

31

The presumption of second degree murder, however, arises only "if a homicide is proven beyond a reasonable doubt." This must refer to that individual only who is proved to have been responsible for the killing. Allowing for the moment the assumption of the prosecution that Barnett or Davis shot Grimm, proof of such shooting raises a presumption of second degree murder against Barnett or Davis only and against none of the other I.W.W.s until their responsibility is shown. The prosecution sought to implicate the others on the theory of conspiracy, which presupposes premeditation. But proof of this theory would make a second degree verdict impossible.

The brief for the State on appeal argued: "If the defendants committed murder, as a result of a conspiracy, manifestly they were guilty of murder in the first degree." In order, however, to uphold the conviction on appeal the prosecution was forced to offer some justification for the second degree verdict. It attempted to sustain the verdict on the ground that the defendants were "aiders and abettors." An instruction was given on this theory by the trial court but a careful reading of the evidence at the trial leads to the conclusion that the only real contention of the prosecution was that the defendants were conspirators, with the possible exception of John Lamb. None of the nine jurors interviewed suggested any such theory as that of "aiding or abetting," and the Supreme Court did not mention it in its opinion.

On April 14, 1921, the Supreme Court of the State of Washington unanimously affirmed the judgment of the lower court. (State v. Smith, 115 Wash. 405, 197 Pac. 770.)

Comment on the Verdict

According to the aforementioned pamphlet* prepared by the American Legion, "Grays Harbor County and the entire Pacific Northwest" declared the verdict to be "an impossible, monstrous miscarriage of justice. Both State and defense," it said, "were agreed, for the once, that but one of two verdicts could logically have been returned—guilt in the first degree, or acquittal. And local belief declared that unworthy fear of I.W.W. reprisals, together with a desire to placate public sentiment, led that incomprehensible jury toward a verdict which its members considered a compromise."

"Later it was to be known," continues the pamphlet, "that two jurors were violently radical, and that a third favored their attitude—

* See page 15.

these three holding out for acquittal. Nine Americans, therefore, against their own belief in the extreme guilt of the accused, permitted the prejudiced opinion of openly avowed radicals to force them into a shameful and illogical decision."

Editorials in the Portland *Oregonian* for March 15 and 16, 1920, and the Seattle *Post-Intelligencer* for March 16 should have careful consideration. Only brief extracts can be given here.

"The Montesano verdict violates both justice and common sense." "The men accused were either guilty of premeditated murder—murder in the first degree—or they were innocent. . . . Here is a clear case of jury incompetence—of a verdict born of compromise or of fear of personal consequences, or of plain lack of comprehension, or of reluctance to accept a sworn responsibility. . . . The jury finds that it was murder without premeditation. As well have held that Grimm committed suicide. . . . Fear of personal consequences can only be inferred. . . . Lack of comprehension was revealed by the jury's invidious discrimination between conspirators." *Oregonian,* March 15.

"Grotesque miscarriage of justice. . . . The travesty of the Montesano mistrial consists in the fact that it is judicial compromise with crime in its blackest form. If not that, it is conviction of innocent men. Who pretends that the seven were innocent men?" *Oregonian,* March 16.

(After a reference to the general spirit of dissatisfaction): "Is it then to be supposed that such a verdict must necessarily be the result of jury-room compromise, of indifference to the evidence and the court's instructions on the law? . . . If we are to continue to have faith in the virtues of our scheme of administering justice we must show a measurable willingness to accept the results of fair and well-fought trials." *Post-Intelligencer,* March 16.

Prosecutor Allen before announcement of the verdict had filed an information against the defendants charging them with the murder of McElfresh. Smith and Sheehan were rearrested immediately on their acquittal. Allen said that "the verdict is a travesty on justice. We shall continue to prosecute these men until a proper conviction is procured." Attorney Abel was "absolutely astounded" and said he would cheerfully undertake the prosecution again. Attorney Cunningham was quoted in the Centralia *Daily Chronicle* of March 16 as saying, "You may be certain they will be tried. Centralia will insist upon it and back of Centralia stands the good citizenship of Washington and of the country at large." Two weeks later he was again reported as stating, "I would gladly try the entire case over again with all the work entailed to bring to exact justice the men who murdered Warren O. Grimm and his fellow victims of Armistice Day."

The American Legion made a "quiet determined resolve" to insist on further prosecution, in order that the crime should not go "inadequately punished."

Motion for Retrial

These declared intentions, however, were not carried out. By a motion for a new trial Vanderveer afforded an opportunity to the prosecution to secure what it would consider a "proper conviction," under the rule in the State of Washington that a prior conviction for a lower degree of crime does not preclude a conviction of higher degree on a new trial. Nevertheless, this motion and the appeal to the Supreme Court for reversal and a new trial were, in fact, strenuously resisted by the prosecution. The motion for a new trial was denied.

A new trial might conceivably, of course, have resulted in acquittal. The State had secured a conviction which, under the law, required a sentence of at least ten years. A method exists by means of which the State could have maintained the conviction secured and at the same time could have sought a first degree verdict, namely, trying the defendants for the murder of McElfresh or another of those killed. The State took the position that constitutional protection against double jeopardy would not preclude such a trial. In any event the issue could be tested in court. For that matter, a charge of murder can still be prosecuted at any time.

The new charge was never pressed, however, not even against Elmer Smith and Mike Sheehan, who had been acquitted. One reason may have been the expense involved. According to the auditor of Lewis County the Montesano trial cost about $65,000, and an unsuccessful effort was made to have the State assume the cost. It is the opinion of all interviewed on the question that no trial will be had again for the Armistice Day shooting. This is pertinent in connection with the question of parole.

In this connection the question inevitably arises why the prosecution settled upon the charge of the murder of Grimm as the basis for its case against the defendants in preference to a charge of the murder of McElfresh or of Casagranda. There is a possibility that it might be proved that McElfresh was actually attacking the hall when shot. The evidence tends to indicate that Casagranda was shot by Everest when the latter was escaping. It would seem, therefore, that the prosecution had based its case on the charge which seemed most susceptible of proof and most likely to result in a conviction. This, of course, is the general practice in prosecution.

The Sentence

Each of the men convicted was sentenced to imprisonment for a minimum term of 25 years and a maximum of 40 years. The court apparently disregarded the jury's petition for leniency. This was, of course, its legal right. Nevertheless, some of the jurors expressed great astonishment at the severity of the sentence.

The Washington statute provides that the punishment for second degree murder shall be imprisonment for "not less than ten years." The position taken by the court was that this vested in it discretion subject only to the limitation that the minimum sentence must be not less than ten years' imprisonment. The indeterminate sentence law provides that where, as in this case, the statute does not definitely fix the sentence for a felony the court shall direct imprisonment "for a term not less than the minimum . . . prescribed by law" (nor greater than the maximum—with which we are not here concerned). An earlier decision (1917) of the Supreme Court involving an analogous statute supports the construction of the law made by the court in the Centralia case. (State v. Clark, 98 Wash. 81, 167 Pac. 84.)

It is strongly contended, to be sure, by the Centralia Publicity Committee, working for the release of the prisoners, that a minimum sentence in excess of ten years is void and that under the parole system the prisoners were entitled to parole on April 5, 1930, ten years from rendition of the sentence. Attorneys are divided in opinion on this question, and the Committee has been planning to test the matter in the courts.

The "Labor Jury"

Official representatives were sent to the trial by labor councils of the larger cities nearby. The "labor verdict" of this group found that the defendants were "not guilty," that there was a "conspiracy to raid

35

the I.W.W. on the part of the business interests of Centralia," that the I.W.W. hall was "unlawfully raided," that Grimm was "a party to the conspiracy of raiding the I.W.W. hall" and "participated in the raid," and that the defendants did not "get a fair and impartial trial."

The American Legion pamphlet before referred to claims that "these men were the representatives of the most drastically radical element of organized labor. The verdict of exoneration later returned by the 'labor jurors' was wholly in keeping with the intent which dispatched them to the Grays Harbor capital." On the other hand, bitter rivalry existed between craft unions and the I.W.W., an industrial union. It is true that the radical element predominated at that time on the Pacific Coast. Opposed to the influence of this rivalry in the minds of these men, however, would be the common cause of labor. The weight of the "labor verdict" depends upon which of these two sympathies was stronger.

A Class Trial?

The fact that the labor jurors were present indicates that the trial was regarded by labor as a class trial. On the other hand, the court definitely instructed the jury that "the I.W.W. is not on trial" and that its economic and social theories must not be allowed to prejudice them as against the defendants. The court on another occasion said, "The issue in this case is murder." It has been asserted, however, that the trial involved other issues: the question of patriotism, with the American Legion as the opponent of the I.W.W.; and the conflict between capital and labor, with capital represented primarily by the "lumber interests" and by the business men of Centralia.

From the beginning of the trial, Vanderveer emphasized the class element, making frequent reference to "lumber trust counsel." In his argument to the jury he said, "I am asking you to decide the fate of organized labor." According to the Portland *Oregonian*, Vanderveer spoke with apparent directness to certain jurors, charging them to acquit "or forever-after keep silent on protestations of belief in the cause of radical labor."

Juror Torpen made affidavit, as follows, "I verily believe . . . that if these men had not been affiliated with the I.W.W. organization they would never have been convicted." Juror Sweitzer made a statement to the same effect. Jurors Inmon and Samuel Johnson stated that membership in the I.W.W. was a factor in the conviction. Juror Robinson also asserted that the matter of the I.W.W. entered into the deliberations. Sellers differs from Torpen in denying that the former was influenced by the affiliations of the defendants. The lumber companies and the Citizens' Protective League contributed to the American Legion Fund.

The prosecuting attorney in his official statement to the prison authorities, made at the time the prisoners were transferred to the penitentiary, remarked that James McInerney was still an I.W.W. enthusiast and recommended that "if, after the expiration of his minimum sentence he has not assumed a different attitude . . . he should be retained in the penitentiary for the full maximum term." Similar statements were made with respect to other prisoners.

7. THE PART PLAYED BY THE CHURCHES

Prior to Armistice Day, 1919, and even on that day, the tense social situation seems to have escaped serious attention on the part of the churches and the ministers in the town and neighborhood. If any of them knew of a plan to raid the hall they took no measures to prevent it. There is no evidence that in the strenuous hours following the shooting any minister attempted to calm the hysteria or to prevent the lynching. The body of Wesley Everest was buried without religious rites of any kind.

The Centralia *Daily Chronicle* makes reference to sermons concerning the tragedy, but nothing of particular significance is recorded except one sermon which began with a defense of the use of force. The speaker was reported to have said: "How then shall we blot out this I.W.W.ism? I mean not for today only, but for tomorrow as well. How shall we rid ourselves for all time of this accursed poison? . . . Let us cut out this cancerous growth. If we have laws, then enforce them. Apprehend every murderer; send them to the gallows. This is God's law and it is necessary for self-preservation today. This is the place of force, and let force with all its power do its work. The tragic thing about it all is that the vast majority of our citizens are perfectly willing to stop there. After force has done its work, they are ready to go to sleep. But nothing constructive has been done. No healing power is manifest. The heart is left the same."

8. THE QUESTION OF PAROLE

Under the Washington law, prior to the expiration of the minimum sentence release may be afforded only by the action of the Governor, who may pardon or parole. He usually relies on the recommendation of the Parole Board. Since the minimum sentence in this case is 25 years, unless the Centralia Publicity Committee succeeds in its effort to establish the illegality of a minimum sentence in excess of 10 years, nothing can now be done to reduce the time actually served by the prisoners except through action by the Governor.

Since the trial, the hysteria and bitterness have abated considerably. Several committees and organizations have been working independently for the release of the prisoners: (1) the Centralia Publicity Committee, originally organized by the I.W.W. but later independent; (2) the General Defense Committee of the I.W.W. organization with headquarters in Chicago, a Washington Branch in Seattle, and another branch in New York City; (3) the Washington Conciliation Committee in Seattle, affiliated with the Civil Liberties Union; (4) the Communist Party with its International Labor Defense organization and its Centralia Liberation Committee; (5) the Seattle Citizens' Committee, with the Rev. James Crowther as chairman, which prepared an appeal to the Governor in 1925 but which is no longer functioning.

The methods of the Communist Party have been extreme and are generally considered more harmful than beneficial. Five of the prisoners have deliberately repudiated its efforts.

The General Defense Committee has been accused of using the Centralia prisoners' situation for propaganda. It states, however, that their imprisonment is not an asset to the I.W.W. but a reflection upon its strength.

In spite of the rivalry between themselves and the radical I.W.W. organization, regular labor unions have worked for the liberation of the prisoners. Numerous trade unions and the Washington State Federation of Labor have passed resolutions favoring release. Seven of the twelve jurors, and the remaining alternate juror, who heard the testimony, have sought the freedom of the prisoners. They have signed affidavits and written letters to the Governor and five of them have appeared before him personally to request executive action.

There is a considerable amount of opposition to parole. Many individuals, including some ministers, feel strongly that any clemency would be a mistake. The State American Legion Convention in 1928 passed a resolution opposing pardon for the prisoners. The Legion, however, refused to send a representative to oppose application for parole.

Reasons given for objecting to parole include the fear of further bloodshed and the fear that the men when released will pose as martyrs, giving propaganda material to the I.W.W. The prevalence of crime is given as a reason for exacting the extreme penalty under the law. Some of the men are still enthusiastic radicals and would not obtain their freedom at the cost of foregoing the right to work for what they consider a better society. Others are through with radicalism and wish to procure work and "settle down."

Some of the prisoners, with apparent sincerity, profess to have no personal animosity against anyone responsible for their imprisonment. A marked spirit of reasonableness is found also on the part of certain American Legion representatives. Many ministers and other leaders in Washington are earnestly seeking to know whether or not justice was done in the Montesano trial.

II.

CONCLUSIONS

The foregoing completes the statement of fact in the Centralia case. What follows represents an effort impartially to interpret the facts and to draw conclusions from them.

1. RECONSTRUCTION OF EVENTS

Following the discussion of so many details it may be well briefly to reconstruct the events as we believe they probably happened.

A definite drive was in progress against the I.W.W.s in Centralia. Newspaper statements supplied sufficient ground for the expectation of a raid and the fact that a raid had occurred in connection with a parade a year and a half earlier made this assumption reasonable. Elmer Smith believed that such a raid was planned and, as their attorney, warned the I.W.W.s on the morning of Armistice Day.

The I.W.W.s planned to defend their hall with firearms both from inside and outside the hall. Becker, McInerney, and Britt Smith, who remained in the hall, were party to the agreement and were armed. Faulkner, Morgan, and Sheehan, also in the hall, were unarmed and may or may not have known of the agreement. Bert Bland, Hanson, and Roberts were stationed on Seminary Hill and Davis in the Avalon Hotel, all parties to the agreement and armed. O. C. Bland and Lamb were in the Arnold Hotel, Bland a party to the agreement and armed while Lamb may or may not have known of the plan and was probably unarmed. Barnett was in the I.W.W. hall during the morning but left before the parade began. His participation in the event is referred to below. The arrangement was that those outside should fire when they heard shots coming from the hall or saw a move against it.

The halting of the Centralia contingent in front of the building was probably by design, since some of the Legionnaires immediately interpreted it as a signal for hostilities and offered to rush the hall. Such a move was probably made before any firing occurred. It is possible, of course, that, seeing paraders bunched in front of the hall, some one of the waiting I.W.W.s, either inside or outside the hall, precipitated the affair by firing sooner than his comrades in the hall expected or intended. At the distance of Seminary Hill it would be easy to confuse a bunching of men in the street with an actual attack upon the building.

The shooting precipitated excitement and fury. At the time of the rush on the hall McElfresh was shot from Seminary Hill. Casagranda was mortally wounded some time after the first rush and at some distance from the hall. It is probable that Grimm, for whose death the men were tried, was shot from the Avalon Hotel and while he was standing in the street at the head of his contingent. Whether he was deliberately picked off or not is not clear. It is probable that Barnett was not in the Avalon but in the Roderick Hotel, and therefore, that he did not shoot Grimm.

The I.W.W.s found in the building were taken prisoners; Everest made his way out and, some distance away, wounded Dale Hubbard in attempting to elude pursuit. Everest was lynched early that evening.

2. QUESTIONS OF FACT

The crucial questions of fact in this case are, (1) Did the rush on the hall or the shooting occur first? and, (2) What agreement had been made concerning the defense of the hall? The fact that the men were tried solely for the murder of Grimm raises further questions: Was the shot which killed Grimm fired from inside or outside the hall? Was Grimm a party to the attack on the hall?

As to the first question, no exact answer is possible. It seems likely that some actual move toward the hall on the part of the paraders occurred before any shots were fired. The most that can be said with assurance is that the movements of the paraders in front of the hall made it appear to the waiting I.W.W.s that an attack was commencing, or, at least, was imminent.

As to the second question, it was admitted by the defense and may be regarded as certain that the I.W.W.s had formulated a plan of defense involving the use of firearms both inside and outside the building.

As to the other questions, there is a strong probability that the shot which killed Grimm was fired from the Avalon Hotel. The evidence indicates that it came from the 38.55 caliber gun which "John Doe" Davis took to the Avalon Hotel. The most credible evidence at the trial was to the effect that Grimm did not personally participate in the attack. It is true that affidavits have been offered to prove that Grimm was among the raiders, but certainly the weight of the evidence at the trial was against this contention.

As to the contention of the prosecution that Barnett fired the fatal shot from the Avalon, this was not definitely established and does not seem to be in accord with the facts. As already stated, the weight of the evidence tends to support his own contention that he was in the Roderick Hotel and unarmed rather than the contention of the State.

3. QUESTIONS OF LAW

The shooting of Grimm from an outside station was without legal justification. Under the Washington statute defense of property is lawful, even with firearms, when danger to property involves danger to person. The Supreme Court has held, however, that armed defense of another person (except perhaps a member of one's family) is lawful only when it takes place "in the presence of such other person." In this case the court held that the men who were stationed at a distance from the hall were not "in the presence" of those they sought to defend, within the meaning of the statute. This interpretation was upheld by the Supreme Court.

If the statement of the trial court that a second change of venue is not permissible in a criminal case is correct, this settles the matter. The statute does not in terms permit a second change; it does, however, permit a change generally, in the event of "excitement or prejudice." If no second change of venue is permissible a gross miscarriage of justice may result from the fact that the court and not the defense decides on the county to which the case is moved; it might conceivably change the venue to a county where prejudice was greater than in the original county and the defense would be without redress. A fundamental rule of statutory construction is that such construction shall be reasonable. This decision against a change of venue was a great blow to the defense and prevented holding the trial in an atmosphere that even approximated impartiality.

In sharp contrast with Judge Wilson's handling of this matter is the action of Judge Jurey of Seattle in the Cunningham Criminal Syndicalism case. In the latter case the jury was discharged on the motion of the State after all the evidence was in. The action was based on the presentation of a mimeographed letter purporting to have been signed by Sherman Rogers, industrial editor of *The Outlook*—repudiated by him, however—which had been sent to prospective jurors and which contained denunciations of prominent labor leaders, warnings of anarchy and adjurations to the jury to "do their duty" in criminal syndicalism cases.

In connection with the arrest of witnesses for the defense during the progress of the trial it may be well to consider the judicial attitude in similar circumstances. The latest judicial statement concerning such action is that of an appellate federal court in November, 1929, as follows: "The practice of arresting witnesses during the progress of a trial is not to be commended. If it is done for the purpose of intimidating witnesses, or influencing the jury, it is a plain attempt to obstruct the administration of justice, and should be punished as a contempt." (Powell v. U. S., 35 Fed. (2) 941.) The significance of these arrests in the Centralia case is accentuated by the fact that witnesses for the State who were discredited by their own statements were not subjected to similar treatment.

The true function of the prosecution in a trial is not primarily to secure a conviction, but to do justice. In this case the prosecution attempted to keep the trial in Lewis County where the clash occurred and where prejudice was intense, brought federal troops to the scene of the trial, and had two defense witnesses arrested for perjury. The prosecution's brief on appeal asserted in substance that the testimony of any I.W.W. sympathizer might be disregarded as presumably false.

Waiving legal technicalities, it is difficult to see how the exclusion of evidence concerning the raid on the I.W.W. hall which had occurred during the year previous could be other than prejudicial. Obviously, this event had a very great bearing on the attitude of the members of the organization. The same may be said of the exclusion of evidence concerning the activities of the Citizens' Protective League and the employers' meeting of October 20. By judicial ruling matters of the utmost significance in interpreting the acts of the defendants were excluded from the trial.

Since the court did not disclose the information upon receipt of which it refused to have the federal troops who were stationed in the vicinity of the court house withdrawn it is impossible to assert with finality that they served no useful purpose. It is difficult, however, to see any necessity for their presence and quite as difficult to avoid the

43

impression that they must have created an atmosphere that was not conducive to the rendering of impartial justice.

The theory of the prosecution was, of course, that the plan to use firearms was a conspiracy to kill. The contention of the defense was that it was a lawful plan to defend the I.W.W. hall. The jury were required, in law, to convict of first degree murder all who were party to a conspiracy to kill. Under the Washington statute above referred to an agreement to defend the hall with firearms from outside was in effect such a conspiracy. The jury were also required to acquit all who were found not to have been party to such agreement, and who were not found to be responsible for the fatal shooting. The jury were apparently unwilling to find any guilty of first degree, which under the Washington statute, would involve the death penalty or life imprisonment, in the jury's discretion. They were likewise apparently unwilling to let all of them go free. The court afforded a way out in its instruction to the jury at the request of defense counsel that a finding of murder in the second degree was permissible. In bringing in a verdict of second degree murder against all seven, however, the jury acted in a manner inconsistent with any legal theory which applies to the facts. They did, on the other hand, bring in a verdict which would, they apparently thought, assure a punishment that would fit the offense. The theory underlying the verdict seems to have been that the prisoners had not conspired to kill wantonly but had intended to defend their hall from attack, but that, on the other hand, they were acting illegally in placing armed men outside the hall. Thus the verdict appears to have dealt what the jurors, in their own minds, considered to be rough justice.

Seven I.W.W.s were found guilty of second degree murder which involves unpremeditated but intentional homicide. This is the crime for which the men were given a sentence of from 25 to 40 years' imprisonment. Question has been raised as to the legality and judicial propriety of this sentence. On legal grounds alone it cannot be said that a sentence of from 25 to 40 years for second degree murder is unjustifiable. Court practice in sentencing for second degree murder varies widely. Nor can objection be made on strictly legal grounds to the disregarding of the jury's recommendation of leniency. Under the Washington law discretion in this matter is a prerogative of the court. On the other hand, the long sentence raises an important moral question which will be treated in the next section.

It is impossible to exclude from consideration the many acts of violence against the I.W.W. for which no one was prosecuted. The earlier raid on the I.W.W. hall, the destruction of that organization's property on this occasion, the deliberate lynching of one of their number, the violence of the man hunting, as well as earlier acts of violence, have gone without investigation or punishment. Neither were the deliberate attempts to influence the jury investigated. Proceedings for contempt of court were not brought against those responsible.

The lynchers of Everest have never been prosecuted. This killing, committed four hours after the shooting and after nightfall and some hours before the death of the man he shot, was a peculiarly revolting affair. The reason assigned by the prosecuting attorney for not prosecuting is that the perpetrators are not known. There is evidence, however, that the names of some who took part could be ascertained. The severe treatment accorded this little group of radicals considered alongside the immunity given to those who committed crimes against them makes a deadly parallel.

4. QUESTIONS OF MORALS

In considering the course of events which immediately led up to the Centralia tragedy, the business men's meeting three weeks before, at which was formulated the plan to use private and violent methods to eliminate the I.W.W.s from the town and to wreck the I.W.W. hall, stands out as the beginning of this series of tragic events. The action taken at this meeting was unjustifiable and lawless.

The mood of revolt which had come over these I.W.W.s was fortified by a deep sense of social injustice and economic disadvantage and the plan to deal with them by violence only deepened their resentment and goaded them to violent resistance. Admittedly, the I.W.W. hall was to the business men of the town a symbol of open opposition to their economic and social beliefs and to their patriotic sentiments, as well as a menace to industrial equilibrium, to their own economic security, and to their mental serenity. They looked upon it both as a danger and an insult to themselves, the community and the nation. No legal way existed, they had been told, by which they might destroy it. Yet the I.W.W.s had a right to their beliefs. Violence against them was without justification. And the fact that private violence was required to accomplish the end sought should have deterred the employers and Legionnaires from their purpose.

It is understandable that the police officials may have been unable to give adequate protection to the I.W.W. hall in the general situation which followed the meeting of the business men. But denial of protection and, above all, the failure to give protection to the hall during the parade, was neglect of duty. The probability of a raid was known; the parade was to pass the hall; the tenseness of the community also was known. The situation was explosive even if the police knew of no definite plan to raid the building that day—which is doubtful. The officials appear to have been seriously recreant in the performance of their duty.

The planning of the raid was wrong even if the probability of bloodshed could be eliminated. But in the situation which existed that day, the probability of serious casualties could not be eliminated, and should have been foreseen.

These Legionnaires were returned soldiers commemorating the first anniversary of the end of the war. Their emotions were intense, having been fanned during the war and afterward by national and local patriotic propaganda, in which was mingled agitation against the I.W.W.s as pacifists during the war. The attack was probably quite spontaneous on the part of many of them. But those of their leaders who took part in the planning of violent measures against the I.W.W. must have known that they were allowing the patriotic impulses of the Legion to be exploited in the interests of lumber operators in a way that concerned many of the Legion members not at all and might even militate against the welfare of the humbler ones among them. This attack was no noble patriotic demonstration. The motives were manifestly mixed. Economic interest and class solidarity were powerful and obvious influences in the tide of feeling which broke into hysteria and fury on that Armistice Day. The leaders were definitely wrong in allowing their organization to be led, by appeal to its fraternal and patriotic sentiments, into attempting to handle matters with which none should interfere save the people's duly selected representatives. Again, the fact that the desired result could not be arrived at by proper and legal measures should have been an effective deterrent to men of patriotic spirit.

The situation of the I.W.W.s was difficult. Since they expected a raid at the hands of a much stronger party of determined men, they might have made one more earnest effort to secure police protection on Armistice Day and if it were refused them, rather than incur the risk of a deadly encounter, they might better have removed their effects for safe keeping and abandoned the hall. This would have been in accordance with the avowed creed of their organization. The hall was in effect their property, by virtue of a lease, and their meeting place, with all that that meant to them as casual laborers and social outcasts. It was the symbol of their ideal of a new society. But bloodshed and even loss of life were likely to result from armed resistance. Their own plans of defense from inside and outside the hall made bloodshed practically certain. Where it would end no one could tell. Another meeting place could doubtless be found if this one should be destroyed. The course they took, involving as it did an almost certain loss of life on both sides was clearly wrong. It resulted, as might have been foreseen, not only in the loss of several lives, but also in the loss of their liberty, the closing of their hall and suspension of the activities of their organization. They completely frustrated their own purposes.

The verdict of the jury was manifestly a compromise; they were apparently seeking the closest possible approximation to justice. Their effort, however, was thwarted by the court in the infliction of so long a sentence. It is at this point that the disinterested student of the trial gains the strongest impression of injustice, an impression which is sharply accentuated by the fact that shameful crimes against the I.W.W.s have gone unpunished to this day. In view of the wide latitude allowed the court in the matter of sentences for second degree murder, the moral responsibility resting on the judge was very great.

Throughout this whole tragedy passion reigned. Business men, raiders and I.W.W.s alike were in a state of mind which does not lend itself to reason. The fury of the lynching, the hunting down of the I.W.W.s, the killing of a posse member and the plea that such killing was accidental and even justifiable because the man was mistaken for an I.W.W., the policing of the city by Legionnaires, and the conduct of the trial, are indications, after the event, of the state of mind which led to the tragedy. The outstanding feature of this whole series of events was the passion of the community, which made sound moral judgments impossible. Both sides used social dynamite and neither seems to have realized the magnitude of its offense.

The Centralia story is a vivid warning of his duty to the man who feels the pull of a current of mass excitement and the quickening of the pulse that heralds the surrender of reason to mob passion. Those who feel the rising tide of passion, who lend themselves to its increase, or make no effort to lessen its force, are far from guiltless of the consequences. The six I.W.W.s in Walla Walla Penitentiary are paying the penalty for their part in a tragedy the guilt for which is by no means theirs alone. They alone were indicted; they alone have been punished.

APPENDIX

NOTES CONCERNING THE PRINCIPALS IN THE CASE

DEFENDANTS

EUGENE BARNETT. Charged with the actual shooting of Warren O. Grimm. Much doubt exists regarding his implication.

RAY BECKER. One of the armed men in the I.W.W. hall. Not proved to have actually done any shooting.

BERT BLAND. One of the younger members of the I.W.W. Admitted shooting from Seminary Hill.

O. C. BLAND. One of the men in the Arnold Hotel. Claims that he disabled himself in preparing to shoot and did not fire.

BERT FAULKNER. One of the men in the I.W.W. hall; the youngest involved. A former service man. Dismissed by the court at the close of the State's direct case because of insufficient evidence.

JOHN LAMB. Companion of O. C. Bland in the Arnold Hotel. Unfamiliar with the use of firearms; his participation in the shooting is in doubt.

JAMES McINERNEY. One of the men armed in the I.W.W. hall. His participation in the shooting not proved. Died August, 1930.

TOM MORGAN. One of the men in the I.W.W. hall. Turned State's evidence.

LOREN ROBERTS. Was on Seminary Hill and participated in the shooting. Was declared by the jury guilty but insane. Confined in asylum and later in prison. Released August, 1930.

MIKE SHEEHAN. One of the men in the I.W.W. hall. Acquitted.

BRITT SMITH. Secretary of the Centralia I.W.W. Local. Was in the I.W.W. hall, armed. Participation in the shooting not proved.

ELMER SMITH. Centralia attorney, counsel to the I.W.W. Tried for complicity in the plan to shoot from outside stations. Not in the vicinity of the hall at the time of the shooting. Acquitted. Disbarred from Washington State courts.

ESCAPED

"JOHN DOE" DAVIS. Was stationed in the Avalon Hotel, armed.

OLE HANSON. One of the three men on Seminary Hill. Participated in the shooting.

KILLED

BEN CASAGRANDA. Legionnaire. Bootblack. Was shot some distance from the hall.

WESLEY EVEREST. Was in the I.W.W. hall. Killed Dale Hubbard while attempting to escape. Lynched by a mob. Buried without ceremony.

WARREN O. GRIMM. Commander Centralia Post of the American Legion, for whose killing the defendants were tried on a charge of murder. Attorney. College football star. Killed by a shot which probably came from the Avalon Hotel.

JOHN HANEY. Killed by a posse which was conducting a man hunt.

DALE HUBBARD. Legionnaire. Shot by Wesley Everest while attempting to prevent the latter's escape.

ARTHUR McELFRESH. Legionnaire. Was shot from Seminary Hill.